Joseph Tuckerman
and the Outdoor Church

Princeton Theological Monograph Series

K. C. Hanson, Charles M. Collier, and D. Christopher Spinks,
Series Editors

Recent volumes in the series:

Ilsup Ahn
Position and Responsibility: Jürgen Habermas, Reinhold Niebuhr, and the Co-Reconstruction of the Positional Imperative

Budden
Following Jesus in Invaded Space: Doing Theology on Aboriginal Land

Eliseo Pérez-Álvarez
A Vexing Gadfly: The Late Kierkegaard on Economic Matters

Elaine A. Heath
Naked Faith: The Mystical Theology of Phoebe Palmer

Bernie A. Van De Walle
The Heart of the Gospel: A. B. Simpson, the Fourfold Gospel, and Late Nineteenth-Century Evangelical Theology

Oscar Garcia-Johnson
The Mestizo/a Community of the Spirit: A Postmodern Latino/a Ecclesiology

David C. Mahan
An Unexpected Light

Samuel A. Paul
The Ubuntu God: Deconstructing a South African Narrative of Oppression

Jeff B. Pool
God's Wounds: Hermeneutic of the Christian Symbol of Divine Suffering, Volume One

Joseph Tuckerman and the Outdoor Church

JEDEDIAH MANNIS

☙PICKWICK *Publications* · Eugene, Oregon

JOSEPH TUCKERMAN AND THE OUTDOOR CHURCH

Princeton Theological Monograph Series 122

Copyright © 2009 Jedediah Mannis. All rights reserved. Except for brief quotations in critical publications or reviews, no part of this book may be reproduced in any manner without prior written permission from the publisher. Write: Permissions, Wipf and Stock Publishers, 199 W. 8th Ave., Suite 3, Eugene, OR 97401.

Pickwick Publications
A Division of Wipf and Stock Publishers
199 W. 8th Ave., Suite 3
Eugene, OR 97401

ISBN 13: 978-1-55635-551-6

Cataloging-in-Publication data:

Joseph Tuckermann and the outdoor church / Jedediah Mannis.

   Princeton Theological Monograph Series 122

   xii + 230 p. ; 23 cm. — Includes bibliographical references.

   ISBN 13: 978-1-55635-551-6

   1. Tuckerman, Joseph, 1778–1840. 2. Unitarianism. I. Title. II. Series.

BX9869.T8 .M30 2009

Manufactured in the U.S.A.

*For Joyce Hartweg Mannis,
with love and gratitude*

Contents

Acknowledgments / ix

1. Introduction / 1
2. Joseph Tuckerman / 14
3. Tuckerman's Ministry at Large / 32
4. The Outdoor Church on the Cambridge Common / 45
5. The Outdoor Church in Porter Square / 70
6. The Outdoor Church in Harvard Square / 98
7. The Outdoor Church in Central Square / 113
8. Covenant and Church / 128
9. The Lord's Supper / 160
10. Death / 181
11. Salvation / 193
12. Conclusion / 212

Bibliography / 225

Acknowledgments

My ministry to the homeless was shaped by two clergy, Deborah Little Wyman and Carl Scovel. Debbie, the founder of Common Cathedral, an outdoor church for homeless people in Boston, gave me my first opportunity to learn about homelessness as a lawyer and then, later, as an aspiring minister. Her quiet courage and perseverance have sustained me throughout, especially when what I saw and heard on the street threatened to overwhelm me. Carl, then the Senior Minister at King's Chapel in Boston, helped me with endless forbearance and great wisdom to translate my work with Debbie into a sense of ministry as discipleship. He has become a close friend, a wise and empathetic mentor, and a faithful member of the Outdoor Church. More than any other person, my ministry reflects his patience, generosity, and boundless spiritual gifts.

The Outdoor Church would not exist but for the initiative of Robert Tobin, the former Rector of Christ Church Cambridge (Episcopal). During his tenure at Christ Church, Bob had been deeply involved with Common Cathedral and opened the church to homeless men and women who needed a cup of coffee, a bathroom in which to wash up and a warm, dry place to rest for a few moments. Impatient to translate this liberal policy into some form of outreach before he retired, Bob invited me to talk with him and Pat Zifcak, an Episcopal deacon and then the head of children's religious education at Christ Church, about the possibility of an outdoor church in Cambridge. With that, we were launched.

Scott Campbell, Senior Minister at Harvard-Epworth Church, agreed to lead our services on the Cambridge Common once a month. He still does. Scott has written about the Outdoor Church, encouraged members of Harvard-Epworth to join as volunteers, provided us with office space and committed Harvard-Epworth to a level of financial and spiritual support for our work that is essential to our continuing commitment to the homeless.

Mary Luti, Director of Wilson Chapel and Visiting Professor of Worship and Preaching at the Andover Newton Theology School, served as liaison to the Committee on Ministry during my ordination process. The seriousness and rigor with which she addressed questions of theology and polity survives in our commitment to bring a fully realized church outdoors to those who cannot or will not go indoors.

Tom Clough, pastor and teacher of the Edgecomb Congregational Church, United Church of Christ, Edgecomb, Maine, and former Associate Conference Minister, Massachusetts Conference, United Church of Christ, was another member of that committee. His enthusiasm for the idea of the Outdoor Church encouraged the committee to consider my intended ministry to the homeless as an ordainable call, evidence of the UCC's continuing commitment to social justice and outreach.

In my last year at the Harvard Divinity School, I completed an internship under the supervision of Dudley Rose, Associate Dean for Ministry Studies and Lecturer on Ministry and Minister of North Prospect Union Church, UCC, in Medford, Massachusetts. Tom Lenhart, senior minister at First Church of Chappaqua, New York, and Kevin Smith, senior minister at Almaden Valley United Church of Christ in San Jose, California, did their internships there at the same time. With Dudley's support, the three of us spent a very long and very cold winter extending the reach of the Outdoor Church to Porter Square in Cambridge.

Frances O'Donnell, the Curator of Manuscripts and Archives at the Andover-Harvard Theological Library, gave me patient assistance in accessing, copying and reading Tuckerman's papers archived at the Harvard Divinity School. Various staff members at the Congregational Library in Boston allowed me to use the library's resources to supplement Tuckerman's papers at Harvard. Galen Wilson, with whom I co-edited a book of civil war letters, provided a typically meticulous and sympathetic reading of some of the early chapters. Robert Orsi, Professor of Religion, Grace Craddock Nagle Chair in Catholic Studies, Department of Religion, Northwestern University and my senior thesis advisor at the Harvard Divinity School, helped shape the chapters on Joseph Tuckerman. Ongoing conversations with Stanley B. Marrow, Professor of New Testament at the Weston School of Theology in Cambridge, Massachusetts, informed the sections of the book that focused on Tuckerman's theology.

The Outdoor Church is sustained by the dedication, wisdom and strength of Pat Zifcak and Jean Chapman, my fellow clergy and partners in the Outdoor Church's ministry. Their unflagging enthusiasm for our mission, despite its many difficulties and challenges, has ensured its success.

The idea for this book originated with my wife, Joyce, who each Sunday evening patiently listened to my stories and anecdotes about people I had encountered on the streets of Cambridge. She read every draft and offered extensive and constructive editorial suggestions. Her faith in the essential goodness of the people whose stories fill this book flows directly from the distinctly Unitarian impulse that informed Tuckerman's Ministry-at-large.

1

Introduction

> While at New York, I sometimes was much affected with reflections on my past life, considering how late it was before I began to be truly religious; and how wickedly I had lived till then; and once so as to weep abundantly, and for a considerable time together.[1]

I WISH I COULD SAY THAT I HAD AN EPIPHANY ABOUT HOMELESS PEOPLE, a conversion experience like Saul on the road to Damascus, but I didn't. I just tripped and fell down.

I was walking down Boylston Street, next to the Granary Burial Ground, where Ben Franklin keeps company with Samuel Adams, John Hancock, Crispus Attucks, Paul Revere, and Mother Goose.

It was a bitterly cold and windy November afternoon and I was hurrying from the motions session in Suffolk Superior Court toward the Park Street subway station. My shoe caught on a crack in the pavement and I sprawled across the sidewalk, attaché case skidding into the gutter. Feeling extremely self-conscious, I looked around to see if anyone had noticed and found myself looking up into the eyes of a homeless man with a McDonald's coffee cup and a handwritten sign that said, "Sober Vietnam Vet needs help." But the homeless vet was not looking down at me—he was staring over me, straight ahead at the evening traffic on Tremont Street. His lips, which were covered with a white flaky crust, moved slightly. His face was covered with little cuts, he had a black eye and his hair hung in filthy clumps on each side of his head. I struggled to my feet, groped in my pants pocket for something to give him and came up with a quarter. I put it in the cup. There was a tear in the right knee of the pants of my best suit. The homeless man didn't move, didn't

---

1. Marsden, *Jonathan Edwards*, 88.

say anything and didn't look at me. This was the first homeless man I had ever encountered in Boston.

I don't mean that I had never *seen* any homeless people in Boston. There were plenty of homeless people to see. You could hardly walk along a downtown street without stumbling over someone with a cup or a sign or just staring vacantly into space. I had been living and working as a lawyer in the Boston area for more than twenty years, and I had spent a lot of time walking around Boston during the work day. I hadn't lacked for opportunities to see homeless people. I am sure I saw scores of homeless men and women there. I probably had seen *this* guy too. And yet, somehow, I had never *noticed* a homeless person before.

(But the Rev. Joseph Tuckerman, the great nineteenth-century Unitarian minister whose Boston street ministry became the inspiration for mine, had noticed as soon as he began to visit the poor in their homes: "The traveler, having heard of the depression of the lower classes ... may ask," he wrote, "where are those ravenous and wretched beings. ...? The answer is, you see them not, because they are kept in the back ground by a power which is effectual for keeping them there; or, not a few may be near you, and you may not see them, because all your thought and interest are kept in constant excitement by the displays of wealth and greatness which are everywhere soliciting your observation."[2])

Two years earlier, I had cut out and filed away a *Boston Globe* magazine article about an Episcopal priest, Debbie Little, who had started Common Cathedral, an outdoor church for homeless people in Boston. The church met every Sunday near the Brewer Fountain on the Boston Common, steps away from the Park Street subway station. Why not stop by?

It had been a long time since I had done anything "good"—I had come up to Boston to help set up a black venture capital company, but my role there petered out and—other than a few antiwar demonstrations—I really hadn't done much since. And what I had done was all in my own back yard.

I had been attending King's Chapel, just two blocks further down Tremont Street from the Granary Burial Ground. So I didn't have to go far out of my way when I went looking for Common Cathedral one December morning, an hour before the service at King's Chapel be-

---

2. Tuckerman, *Sermon (Barnard and Gray)*, 30.

gan. No one was there. No one knew where Common Cathedral was or *what* it was. I went off to King's Chapel and, on way back to Park Street Station, an hour later, I stopped by again. This time, there were people there, all bundled up against the cold, standing in a circle near the empty fountain—they were from a Unitarian church in Concord. A makeshift wooden cross leaned against a shopping cart. Across the shopping cart lay a board, covered with a white cloth and there were a Bible, bread, a bottle of grape juice and little plastic cups on the white cloth. Some elderly men and women slumped on the park benches that circled the fountain. Others stood around in a small circle. And there was Debbie in the middle of the circle, a slender blond woman with a stole and a clerical collar, swaying back and forth against the cold. There were some prayers and chants I had never heard before. When it was over, the homeless men and women on the benches lined up in front of the shopping cart, now stripped of the white cloth, and the people from Concord served them a hot meal on plastic plates. It was bitterly cold, with a steady wind coming off the Common. I was dressed for church indoors, not outdoors, and my ankles went numb. I tried, to no avail, to regain some circulation in my feet by rocking back and forth.

No one in my family had ever been homeless. I didn't know anyone who was homeless. But I was deeply touched nonetheless. I introduced myself to Debbie and—imagining that I would hand out steaming cups of chicken soup and smile benignly on homeless people shuffling past me—I volunteered to help. Debbie didn't need more people to hand out cups of chicken soup, but she was very interested in the fact that I was an attorney. Would I volunteer my services as a lawyer for any homeless person attending her service?

I was then, and am now, a real estate lawyer, preserving open space throughout Massachusetts using limited development as a preservation tool. Open space preservation is about as far removed from the legal problems of the homeless in Boston as admiralty law. Homeless people have problems with obtaining and maintaining Social Security disability benefits, with bad debts, with Federal and state income tax deficiencies, with leases and tenancies and evictions, with all kinds of low level criminal problems to which the public defender program doesn't extend and with a seemingly endless array of other issues that I had neither studied nor practiced. My office was in my home in Winchester. Would homeless people come there? How would my wife feel about that? But without even the presence of mind to say that I'd think about it, I said yes.

I set up shop on the periphery of the circle of homeless people who gathered every Sunday at 1:00 to worship with Debbie. Debbie wanted the people who managed to get to the Brewer Fountain to pray, not to talk about their latest eviction notice. But it was the easiest way to meet my new clients and, in time, I learned to blend into the noise and movement at the edge of the prayer service. When it was pouring or sleeting or the temperature dropped below twenty degrees, we would talk at one of the tables in the basement of *Finagle a Bagle* across Tremont Street. Office hours were from 1:00 to 3:00 PM on Sundays, or until I could pull myself away. I invested in thermal underwear.

And my clients! Some I couldn't understand at all. Some had stories that they thought were legal problems, but were really stories about their descent into hell. Some were always drunk. Some were drinking and using drugs at the same time. Some were deranged and some were fugitives. All of them were broke. Most of all, my clients needed an attorney who would leave his office and come to *them*—just as they needed someone to bring them food and clothes and medical assistance and everything else that a human being needs to subsist from day to day—rather than expecting people who couldn't manage any part of their lives to go indoors to keep an appointment.

So long as I was prepared to practice law outdoors, I could see—and hopefully help—anyone who showed up for Debbie's church service. My practice began to resemble a jacked up, steroid fueled small town general practice. I handled everything under the sun, except for open space and admiralty problems. I had clients with patent problems and tax problems and sex offender registry problems and Social Security problems and Asperger's Syndome problems and problems in areas like cannon law that were utterly foreign to me.

It was easy to feel heroic helping chronically homeless men and women escape credit card debt and defending them against income tax deficiency assessments. With the help of two very fine accountants, one client expunged more than $250,000 in outstanding federal and state tax liabilities, although he developed dementia before he could take any satisfaction in it. Often, simply showing up in court made a tremendous difference. Creditors' attorneys—credit card debt collectors especially—handled twenty or thirty cases every day in the Suffolk or

Middlesex small claims courts. Almost any defense would work if an attorney presented it.

As my client list expanded, the very practice of law began to redefine itself. Issues of confidentiality and disclosure and conflicts of interest, to which I had paid virtually no attention before, came to take on meaning framed by the extraordinary collaboration among social workers, priests, lawyers, doctors, nurses and others who sought to ameliorate the suffering of the homeless men and women who attended Common Cathedral. I consulted experts in legal ethics and read extensively in the Christian or moral practice of law. I found new and more effective ways to work with other caregivers without compromising my professional ethics. My new legal practice was burnished by legal theory as well as heroic purpose.

I began to see that much of the time people who thought they had a "legal" problem or needed to talk to a lawyer only wanted to tell me a story about themselves. The framework for the story often had legal overtones—many people ascribed their homelessness to siblings or other relatives who had cheated them out of a rightful inheritance—but the claims often proved to be illusory. I would hear the same account over and over again and no amount of legal advice could shake people's conviction that they had been wronged. These were narratives that gave meaning to a person's life on the street and the people who related them wanted someone to listen to them and validate them. I couldn't justify spending time as a lawyer listening to the same people tell me time after time that they only needed to find a copy of their mother's will in order to claim their just portion of their parent's estate from their conniving brothers or sisters.

But I found that I was willing to listen anyway and give people the satisfaction of having an audience, so long as I wasn't depriving someone else of representation for a legal problem that could be defined and resolved as such. I began to think that I ought to add another arrow to my quiver—a role for myself in which providing such a presence was my primary purpose. I began to think, in short, that I was as much a minister who happened to be trained as a lawyer as I was a lawyer who wanted to help homeless people.

· · · · ·

My decision to become a minister didn't come out of nowhere. It just seemed that way. I grew up in a completely non-observant Reform Jewish household. My parents were classic second generation Jews whose own parents had emigrated from the Ukraine. They were eager to escape from Brooklyn and all things Russian and Jewish and they succeeded completely. Other than a Bar Mitzvah to satisfy my grandmother and the year of Hebrew school that preceded it, I grew up innocent of Judaism as a religion. This fit nicely with my father's abiding embarrassment at being Jewish. When I went to Yale, I arrived a blank slate regarding religion. I stayed that way for many years after. But now I see that Yale laid a foundation for my religious convictions.

The only person I knew at Yale when I arrived was Steve Wolfe, who had graduated from Manhasset High School two years ahead of me. Steve was going bald, even in high school, and walked with a sailor's roll. I did lots of things because Steve did them—played on our hapless tennis team and joined the dramatic club in high school, sung in the Apollo Glee Club and New Haven Chorale at Yale.

Steve had joined a charismatic group that met weekly in a small chapel at the base of the Harkness Tower to pray and speak in tongues. He urged me to take a course with Hans Frei, in which, improbably, I fell in love with Adolf Harnack's *History of Dogma* because it sounded as magisterial as *The Rise and Fall of the Roman Empire*. Steve was gay at a time when students at Yale didn't talk much about being gay. He joined Bankers Trust in New York after graduation and died of AIDS in the eighties.

Yale was where I experienced faith as aesthetics: faith expressed in painting, faith expressed in architecture, faith expressed in music. That was how I first understood faith. I understood faith that way—sensed it, really—listening to Monteverdi's Vesper setting of Psalm 147 at Evensong in King's College Chapel at Cambridge, England, late afternoon sunlight igniting the brilliant colors of the stained glass windows. I sensed it that way, much later, at the Church of the Advent in Boston, gazing up at the enormous crucifix suspended over the sanctuary, almost feeling the fabric of the priests' vestments as they processed by me.

Yale was also where I learned about faith as mission: faith as discipleship and faith as calling. In the early sixties Yale was a wonderful place to be for that. Between William Buckley and William Sloan Coffin,

Yale encouraged a muscular form of religious activism that had its roots in its founding as a theologically conservative alternative to Harvard. I had never before seen faith taken so seriously, much less serve as the basis for a vocation. As it turned out, these two ideas—faith as aesthetic expression and faith as mission—would come to frame a ministry that I wouldn't begin to imagine for another thirty years.

• • • • •

And for thirty years that was where things stood, until John Wortmann asked me to join him in a whirlwind tour of churches in and around Boston. John and I had become good friends while sitting on the Winchester Conservation Commission together. He was unhappy with his church, Second Church of Winchester, because it refused to become an Open and Affirming Church. He was determined to find another church and asked if I would go with him as he visited different churches in the area. In time, John lost his appetite for visiting a new church each Sunday, so I soldiered on alone. I was intrigued by each church's unique tone and style, by the radically different liturgies, by the different kinds of music and preaching I heard from week to week.

King's Chapel was the tenth or twelfth church I visited. Nominally Unitarian, King's Chapel uses a version of the Episcopal Book of Common Prayer. Instead of pews, it has boxes that can seat six to eight people. Benches run around the interior of the boxes so that some people were facing toward the pulpit and some people were facing toward the organ and choir at the rear of the church. When there weren't many people in church, you could face the pulpit for the sermon and then switch benches to face toward the organ when the choir sang an anthem. John found the boxes confining and isolating; I thought they were intimate and private. The music tended toward fifteenth-century English polyphonic composers. I especially liked the minister, Carl Scovel, whose preaching was both erudite and accessible. He had mastered the art of sounding, as he preached, as if he were having a conversation with you and you alone. I decided to stay.

Carl in person was as accessible as his preaching, although at first I was in awe of him. I talked with people only when I shared a pew box with them, and concentrated on getting it right: when to stand and when to sit, how to take communion. The Federal architecture, the congregational musical responses and the professionally performed music were transporting but intensely private. Small sensory experiences—feeling the hem of Carl's robe and hearing his whisper as he administered communion, being transported by the entire Holy Week liturgical experience—began to shape my experience of King's Chapel. I had never been in a church that appealed to me in so many ways.

•••••

I had found a vocation—providing *pro bono* legal services to the homeless. I had found two mentors—Debbie and Carl. I had found a church. And, much earlier, I had found a call to ministry, too.

The call had been there for a long while, but I didn't recognize it as a call. It didn't come nicely packaged or clearly labeled. I didn't see it because I wasn't ready to look.

I was walking through Grand Central Station one day, along one of the tunnels leading to Vanderbilt Avenue, on my way to a gathering at the Yale Club. It was a little after five and a constant stream of commuters poured through the tunnel. I was walking right along with them until I happened on an old black woman crouching in a small alcove. Her lined face was scrunched up, as can happen to people who have no teeth and no dentures. Her eyes were wide open and shifted rapidly from side to side as the crowd flowed by. She had been crying and her tears, where she had wiped them away, had relieved some of the grime on her cheeks. She was wrapped in a stained gray blanket; her feet, with socks but no shoes, poked out from the edge of the blanket. She was trying to get out of the alcove but she was too slow, too weak, too intimidated. The relentless pace of the passersby kept her pinned against the wall. I hesitated, and then I walked by.

Shortly after this, I saw a photo in the *New York Times* that powerfully evoked that experience of walking past the homeless woman. The photo is of a young woman in Pennsylvania Station in New York, shortly before the 1992 Democratic National Convention. She is sitting on the ground, cross-legged, her back against a wall. She is pretty, but distracted, and looks down at her lap. Commuters stream by her, paying her no attention. Her mouth is slightly open. She is having a conversation with herself. The young woman is not trying to make eye contact with the people walking by. Her hand makes a gesture of emphasis, as if she were arguing with herself. Who else should she talk to? No one will stop to talk to her. The young woman is wearing a cross. She is a

Christian. There are other Christians in the picture, but they are just walking by.

Like me. That is what I was doing in Grand Central Station. Just walking by.

But I was ready now. I had been out on the Common for four years. Now I could see people I hadn't seen before—people sitting in the slush in front of the Granary Burial Ground, people living under the bridges over Memorial Drive, people sleeping on the benches near the Frog Pond. I could see them and I could hear them and I wasn't afraid to get close to them. This was the call: I was called to stop, and not just walk by.

I just hadn't heard it clearly yet. But I began to hear it over time—see it, actually—talking with my homeless clients on the Boston Common.

I became aware, standing outdoors near the Brewer Fountain, that most people walked past Debbie's service, just as I had, without seeing anything. People—large Latino families taking their kids to wade in the Frog Pond, young adults holding hands on their way to the Public Garden, Gypsies selling rosettes—streamed by but, when I tried, I couldn't make eye contact with any of them. I remembered the old homeless woman in Grand Central Station and the young homeless woman in Penn Station. It was like being at the bottom of a deep well and looking up at the surface, where other people walked by.

Members of King's Chapel were also walking by. King's Chapel is located at the corner of School Street and Tremont Street, while its parish house is located on the other side of the Common. To get to the parish house for a reception or a meeting after services, you have to walk past the Brewer Fountain. People who knew me by name or by sight in church walked right past me on the Common without seeing me, because I was standing with a group of homeless men and women.

I had become as invisible as my homeless clients.

It was clear now. I was deeply shaken. I had, for that moment, fallen out of the world. Like Nathan Cole riding to Middletown to hear George Whitefield preach at the height of the Great Awakening nearly two hundred and fifty years ago, "by God's blessing, my old foundation was broken up, and I saw that my righteousness would not save me."[3] Education, experience, family and networks of friends and colleagues

---

3. Cole, *Spiritual Travels,* 89–92.

counted for nothing when I took on the aspect of a homeless person. But in the eyes of the world, my homeless clients were always invisible.

I decided to become an ordained minister and start an outdoor church in Cambridge.

· · · · ·

This book is about the Outdoor Church of Cambridge, viewed through the prism of the life, thought and ministry of the Rev. Joseph Tuckerman, a Christian Unitarian minister in nineteenth-century Boston. More and more, I have come to use Tuckerman's outdoor ministry to the poor of Boston as a way to think about all of us at the Outdoor Church and all of the homeless men and women who join us to pray, to speak and hear scripture and to administer and receive the sacraments.

Tuckerman, like me, decided late in life to take his ministry to the streets of Boston, the better to reach the poor, the homeless and the dispossessed. Tuckerman's career spanned the Unitarian Controversy. Although he was a close friend of William Ellery Channing, minister of the Federal Street Church in Boston from 1803–1842, and spokesman for the liberal churches in Massachusetts at the beginning of the nineteenth century, and although he knew most of the participants in the Controversy, Tuckerman's interests lay elsewhere: in the amelioration of the condition of the poor of Boston.

Immediately after concluding a career as the minister of the Congregational church in Chelsea, Tuckerman was asked by Channing and other Unitarian ministers to serve as the fledgling American Unitarian Association's first Minister-at-large to the poor. Tuckerman's career as a minister in Chelsea had been quiet and uneventful. Little in his academic, social or professional life suggested that he would do anything other than attempt to restore his failing health after retirement. But on assuming the Ministry-at-large, he immediately developed an intense and consuming interest in the social, economic and cultural conditions in which the poor of Boston lived and how those conditions hindered their progress toward the complete realization of their potential as human beings. Having no examples on which to model his ministry, Tuckerman walked the streets near the Boston docks, visiting people in their homes and talking with them about their circumstances, problems and hopes. He called this "friendly visiting." In the first two years of his ministry to the poor, before chapels were built to accommodate the throngs of poor people who flocked to him and his ministry, Tuckerman was a minister called to serve not a congregation meeting in a physical church but impoverished men and women, wherever they were, who needed his attention and care.

Tuckerman's ministry was not just anomalous, it was radical. He located the heart of Christian Unitarianism in the Great Commandment—to love God with all your heart and to love your neighbor as yourself—which pointed not just toward the Social Gospel movement but also toward radical Christian discipleship. He eschewed church, social distinction, denominational boundaries and political imperatives in his single-minded pursuit of love for the unlikable. But despite its echo in the Social Gospel movement and the subsequent phenomenal growth of the Unitarian Benevolent Fraternity of Churches, Tuckerman's ministry, which was intensely personal, died with him.

• • • • •

Tuckerman was not an obvious choice of a model for me. His path to a ministry to the impoverished and destitute was very, very different from mine. Born into an established Boston family, Tuckerman roomed at Harvard with Channing and Joseph Story, later to become Chief Justice of the Massachusetts Supreme Judicial Court. Throughout his life, he was one of the leading clergy of antebellum Boston and liberal Unitarianism. He was dull, stiff and largely uninterested in anything other than the social and religious issues which preoccupied him.

But I *liked* Tuckerman. I liked his willingness to start all over again when he could have retired in peace and comfort. I admired his ability to ponder new experiences and accept new ideas at a time in his life when most people avoid such challenges. I liked his use of his actual experience with the poor as the foundation of his ministry and I liked his confidence in the cogent and coherent practical theology that emerged from it. I liked the way he moved without hesitation from the most mundane pulpit ministry to the most radical street ministry simply by taking account of the evidence of his eyes. I liked his personal integrity and his courage in following the imperatives of his theology no matter where they led him. He didn't deny who he was in order to do what he needed to do; he was true both to his heritage and to his vocation. The poor people to whom he ministered sensed his love for them and respected him for his personal honesty and his commitment to their well being. I liked his equanimity in the face of such an emotionally challenging ministry: he didn't, as I am so prone to do, take personally the disappointments and failures of his ministry.

But I especially liked his seamless integration of a conservative character with a radical ministry. It made sense to me personally and it made sense to me theologically. I am cautious by disposition, not given to dramatic moves that might put me at variance with those whose approval I value. I know that it annoys people when I say that my ministry seems to me entirely normal and unexceptional. But it is important to me that I feel that way. That how I *want* to feel: normal and unexceptional, as if to say: it's not my fault that Christ's command is so clear. *I didn't write the stuff.* Without hesitation or qualification, Tuckerman created a ministry that is still radical today while remaining true to himself. That is what I most liked about him.

· · · · ·

In order to recommend me for ordination, my Committee on Ministry had to liberally construe the United Church of Christ requirement that every candidate for ordination have an ordainable call—and not coincidentally, a paying job—before she can be ordained. This was a great vote of confidence in my intended ministry. The same liberal impulse that propelled my ordination also encouraged me to build a practical theology for the Outdoor Church in a setting that could not have been anticipated by the ministers, theologians and teachers who shaped congregationalism. I was free to shape a congregational church in response to the lives of chronically homeless men and women and still remain comfortably within the congregational tradition.

Congregational tradition gave me all the theology I would need to make sense of my intended ministry, but it didn't provide me with many role models. I didn't know any United Church of Christ minister— actually, apart from Debbie, I didn't know any *person*—who was doing what I intended to do. Most of the clergy I admired came from apostolic, not congregational, denominations. There was something about the Episcopal Church and the Roman Catholic Church that encouraged ministries that seemed to be at variance with conventional church practice yet remained faithful to a core theology.

For me, Tuckerman would be that role model. His life before he began his Ministry-at-large to the poor of Boston was unexceptional and his ideas were general and unfocussed; his impulse to minister to the poor lay dormant for years. But when, by circumstance as much as by design, he was empowered to create a ministry for the benefit of rich and poor together, he instinctively chose a form of ministry—visiting the poor in their homes and on the streets—that balanced a radical ministerial practice with a very traditional theology. Almost immediately, his ministry encouraged great trust and affection in the people he visited. As his experience among the poor increased, his theology took on more substance, shape and direction, so that his experience and his thinking became so interdependent as to be indistinguishable. His theology seemed no different than the contemporaneous teaching of Harvard's moral philosophers; but his work on the streets of Boston transformed his Unitarianism into a form of discipleship.

• • • • •

Confident as he was, though, Tuckerman couldn't save himself (or me) from the physical and emotional impact of this kind of ministry. I went to the Harvard Divinity School to learn a language that would inform my commitment to minister to the chronically homeless men and women in Cambridge. I thought I had it. Anyone who can burst into tears reading about the Puritans' idea of sanctification has got *something*. But, although I now have a language—among the most beautiful and evocative ever used to describe human despair and human hope—I struggle to use it. I feel that—in my mind and heart—I am stuttering when I try to explain to myself and to others what I am trying to do.

And sometimes it is so terrible out there that I can't even talk about it. Sometimes, when I finally get home on Sunday night, it is as much as I can do to make a fire in the fireplace and watch something mindless on television. Sometimes I stammer when I describe my church; my preaching can be halting. Yet both the Old and New Testaments are full of people, like Jonah, whose words failed them. It is a weakness, but not a fatal one. I take heart in knowing that Paul found courage in this very weakness. "And I, brethren," he wrote to the Corinthians, "when I came to you, came not with excellency of speech or of wisdom, declaring unto you the testimony of God. For I determined not to know any thing among you, save Jesus Christ, and him crucified. And I was with you in weakness, and in fear, and in much trembling" (1 Cor 2:1–5).

2

Joseph Tuckerman

> The highest maxim of the most philanthropic statesman is, the greatest good of the greatest number. Human legislation can look no further. The characteristic rule and object of Christianity is, the greatest good of every individual. And its means are competent to its ends.[1]

JOSEPH TUCKERMAN WAS BORN IN 1778, THE SON OF EDWARD TUCKERman, a prominent baker and land owner.[2] Tuckerman and his college roommates, Joseph Story and William Channing, graduated from Harvard in 1798. Both Story and Channing had a low opinion of Tuckerman's prospects. An indifferent student, Tuckerman seemed to have no interests and no motivation. According to Channing, Tuckerman "had no serious view of life. Three years he passed as a holiday..."[3]

Despite his seeming lack of focus, Tuckerman was called to a ministry in Rumney Marsh (now Chelsea) where he served faithfully for twenty-five years. Among his parishioners he was remembered with affection and fondness for his unflagging pastoral activities.[4] Tuckerman's years in Chelsea were untroubled and unremarkable.[5] After many peaceful and pleasant years, Tuckerman could reflect: "It is a circumstance to excite strong emotions of gratitude and happiness,

---

1. Tuckerman, *Sermon (Barnard and Gray)*, 25.

2. "'I remember his telling me,' a friend informs us, 'that his father was a baker, who kept three hundred men at work.'" Carpenter, *Memoirs*, 2.

3. Channing, *Ministry for the Poor*, 27.

4. Carpenter, *Memoirs*, 13–14.

5. "Dr. Tuckerman was minister for twenty-five years, rendering faithful and useful service, but without accomplishing anything to distinguish himself from many other country ministers." C. R. Eliot, "Chapters in a Biography," 6.

that for twenty years we have lived together in uninterrupted union. Not a question has come before the church on which there has been division of opinion."[6] Not only the Unitarian Controversy, but also the extraordinary changes in Boston itself, and particularly its changing demographics, had little evident impact on his thinking.[7] Incipient throat cancer made it extremely difficult for Tuckerman to give two sermons every Sunday and he reluctantly resigned his pulpit in 1826.

As Tuckerman was contemplating retirement, Boston was undergoing a radical transformation. Prior to 1820, Boston had been a relatively homogeneous city of approximately 13,200 families, of which only 5,000 could not claim to have a church membership.[8] Shipping had fuelled Boston's growth since the Revolution. But, in the 1820's, Boston's commercial base shifted from shipping to industry. The sudden availability of many semi-skilled factory jobs drew immigrants from Ireland and encouraged young men and women to leave country farms all over New England and come to Boston. The industrialization of Boston also accelerated and deepened the division between Congregational churches adhering to the Orthodox Calvinist tradition and the more liberal, Arminian churches—soon to become Unitarian—with which Boston's new business elites were more comfortable.

With urbanization came urban problems. Although Boston was still a small city, it was now beset by big problems, including slum conditions, intemperance and neglected children. Immigration was increasing rapidly and brought with it a new urban lower class that included free Negroes, widowed and unwed mothers, the sick and crippled, alcoholics and prostitutes.[9] Along the waterfront, where immigrant families congregated, single cellar rooms housed families of three, four, five or more. Children of all ages lived on the streets, sent out by their parents

---

6. Tuckerman, *Sermon (Twentieth Anniversary)*, 12–13. For a description of the controversy between the liberal and orthodox wings of the church in Chelsea that broke out after Tuckerman's departure, see McColgan, *Tuckerman*, 304 n. 48.

7. Christopher Rhodes Eliot describes the apparently somnolent Tuckerman in Chelsea as a "High Arian, that is, a Unitarian of the most conservative type." C. R. Eliot, "Chapters in a Biography," chapter IVB, 5.

8. F. G. Peabody, "The Place of Joseph Tuckerman in the History of Philanthropy," 1133.

9. C. R. Eliot, "Joseph Tuckerman," 5.

to beg or sell their bodies.¹⁰ But for its lower density, Boston was beginning to look like Dickensian London.

The substantial increase in the number of Boston's poor directly impacted the churches of the Standing Order. By the 1830's, the population of Boston had reached 61,392. Poor immigrants made up almost all of this increase.

Boston responded to the wave of poor immigrants in a number of ways. It began to adopt poor laws modeled on regulatory schemes that had become prevalent in Europe, but cautiously, for fear that such legislation would institutionalize, even encourage, poverty. Its various denominations established privately funded benevolent societies. And it attempted, without success, to encourage immigrants to return to their towns or countries of origin.

Although at first Congregational churches were slow to recognize an opportunity for social outreach and evangelism, there were exceptions. As early as 1816, a conservative Congregational church, Old South, responded to the growing number of the poor in Boston. Old South had discovered that "the heathen were at our door" and that in certain parts of Boston (notably between Beacon Hill and the Charles River) there were "dance halls, grog shops, gaming houses and all the multiplied engines of Satan, in full and vigorous operation." Under the leadership of its minister, the Rev. William Jenks, Old South established Sunday Schools, distributed tracts, opened a school for blacks, provided preaching services and maintained a Bethel boarding house for sailors. But by 1826, Jenks had withdrawn to a more conventional church.[11]

The initial indifference of the Congregational churches to the growing numbers of the poor paralleled an unwillingness to incorporate the poor in their membership. If the newly arrived poor managed to find their way to the doors of the churches of the Standing Order, they were often isolated in easily identifiable parts of the sanctuary; since pews were normally rented or sold, when poor people did attend church they were relegated to humiliating "free" galleries, a practice that Tuckerman found odious.[12]

---

10. C. R. Eliot, "Chapters in a Biography," 5.
11. Ibid., 11, 12–13.
12. Tuckerman, *Principles and Results*, 47–55.

It required a growing awareness of relief programs run by Roman Catholic, Orthodox and Baptist churches to spur the Congregational churches to action. The idea of a Unitarian minister to the poor originated with an informal group of ministers who met for the first time on October 2, 1822, at the Brattle Square home of Madam Turrell, a philanthropist and adoptive grandmother of Frederick T. Gray, who would later join Tuckerman as an associate minister in Tuckerman's future Ministry-at-large. The group, "The Association for Religious Improvement," undertook the establishment of a Sunday school and a series of lectures for those poor who had not joined an existing church. The Rev. Henry Ware, to whom the phrase "Minister-at-large" is attributed, provided the preaching. In January 1823, a committee was formed to build a chapel and another committee formed to procure the services of a Minister to the Poor, but both efforts foundered when Ware's health declined.[13]

At the same time, and working more or less in parallel, Channing had organized a similarly informal group in February, 1822, called the Wednesday Evening Association, which sponsored a wide variety of charitable works. Tuckerman participated when his health permitted. The liberal ministers represented by the Wednesday Evening Association—especially Ezra Stiles Gannett, Henry Ware Jr., and James Walker—had become increasingly alarmed at the influx of poor Catholic and rural immigrants, most of whom clustered by the docks near what is now Boston Garden. They were equally concerned at the apparent indifference of the liberal churches, especially in light of the orthodox churches' efforts to evangelize Boston's poor.

In response, the American Unitarian Association was formed in 1825. The structure of the AUA generally followed the structure of other missionary organizations established by coalitions of the more conservative churches. The primary purposes of the AUA were the publication of tracts and the financial support of new and struggling churches.[14]

Channing had been involved in the stalled efforts to create a Ministry-at-large and participated, if peripherally, in the planning and organization of the AUA. He urged the AUA on May 17, 1826, to hire a

---

13. McColgan, *Tuckerman*, 308 n. 58.
14. Wright, *Congregational Polity*, 124–38.

minister for the poor.¹⁵ With Tuckerman already in mind, and encouraged by the board's response, Channing met with Tuckerman over the summer to propose that Tuckerman consider a position with the AUA once he retired from his pulpit in Chelsea. Tuckerman was interested, if uncertain about what precisely Channing was proposing. "In a favored hour," Channing wrote, "the thought of devoting himself to the service of the poor of this city entered his mind, and met a response within which give it the character of a divine monition."[16] Not content with divine monitions, Channing conveyed Tuckerman's interest to Gannett, then serving as Secretary to the AUA. In August, Gannett proposed that Tuckerman spend three months in a preaching tour in the western part of Massachusetts. Tuckerman declined, citing the difficulties of extensive travel in light of his ill health. The AUA again tried to engage Tuckerman. Roughly one month later, it offered to employ Tuckerman as a missionary to the poor in Boston at a salary of $600.00 a year.[17] Tuckerman accepted immediately.

The Ministry-at-large grew rapidly. By February 5, 1827, Tuckerman was regularly visiting fifty families. At the close of the next three months he had added two score more families; and by the end of twelve months he had assumed the care of a hundred and seventy families.[18] Aided by Moses Grant, a friend, philanthropist and early advocate of temperance, and Frederick T. Gray, soon to become his associate, he documented more than 1,900 visits to poor families in just the first year of the Ministry-at-large.[19]

On December 3, 1826, shortly after Tuckerman began to visit Boston's poor, he undertook a series of Sunday evening lectures in a small room he had rented over a paint shop in the Circular Building at the corner of Portland and Friend Streets. The space was less than ideal; the room was two flights up and difficult for older parishioners to reach. The space had open beams and brick walls. The windows rattled in the wind, and most surfaces were covered with soot. Tuckerman soon found himself exhausted by the preaching—it was, after all, why he had retired

15. McColgan, *Tuckerman*, 68.
16. Channing, *Ministry for the Poor*, 30–31.
17. McColgan, *Tuckerman*, 65.
18. Tuckerman, *Principles and Results*, 16–17; Carpenter, *Memoirs*, 26.
19. McColgan, *Tuckerman*, 120–21.

from Chelsea—but an appeal to Harvard did not produce any additional lecturers. Gray assumed responsibility for most of the preaching while he was organizing the Howard Sunday School for the children of those attending the lectures. The Sunday School also used the rooms at Smith's Circular Building. These meetings, called the 'Pleasant Hour,' were distinctly religious in character and yet astonishingly popular with the children who attended them.[20]

Freed of responsibility for some of the preaching, Tuckerman found the energy to lead the evening services and Sunday School sessions that met in the Circular Building. Increasingly, however, the space could not accommodate all who wished to come and the two flights of stairs remained a challenge for the elderly. Tuckerman urged the establishment of a permanent facility for the Ministry-at-large. At the end of his Second Quarterly Report to the AUA, he wrote, "If we could obtain a cheap building as a permanent place of worship, I think that it would not be difficult to obtain a supply of the pulpit half of each Sunday as well as for the evening service."[21] In response, the Association for Mutual Improvement launched a campaign to build a chapel. A committee managed to raise $2,000, purchased a lot on Friend Street and built a small meeting place.[22] For Tuckerman, this was a milestone: "I have been permitted to see this work completed and so important a stage attained in the work of giving permanence to the office of a ministry for the poor ... I now solemnly renew the dedication of myself, my heart, my life, to Thee and *to Christ in the poor*.[23] The ideas of permanence and continuity had become central to Tuckerman's project; he began to describe his work as a "permanent ministry for the poor of cities ..."[24]

At the same time, Tuckerman involved himself in many other contemporary movements and programs. Even before his retirement from the pulpit in Chelsea, he had attempted, unsuccessfully, to minister to sailors who served the merchant ships that docked in Boston.[25]

20. Ibid., 122.
21. Tuckerman, *First Annual Report*, 11–12.
22. Gray, "Origin of the Ministry-at-Large," 49:204–14; McColgan, *Tuckerman*, 131.
23. McColgan, *Tuckerman*, 131.
24. Ibid., 154.
25. Ibid., 35; Channing, *Discourse on Tuckerman*, 29–30.

He served as a member of the Boston Primary School Committee and urged the inclusion of all young boys and girls over the age of seven who were not yet ready for the Grammar Schools. He concerned himself with adolescent truancy, supported the establishment of the House of Reformation for Juvenile Offenders and campaigned for the employment of Boston's first truancy officer. He promoted a more sympathetic treatment of juvenile offenders in the courts. He helped establish the Farm School on Thompson's Island, where young people at risk of arrest and incarceration could learn practical skills like gardening or farming that might lead to future employment. He served as Overseer of the Poor and as an incorporator or director of innumerable public and private organizations for the elimination of poverty. He campaigned for better wages for female workers, temperance and, later in life, abolition of slavery.

As to temperance, poor farms, job training, education and penal reform—programs that provided for the practical improvement of the poor and eschewed gifts of money or other value—Tuckerman urged greater government involvement and expense. These were programs in which Tuckerman played an active and important role as a citizen of Boston and as a Unitarian minister. But his ministry to the poor sought the *moral* improvement of the poor, through the provision of carefully administered charity. Tuckerman was persuaded that government was incompetent to administer the distribution of alms. "There is no public provision, or associated exercise of charity," he said, "that can be substituted for individual obligations and individual responsibility."[26] He urged that more ministers and lay persons make friendly visits to the poor and develop personal and helpful relationships with them. Tuckerman never ceased to believe that if only private citizens would show more benevolence toward the poor, there would be no need for government intervention.

The expansion of the Ministry-at-large further taxed Tuckerman's fragile health. He again urged Harvard to provide him with students to assist him with the Sunday evening lecture-service, but the response was tepid. As early as November 7, 1828, the ministers of a number of Unitarian churches met to authorize Tuckerman to hire an associate, but it was not until August, 1832, that the AUA hired Charles

---

26. C. R. Eliot, "Joseph Tuckerman," 19.

Francis Barnard, then a student at the Cambridge Divinity School, as Tuckerman's associate. Barnard immediately assumed responsibility for the North End and the area in the vicinity of the Friend Street Meeting House; Tuckerman took the remainder. Frederick T. Gray, who was already deeply involved in the ministry, decided to seek ordination in 1832; after a preliminary trial period, he also was retained as an associate by the AUA in October, 1833.[27]

Tuckerman's health worsened. The AUA persuaded him to take some sabbatical time in England, where he impressed his hosts with his grasp of the theory and practice of working with the poor and with his singleness of purpose. He continued to develop new ways for the Ministry-at-large to help the poor. No sooner did Tuckerman return from Europe than the Ministry-at-large opened an office for a program called Visitors to the Poor in the basement of the Tremont Street Savings Bank. To this office, by the use of tickets, applicants for aid were referred.[28] One minister—after 1835, usually Tuckerman, because of his failing health—manned the office while the others made friendly visits to the families in their charge.[29]

Barnard and Gray were the first of a number of ministers who were retained to assist Tuckerman as he slowly and unwillingly withdrew from the day-to-day activities of the Ministry-at-large. The contributions of the new ministers were characteristically innovative. Barnard, for example, discovered in himself a great love of children, and organized a chapel on Warren Street for a children's ministry that drew on rich and poor children throughout Boston. More than 700 children and their families lined up to join the chapel before its doors even opened. Barnard asked popular guests to visit and developed innovative fund-raising programs, including an annual children's parade around the Boston Common on the Fourth of July at which the children sold flow-

---

27. Gray was surely the only Minister-at-large to have a song composed for him. George Kingsley respectfully dedicated "I Would Not Live Always," to Gray in 1833. The song's cover featured a picture of a dying man surrounded by his family, with the caption "The Christian's Death-bed."

28. McColgan, *Tuckerman*, 260. Typically, by encouraging wealthy church members to refer poor people to the office of the Visitors of the Poor for "investigation before aid was granted," Tuckerman encouraged the participation of the wealthy in the ministry while assuring them that their donations would be effectively and efficiently administered.

29. Ibid., 341.

ers.³⁰ By 1834, the Ministry-at-large consisted of Tuckerman's work in visiting and ministering to the poor in their own homes, two chapels, in which Barnard and Gray preached and conducted their Sunday services and the Tremont Street office of the Visitors of the Poor.³¹

As the AUA became increasingly absorbed in the extension of its administrative mandate and responsibilities, Tuckerman urged that a local coalition of twenty-six Unitarian Benevolent Societies assume exclusive oversight of the Ministry-at-large and its growing number of programs. The final plan of organization called for a central board of delegates representing the cooperating churches and an executive committee composed of five members. Tuckerman was made President and Henry B. Rogers Secretary. On July 21st, 1834, the executive committee of the American Unitarian Association transferred its interest in the Ministry-at-large to the executive committee of the new Benevolent Fraternity of Churches.³²

The institution of the Benevolent Fraternity of Churches coincided with a severe decline in Tuckerman's health. He had gone to Europe in 1834 in order to recover his strength and, while the trip had been professionally stimulating—Tuckerman had talked of nothing except

---

30. Charles Barnard typified the extraordinary character of the ministers who served as ministers-at-large during the first two years of the ministry, before the first chapel was built. Barnard, like Tuckerman, was "never much inclined to religious disputes." He was easily drawn away from his studies to see for himself how Christian charity worked in practice. While in divinity school, he spent a night at the House of Industry, where he shared a meal of rice pudding with the female inmates: "I woke several times during the night and, in spite of the toothache, laughed heartily at the idea of sleeping in an almshouse." Barnard was an innovative thinker and broadly accomplished person; he was one of the founders of the Boston Public Gardens and his successful fundraising for the chapels became a model for the Benevolent Fraternity of Churches. The challenges of the first two years of the Ministry-at-large may have contributed to his increasing instability. His ongoing disagreements with the Benevolent Fraternity of Churches were irreconcilable and he was asked to leave in 1864. He returned to the Ministry-at-large after many years, but his attempt to found a new children's chapel failed. He admitted himself to McLean Hospital in 1884 where he died six months later. See Tiffany, *Charles Francis Barnard*.

31. "By 1834, there were seven such ministers in Boston, of whom three were Unitarians, Dr. Tuckerman, Frederick T. Gray and Charles Barnard. In 1837, a fourth Unitarian was added, Rev. Mr. Sargent. In 1838, there were several other city missionaries at work under the Baptists and Congregationalists. Thus the city was soon fairly covered by this 'ministry-at-large.'" C. R. Eliot, "Chapters in a Biography," chapter V, 8.

32. McColgan, *Tuckerman*, 243.

his ministry to the poor—he returned no stronger than when he had left. He had already ceded the greater part of his preaching and lecturing responsibilities to Grey before he left; now, on returning, he was barely able to deliver the sermon at Barnard's and Grey's ordinations on November 2, 1834. Within the year, Tuckerman's health had forced him indoors.[33] By the end of the decade, he was too weak to continue in any capacity. Despite a number of trips intended to restore his health, he died in Havana, Cuba, on April 20, 1840.

• • • • •

Tuckerman's monument at Mt. Auburn Cemetery is inscribed: "His best monument is the Ministry-at-Large: His most appropriate title, the Friend of the Poor." In the spring of 2004, just before my own graduation from the Harvard Divinity School and a few months before my ordination, I gave a homily at Mt. Auburn Cemetery's annual Memorial Service held at Mt. Auburn Cemetery. America's first "garden cemetery," Mt. Auburn Cemetery is everything its designers could have hoped for, a paean to the natural landscapes for which Olmstead and his studio would become famous. I took a few minutes to look at Tuckerman's monument and stroll along the curved uneven paths. It was a glorious late spring day; a strong breeze blew across the courtyard where folding chairs had been placed in a semi-circle for the memorial and brought the quaking aspens to life.

It is right that the best memorial to an urban ministry lies in a bucolic setting; for, where his contemporaries saw only blight and corruption, Tuckerman found proofs of man's limitless capacity for improvement and self-realization.

• • • • •

As Arminianism gained traction within the Standing Order, the liberal churches became benevolent rather than sacramental communities.[34] The new function of these churches was philanthropy.

---

33. "Dr. Tuckerman passed much of his time in a central office [the Tremont Street office], to which the poor came for information which they wanted and the rich for knowledge of the poor." Carpenter, *Memoirs*, 94.

34. "Traditionally, only the converted members of the church had received the sacrament of the Lord's Supper. But as belief in predestination withered and Arminian ideas of self-cultivation gained acceptance in the vicinity of Boston, the old theological

The idea of the church as an engine for benevolence was formally developed at Harvard, where the liberals had effectively seized power in 1806 with the appointment of Henry Ware, Sr., as Hollis Professor of Divinity and the election of Samuel Webber as President. At Harvard, the benevolent impulse was embodied in a moral philosophy that was to hold sway at Harvard until the Civil War.[35] "You know not what means of personal good and happiness you are disregarding while you neglect . . . Christian benevolence," said Tuckerman. The memory of philanthropy "will bring more gladness to your heart in the prospect of death than a remembrance of all your worldly success."[36]

Unitarian philanthropy sought not material but moral improvement, although material improvement was likely to follow; indeed, material gain was an indicator of moral advancement. For early 19th century Unitarians, chronic or endemic dependence on charity was a disease, like small pox, that society needed to expunge.[37] By encouraging dependency and relieving the recipient of philanthropy of the need for self-regulation, heedless charity encouraged the very behaviors, like intemperance and sloth, that had led him into his pitiful condition in the first place.[38]

Tuckerman's experience in Boston's slums made it impossible for him to dogmatically ascribe poverty to immorality. He saw that complicated webs of duties and responsibilities—a child's dependence on an alcoholic father, or a wife's reliance on an unemployed husband—often precluded simple moral judgments about poverty. Rather than lump all poor people together under one moral heading to avoid such "perplexing" difficulties, he looked to his own direct experience of poverty for guidance:

---

basis for distinguishing the 'elect' from the 'damned' was eroded. When . . . the Liberal meeting houses began to open their communion tables to all, the church was left without its customary special function." Howe, *Unitarian Conscience,* 237. See Laws, "American Unitarian Eucharistic Faith."

35. See generally Howe, *Unitarian Conscience,* 2–120.
36. Tuckerman, *On the Elevation of the Poor,* 139.
37. Ibid., 12.
38. In arguing *against* "soup-houses and two or three depositories of vegetables," Tuckerman cautioned: "The indolent and intemperate will therefore not only obtain their full share of the bounty, but they will sell that which you give them for good for the very means of indulging this intemperance, which is perhaps, above all others, the cause of their poverty and suffering." Tuckerman, *Elevation of the Poor,* 87.

> We say [alms] should not be given to the drunkard. But the wife and children of the drunkard, or of the intemperate man who is not recognized as a drunkard, may be without food, without fuel, without comfortable clothing and wholly innocent in respect to the causes of their destitution. How far, in these cases, should we extend, or withhold our alms[?][39]

Tuckerman concluded that the distinction was in the recipient, not in the alms. "The best resources for improving the condition of the poor," he said, "are within themselves...they often need enlightenment respecting these resources more than alms."[40] The virtuous poor he identified as those impoverished by disease, permanent debility or old age, the temporarily poor, who were doing what they could for self-support but who needed occasional and temporary aid, and the innocent: orphans, deserted children, widows and others whose dependence on others left them helpless and without resources. "Pauperism," on the other hand, was a dependence on alms, evident in the idle but able-bodied, the intemperate and the improvident. These were the undeserving poor, in whom the risk of dependency on the charity of others was especially great.[41] "I am ready," Tuckerman wrote in an 1828 report, "as far as it may be done, to maintain, and to act upon, the principle, 'if a man *will not* work, neither shall he eat.' But if he *cannot* work, or cannot obtain employment—and strange as it may seem to some, this is a very possible case—nor eat, except he obtain the bread of charity, shall it be witholden?"[42]

Tuckerman's distinction was hailed as an extraordinary insight by Baron Gerando, the then acknowledged European expert on public welfare: "[Tuckerman] knew the difference between pauperism and poverty," Gerando wrote admiringly.[43]

Unitarians appreciated the need to accurately distinguish between the deserving poor and the morally debauched. The object of philanthropy was moral uplift. The less deserving (or morally degraded) the recipient of alms, the greater the need for competent supervision of their distribution to ensure that moral improvement, rather than degra-

39. Tuckerman, *Letter on the Principles of the Missionary Enterprise*, 42–43.
40. Tuckerman, *First Annual Report*, 7–8.
41. Ibid., 69.
42. Tuckerman, *First Semiannual Report*, 14.
43. Hale, "Introduction," 7.

dation, would result. The risk was not insignificant: "The thousand evils which certainly follow from reckless distribution of alms are so great that any man of sense or of prudence like Dr. Tuckerman resolutely studies the methods of abating them."[44] The primary reason for the formation of the Benevolent Fraternity of Churches was the perceived need to efficiently and effectively coordinate the administration of the gift of alms by many churches from different denominations.

Such a calculating approach to the dispensation of philanthropy led naturally to an appreciation for "scientific" social work. Tuckerman read widely, traveled to Europe twice to learn about Continental public and private welfare systems, kept extensive records and reported regularly and comprehensively to the American Unitarian Association and, later, the Benevolent Fraternity of Churches. His devotion to scientific methods assured his financial supporters by applying business-like methods to the distribution of material support, implicitly limiting the number of people competent to manage such an enterprise to people like themselves.

The shift of church function from sacramental to benevolent, the application of rational methods to the distribution of alms and the increasing numbers of poor German and Irish immigrants crowding the docks of Boston all prompted an increase in organized philanthropy among the liberal churches. "Men are beginning to feel, as they never did before, that there is an important sense in which every one is his brother's keeper."[45] Many ministers, like the Rev. Nathan Parker of the Liberal South Parish in Portsmouth, New Hampshire, devoted his church primarily to charity. His philanthropic program, which he presented at the Berry Street Conference of 1822, was highly influential.

• • • • •

For most liberal Unitarians, the moral philosophy taught at Harvard at the time of the Unitarian Controversy was the basis for an ethical life; for Tuckerman, it was the basis for a theology.

Tuckerman was not a conventional, systematic theologian. His DD from Harvard recognized his long years of service in Chelsea, not academic achievement. Insofar as he had a theology when he began

---

44. Ibid., 8.

45. J. Walker, "Reason, Faith, and Duty," 237.

his Ministry-at-large, it reflected the same principles of moral philosophy that shaped the thinking and actions of his contemporaries, both in and out of Harvard. Like them, Tuckerman sought to make these moral principles operational. The principles included a belief in the perfectibility of all people, no matter what their circumstance, education or background; the moral responsibilities of the middle and upper classes; the universal creation of men and women in the image of God; and the love of others as the highest achievement of Christian life.[46] He was convinced of the efficacy of the Unitarian message. "Christianity would remove, or enable every individual to surmount, every obstacle in the way to the highest moral completeness within his attainment," Tuckerman insisted. "It would make the servant morally as perfect as his master."

However, unlike many of his peers at Harvard, Tuckerman understood Unitarian moral philosophy to be clearly grounded in theology. "Admit a moral government of the world, and that man has a moral nature," he argued, "and it follows that the moral necessities of those near and around us ... are to be regarded as divine calls upon us."[47]

The substance of that call was a sympathetic benevolence of the wealthy to the poor:

> I think it is contemplated by our religion that the more favored classes should strongly feel that they have a common nature with those in less favored conditions of life; that opportunities and means are responsibilities; and that it is God's will that they should be his instruments for accomplishing the purposes of his benevolence to the poor.[48]

At Chelsea, Tuckerman gave voice to this moral philosophy in conventional terms. He believed in a loving God whose mercy was much more important than his judgment and he believed in the perfectibility of man:

> There is no human being, however, depraved, who is yet totally depraved, no one for whom moral efforts are not to be made as long as God shall uphold him in being. No one, therefore is to be given up, abandoned, cast off as a sinner, whatever may have

---

46. Tuckerman, *Elevation of the Poor*, 106.
47. Tuckerman, *Principles and Results*, 32–33.
48. Tuckerman, *Elevation of the Poor*, 94–95.

been his long continuance, and whatever may be his hardihood and his desperation in sin. This was a first principle of that theory of human nature with which I entered upon my ministry.[49]

Tuckerman never wavered in his belief in the perfectibility of even the most corrupted and dissolute of the poor people he came to know so intimately: "Every human being has a nature by which he is qualified [assuming proper instruction] for endless intellectual and moral progress."[50] The doctrine of perfectibility was the foundation of any effort to reach and save the poor, no matter how disadvantaged or seemingly limited.[51]

The model for that perfection was Jesus, the exemplar of absolute moral perfection. In Tuckerman's theology, all are encouraged to move progressively closer to Jesus' example.[52] "It is the design of our religion," he wrote, "not merely to establish a more perfect system of ethics, than had before been taught, and to bring immortal life to the light of perfect day; but, by its instruction concerning the character and government of God, its warnings and threatenings against sin...to bring man to the highest moral exercises; to the most perfect virtue; to the purest devotion; and to preparation for heaven."[53]

The highest moral exercise was the fulfillment of the Great Commandment to love your God with all your heart and to love your neighbor as yourself.[54] Like his contemporaries at Harvard who taught moral philosophy, Tuckerman found confirmation of God's commandment of love in a law of nature that inspires us to love others as ourselves:

> That man should sympathize with man, that he should feel an interest, deep and strong, in the condition of his fellow-men; and, especially, that we should be affected, and strongly affected, by the wants and sufferings, not only of those around us, but of

49. Tuckerman, *Principles and Results*, 88–89, 106. "Dr. Channing was also convinced that the ministry-at-large was a distinctive product of Unitarian moral philosophy, and, in a rare expression of exclusiveness, opposed co-operating with other denominations in it." Howe, *Unitarian Conscience*, 370 n. 24.

50. Tuckerman, *Principles and Results*, 231.

51. Ibid., 314–15.

52. Tuckerman, *Sermon (Dewey)*, 4, 10.

53. Ibid., 13–14.

54. Mark 12:28–34.

our whole race, I fear not to say is as much a law of our nature, as it is that we should feel a deep and strong interest in those who are immediately connected with us, in the nearest relations of life; or, as it is, that we should love ourselves.[55]

God's command to love others thus demonstrates God's intention that man be the instrument of his love for mankind.[56] For Tuckerman, moral philosophy was a proof text for his theology. He understood Christian charity as a theological rather than a moral duty. "God designs that man shall be his instrument, for imparting the blessings of Christianity to man; and he, who has the means, and the opportunities, thus to benefit his fellow creatures, will be held responsible at the bar of heaven, for the execution of the work which God thus requires of him."[57] He insisted that loving relations are a theological response to God's plan for creation—the "completion of the plans of God, for the moral renovation of the world"[58]—and not simply the response of concerned citizens to social problems. "Christian benevolence will never hesitate upon the question, whether it *shall* act, where it *may* act, for the good of others. It can no more live without this action, than the selfish principles can live without action for its own indulgence."[59]

As Tuckerman's Ministry-at-large continued, his preoccupation with moral obligation intensified. He constantly urged the satisfaction of an obligation to others: ministering to the poor, raising money from his peers, petitioning the state house in support of truancy legislation. His sense of duty to others was palpable. Tuckerman wrote in a letter to "ER": "[O]ur danger lies, not in our liability to erroneous conceptions of Christian doctrine, but in our defective sensibility to Christian obligations, and in our poor and low standard of Christian duty."[60]

• • • • •

Heretofore, Unitarian benevolence had been a one-way street: the wealthy extended charity to the poor because it was their moral ob-

---

55. Tuckerman, *Missionary Enterprise*, 30.
56. Ibid., 31–32.
57. Ibid., 30.
58. Tuckerman, *Sermon (Dewey)*, 12.
59. Ibid., 23–24.
60. Carpenter, *Memoirs*, 93.

ligation to do so. Indeed, because, in Tuckerman's view, Christianity more than any other ethical system required the rich to help the poor, Christianity was the most likely hope of any permanent improvement in the circumstances of the poor or of the prevention of pauperism and crime.[61] But this benevolence was dry and unappealing, a duty with no corresponding benefit or pleasure other than that it had been satisfied. It was no wonder that so few chose to engage in it. Here was the difficulty with the Christian project in a nutshell: the message was simple but its realization nigh unto impossible. Undeterred, Tuckerman, embracing Anselm of Canterbury's dictum that theology is faith seeking understanding, hardly paused to think about what form and direction his Ministry-at-large would take before he set out for the streets of Boston.

Once again, the Unitarians at Harvard gave Tuckerman a morally satisfying basis for his ministry of benevolence. In the view of the Harvard Unitarians, scientific philanthropy did more than fulfill God's injunction to attend to the moral improvement of those in need: it also furthered the moral improvement of the donor. Philanthropy was the most promising means by which the wealthy could incorporate Christian principles in their lives.[62] The rich needed the poor because the poor provided the rich with the most efficient and effective means toward their moral improvement. In short, the rich and the poor depended upon one another for moral improvement.

For Tuckerman, mutuality of dependency created a mutuality of responsibility. The poor were responsible for the moral improvement of the wealthy—expressed as willing participation in the philanthropic project. The wealthy, for their part, were responsible for the moral improvement of the poor—to be evidenced by the scientific administration of alms. The mutuality of responsibility between the rich and the poor was thus the foundation on which progressive Christian life rested.[63]

In philanthropy, Tuckerman found the perfect synthesis of the idea of Unitarian redemption and its realization. Unitarians looked to gradual moral self-improvement as the means to the inward transfor-

---

61. Tuckerman, *On the Elevation of the Poor*, 136–37.

62. Tuckerman, *Principles and Results*, 81.

63. Like so much of Tuckerman's thinking, the idea of the interdependence of rich and poor echoed a much earlier Christianity. See *Shepherd of Hermas*, cited in Johnson, *Fear of Begging*, 25.

mation of the personality. That transformation led the Unitarian closer to Jesus' example and to communion with God. But since character development depended on individual effort, divine acceptance waited on human success; unlike the Calvinists, the Unitarians aspired to raise themselves up to God.[64]

Philanthropic gifts that resulted in the self-improvement of both the donor and the recipient were the means at hand.

In the minds and mouths of socially conservative Unitarians, this symbiosis could seem extremely mechanical and cold hearted. The poor, they argued, were necessary to the order and stability of this world and the next. Their elimination would require a fundamental reorganization of nature itself.[65] At best, it was the subsistence of the poor, and decidedly *not* their transformation, that was the proper object of Christian condescension.

But the need Tuckerman had in mind was spiritual; it was not satisfied by writing out a check. Suppose, he wrote, that welcoming poor people into our churches would bring "great numbers of the poor into our Religious societies, with a view to the alms to be obtained through this connexion? And suppose it should? Might not this very circumstance, if wisely availed of, be made an important means of the best Christian improvement, both of the rich and the poor?"[66] A Christian church should be an association of the rich and the poor, precisely so that their apparent conflicts of interest might be harmonized within the framework of religious practice. Philanthropy began with individual material differences and ended with mutual spiritual gain. The moral improvement of all was insured without having to challenge the existing economic order. In no better way could the virtue of all be so successfully advanced.[67]

---

64. See Howe, *Unitarian Conscience*, 118–19.

65. S. A. Eliot, "Eighth Semi-Annual Report," 124. See Parkman, "Public Charities," 368. Parkman argued: "'The poor ye shall always have with you'—is not only the declaration of him who came to relieve them, but is a part of the established constitution of the world. It is the positive ordinance of God, the will and pleasure of the general moral Governor, that the poor shall never cease from the land." And see generally Posey, "Poverty Encounters."

66. Tuckerman, *Missionary Enterprise*, 31.

67. Ibid., 33–35.

3

Tuckerman's Ministry at Large

> A man must not expect only to live and do good to himself, but he should see where he can live to do most good to others; for, as one saith, "He whose living is but for himself, it is time he were dead."[1]

> When it pleased God in His providence so far to deprive me of health that I could no longer preach twice on Sunday, I left the place and the ministry, and removed to my native city; and there, wishing still to continue the service to which my heart was early consecrated, and not being desirous to take charge of another congregation, I directed my attention to those who were the leavings of the congregation in the city where I had taken my residence.[2]

DESPITE HIS CONVERSATIONS WITH CHANNING, TUCKERMAN INITIALLY had no specific plan for his Ministry-at-large: "I have no set rules to propose to any one," he later said, "for I have none for myself."[3] Having no specific instruction from the AUA about his new position, Tuckerman simply took every available opportunity for social action. He immediately involved himself with preaching to the poor, the plight of "market boys" (truants who loitered in the street markets near the docks), free admission to Massachusetts General Hospital for poor people, prison conditions, a school for juvenile delinquents, employment for discharged convicts, adolescent addiction to alcohol, medical care for drunkards, the advancement of public schools for young children, jobs and job training for unemployed boys and girls and visits to asylums

---

1. Robert Cushman, cited in Heimert and Delbanco, *Puritans in America*, 43.
2. Tuckerman, *Address*, 318 n. 1.
3. Drummond, "Report of the Minister-at-Large," 3.

for the insane and the poor, to prisons, to jails, to poor houses and to schools, among many similar activities.

Tuckerman's approach was distinctly ecumenical. A number of social relief programs had been put in place by other churches before he began working as a Minister-at-large. Their representatives—including Orthodox Congregationalist, Methodist, Roman Catholic, Baptist and Episcopalian ministers and priests—gathered occasionally to promote and coordinate these programs. Tuckerman sought to establish working relations with them. "We met from week to week as fellow-laborers in one cause, to pray together, and freely to communicate with each other."[4] Because so many of the immigrant poor came from Catholic countries, the Roman Catholic church was especially involved in this effort.

At the same time, Tuckerman studied as much of the literature on the poor as he could obtain. He read reports from both American and English penal institutions, and studied the poor laws in both countries. But the most immediate influence on his thinking was the work and writing of the Rev. Thomas Chalmers of Glasgow, Scotland.[5] Chalmers was an implacable opponent of indiscriminate giving to the poor, on one hand, and state intervention in the care for the poor, on the other. Chalmers believed in the essential dignity of each individual and in the possibility of a "scientific" approach to care-giving for the poor, based on the gathering, analysis and use of statistical evidence and actual observation of the impact of charitable programs on their intended beneficiaries. His thinking emphasized local administration, concentration on self help and character building, utilization of neighborhood resources and friendly visiting.[6] It was Chalmers who had first distinguished between "poverty" and "pauperism." He believed that government aid programs discouraged private care for the poor and created a dependency in the poor that prevented them from escaping their poverty. But when Chalmers' philanthropic program was instituted in Glasgow, it failed, perhaps because it required from both government and the church a radically different approach to caring for the poor.[7]

4. Tuckerman, *Principles and Results*, 19.

5. McColgan, *Tuckerman*, 100–101; F. G. Peabody, "Place of Tuckerman in the History of Philanthropy," 1133. And see Chalmers, *Christian and Economic Polity of a Nation*.

6. McColgan, *Tuckerman*, 102–3 n. 21.

7. Tuckerman's interest in the study of poverty and its amelioration continued throughout his Ministry-at-large. He followed his formal study of Chalmers' work

There was much about Chalmers' program that appealed to Tuckerman but its failure in Glasgow made him hesitate to make it the basis for his nascent ministry to the poor. Tuckerman, in any event, began not with a program but with a religious principle. He sought to "call forth in man a Christian sentiment of man—to bring man in every condition before his fellow-man, as Christ has revealed us to ourselves and to each other."[8]

Tuckerman immediately gained a great deal of practical experience with poor people by walking the streets of Boston, introducing himself as a minister and inviting himself to their homes and into their lives to share his ministry with them: "[T]he most important offices of the Christian ministry may be extended to thousands in their homes, who, while their condition shall remain what it is, are not to be collected into religious societies."[9] From the beginning, Tuckerman understood that his ministry depended upon going to where the poor were: in their homes, on the streets, in schools and in jails. "If the mountain would not come to Mohammed, then Mohammed must go to the mountain."[10] The directness and intensity of this experience radically transformed both his practical understanding of ministering to the poor and the theology that underlay it.

Tuckerman went out into the streets of Boston, by the docks near Causeway Street, introducing himself to people he identified by their dress and talk as poor. His object was to render to the poor "any and every service which could be demanded of a Christian pastor and friend."[11] He went door to door, visiting families who appeared to him impoverished and without any connection to a church. Household visits quickly became the center of Tuckerman's ministry.[12] He invited himself into people's homes, spoke at length with husbands, wives and children and returned over and over again, establishing affectionate and

---

with a reading of *Visitor of the Poor* and other works by Baron Joseph Marie Gerando. Ostensibly to restore his health, but primarily to continue his study, he traveled to Europe in 1834–35, where he met Lynnna Baillie, Lucy Aikin, Harriet Martineau, Lady Noel Byron, Elizabeth Fry and other European reformers.

8. Carpenter, *Memoirs*, 105.
9. Tuckerman, *Principles and Results*, 28.
10. Tiffany, *Charles Francis Barnard*, 10.
11. McColgan, *Tuckerman*, 120.
12. Ibid., 119.

continuing relationships. Because he knew intuitively that to intrude on a poor person or family in order to satisfy one's own moral obligations without offering something in return could be, at best, self-serving and, at worst, exploitive, he offered occasional assistance out of what he called his "poor's purse"—a cord of wood, clothing, some money and so on.[13]

Tuckerman was stunned by what he found. He learned more about the poor in his first year on the streets of Boston than he had ever learned in all his years in Chelsea.[14] He gained a first hand knowledge of the grinding poverty in which immigrants lived, saw the ravages that drinking made in family life, saw young children sent out to steal and prostitute themselves and witnessed young widows and old invalids slowly starving to death. He saw the filth and the fetid, unsanitary conditions in which the poor tried to raise their children, the dead animals thrown into the Frog Pond on the Common and the dripping carts of the "nocturnal gold finders" and night soil men who went door to door collecting human waste (even as the new Tremont House offered its patrons indoor plumbing: eight chambers with bathtubs and eight water-closets.)[15] Immediately, Tuckerman sloughed off any preconceptions he had about the poor and developed an understanding of poverty based almost entirely on what he saw and heard.

The poor instinctively recognized Tuckerman as their friend, and "from the first moment, a relation of singular tenderness and confidence was established between them."[16] Visiting with the poor in their homes, Tuckerman brought to bear his respectability, sincerity and openness. He hoped to be welcomed into the spiritual lives of the poor by the poor themselves. The moral, rather than the material, was of the utmost importance. Tuckerman's object was to make better people, although relieving the effects of poverty was not incidental. He was constantly astonished at how much they liked him—probably as astonished as they were to have a minister visit them in their homes. In his lifetime, the number of poor reached by his ministry increased as fast as he and his associates could make visits. Tuckerman was not charismatic—people

13. Tuckerman, *Principles and Results*, 100–103.
14. C. R. Eliot, "Chapters in a Biography," chapter VII, 14.
15. Larkin, *Reshaping of Everyday Life*.
16. Channing, *Memoirs*, 3:384.

didn't flock to him because of the excitement of his presence—but he conveyed a genuine affection for his people that they immediately sensed and appreciated. Improbably, this stiff, reserved and undemonstrative man evoked the deepest affection in those whom he served. Channing eulogized him as one called to love the poor:

> He could not be kept from the poor. Cold, storms, sickness, severe pain, could not shut him up at home. . .It was his delight to relate examples of patience, disinterestedness, piety, amidst severest sufferings. These taught him, that, in the poorest hovels, he was walking among immortals, and his faith in the divinity within the soul turned his ministry into joy.[17]

• • • • •

If the deserving poor were not solely responsible for their poverty, who else were? Tuckerman was not afraid to ascribe responsibility to the wealthy and did not hesitate to claim that the rich were accountable for much of the world's poverty. Tuckerman saw the causes of poverty "in the spirit of monopoly, in the luxury and extravagance and profligacy of the more favored classes, and in the low estimation in which the more affluent hold and have ever held the humbler of their fellow beings."[18] There was a direct connection between the actions of the wealthy and the conditions of the poor: "Nor can [taverns, gambling-houses, the theatre and the brothel] exist and be patronized by the rich without extending their deadly influence to the poor."[19]

Tuckerman reached this conclusion by overlaying his direct experience with the impoverished on a theology that, at least in theory, assumed the moral equality of all.[20] Tuckerman's tenure in Chelsea and his view of Boston as one big parish made it easier for him to see the poor with the same empathy with which he viewed his own peers. The poor, he told his supporters, were no different than him or them; they shared the same qualities, the same instincts, the same moral expectations.[21]

---

17. Channing, *Ministry for the Poor*, 32–33.
18. Tuckerman, *On the Elevation of the Poor*, 101.
19. Ibid., 105.
20. Tuckerman, *Principles and Results*, 246.
21. Ibid., 98–99.

As the poor were similar to the rich, the rich were similar to the poor. Insofar as wealth was inherited, it did not entitle its recipient to any greater moral status than one who had inherited nothing: "Let any one look about him and ask, who were the grandfathers and the fathers of our rich men? And who were the fathers and grandparents of our paupers and criminals?"[22] In the area of moral achievement, the children of the rich held no advantage over the children of the poor.[23]

Tuckerman's convictions that the wealthy and the poor were moral equals and that the wealthy and poor shared responsibility for the economic condition of the poor were mutually reinforcing. Strengthened by his direct encounters with the poor, Tuckerman concluded that this mutuality of obligation implied mutuality of rights: "There is no right that stands out in a clearer or stronger light to my mind, than is that of the intellectually and morally necessitous, who cannot provide for their own necessities, to a provision for those necessities by those who are able to make it . . ."[24] How, after all, could it be otherwise in a Unitarian God's creation, where the pursuit of moral improvement was the functional equivalent of the road to salvation?

In particular, Tuckerman saw the economic rights of the poor as a limitation on the rights of the rich to aggregate wealth regardless of the cost to the poor:

> [The] right to accumulate property is a most distinctly limited right . . . the right to alms by those who *would*, but *cannot* obtain the means of subsistence, and of those who have not *ability* to provide for their own subsistence, and equally the right of those to moral aids who cannot provide for their moral necessities, is in each case a divinely appointed limitation on the right to accumulate wealth for ourselves . . .[25]

Harking back to John Cotton and early Puritan economics, Tuckerman revived the medieval Christian concept of a "just wage" as applied, for example, to the issue of equitable wages for working women

---

22. Tuckerman, *On the Elevation of the Poor*, 125–26.
23. Ibid., 87.
24. Tuckerman, *Principles and Results*, 308.
25. Ibid., 312.

in Boston.[26] Theology, not economics, drove his concern for the material welfare of those to whom he ministered.

• • • • •

Despite the growing respect for his work among his contemporaries, what Tuckerman held together during his lifetime came apart at his death. His health had deteriorated so badly by 1834, the date on which the Benevolent Fraternity of Churches assumed administrative responsibility for the Ministry-at-large, that he was effectively forced to discontinue his own visiting with the poor. Despite Tuckerman's annual pleas for more support from the ministers of his supporting churches, only his immediate associates shared his willingness to visit people in their homes.

Without Tuckerman's constant presence on the street, the Ministry-at-large drifted away from friendly visiting. It came to depend increasingly on indoor programs designed for chapels built by the Benevolent Fraternity of Churches to accommodate all of the poor people who had been drawn to the Ministry-at-large by Tuckerman's friendly visits.

Growing reliance on the chapels virtually insured that those among the poor who would not or could not go indoors—the very people to whom Tuckerman sought to minister—would no longer be served by the Ministry-at-large.[27] By 1870—the height of the Social Gospel movement—the Benevolent Fraternity of Churches had built and was administering five chapels all over Boston, together with a flower farm, a work farm and many other programs of social improvement for the poor. But the ministry had long before ceased to be a ministry to those who were so poor and so distressed that they could not find their way into a chapel or a program:

> [I]n their collective response to poverty in the free chapels, the ministers-at-large, with the exception of John Turner Sargent, largely dismissed those poor who were unable or unwilling to attend Sunday services. These men and women were usually the most needy of Boston's poor, men and women shut in the dank cellars of the city's hovels, to whom Tuckerman had been able to provide at least a ray of hope.[28]

---

26. See generally Tuckerman, *Essay on the Wages Paid to Females*.
27. Posey, "Poverty Encounters," 159f.
28. Ibid., 261.

While it lasted, Tuckerman's Ministry-at-large infused the emerging liberal Protestantism of his era with an urgency and immediacy that could only be sustained by the intensity of religious conviction. Tuckerman was, literally and figuratively, on a mission. But his theology was too radical at base to survive his example. It demanded too much. It required of liberal Protestants a life lived as an overarching Christian vocation, not simply a set of convictions that were subsumed in a larger, more liberal New England character. For Tuckerman, his work was his life and his life was the expression of his faith. He was able to live his theology because his theology had emerged from his life.

· · · · ·

Tuckerman was an enthusiastic supporter of public programs for the poor if they led to the moral improvement of those who received their benefits. He helped organized the Boston Children's Mission and a farm school, originally located on Thompson's Island and later merged with the Boston Asylum for Indigent Boys. Because his encounters with poor families had given him a strong sense of the difficult conditions that discouraged poor children from starting or continuing their education, he worked for the reform of the House of Reformation and urged the appointment of Boston's first truancy officer to encourage Boston's boys to stay in the fledgling public school system for as long as possible. He promoted the incarceration of the deeply insane in lunatic asylums rather than in jails and lobbied for the merciful sentencing of the mentally disturbed. He was active—as were so many of his peers—in the Temperance and Prison Reform movements and—although he was slow to translate an early exposure to the slave trade in South Carolina into opposition to slavery as an institution—he became a forceful Abolitionist. All these were ways to improve the moral condition of the recipients of public and private attention.

However, the distribution of grants, gifts or subsidies—all of which Tuckerman considered "alms"—were, in his view, best left to private, and preferably religious, institutions. For Tuckerman, the distribution of alms was like the distribution of dynamite: they needed to be handled with extreme care by competent, private organizations. Private organizations had a more refined sense of moral purpose and were more likely than government agencies to employ "scientific" methods in their review and management of cases. They were also more likely to encourage financial support from Boston's upper classes and—not incidentally—ensure their continuing supervision and control of a matter of such great economic and moral import. In his periodic reports to the American Unitarian Association on his Ministry-at-large, he inveighed constantly against government participation in the amelioration of poverty. He even urged a *reduction* in government assistance to the poor, opposing—unsuccessfully—the continuation of public assistance for housing for the poor. "I should rejoice, therefore, in the repeal of all legal enactments for the support of the poor, if from no other cause, for the very reason that it would do something and would probably do much, to bring the question before the public at once as an individual and general concern."[29] So committed was Tuckerman to this extreme voluntarism that he felt compelled to support the repeal of the long-standing Massachusetts law, based on the English system of parish support for the poor, requiring each township to provide for its own indigents.[30]

Tuckerman's opposition to public welfare programs was, even in the first half of the nineteenth century, a lonely one. Virtually all of his attempts to limit government's participation in social welfare programs for the poor were unsuccessful.[31]

• • • • •

The Outdoor Church doesn't share Tuckerman's ideas about the role of government in caring for the poor, but neither are we are hopeful about the efficacy of public assistance programs for the chronically homeless men and women to whom we minister.

There are approximately 350 homeless men and women in Cambridge. Most are just a step away from getting off the street: a job, a rent deposit or a successful adjustment to being back in the world after a long hospitalization or prison sentence. These men and women are well served by the myriad of social service programs provided by the City of Cambridge, by private non-profit agencies and organizations and by religious organizations. They need a lot of help—getting off the

---

29. Tuckerman, *On the Elevation of the Poor*, 185.
30. Collison, "True Toleration," 219.
31. McColgan, *Tuckerman*, 192–98.

street and back to conventional society is an exhausting, frustrating and time consuming task—but they are competent enough, sober enough and committed enough to make good use of that help.

Sometimes we encounter homeless people like this—at meals programs, at food pantries or in shelters. But the mission of the Outdoor Church is to serve the *other* homeless men and women in Cambridge, those chronically homeless people who, because of mental instability or substance abuse or both, can make little or no sense of the social services available to them. We want to help those who are beyond everyone's help except God's.

So it is not that public programs to end homelessness don't work; it is that they don't work well for most of the people to whom we minister. There are many causes of chronic homelessness other than economics. However much financial difficulties play a role in their homelessness, our congregants are on the street primarily because of substance abuse, mental illness and, often, both.[32]

The people we encounter on the streets of Cambridge have great difficulty managing their lives. Many are often too befuddled, too drunk or too sick to get to a shelter in time to obtain or reserve a bed, find a church where a free meal is being served or understand, much less afford, the public transportation system. They are especially bad at doing the things that social service programs necessarily require them to do in order to secure benefits: fill out and submit forms; keep appointments; obtain needed documentation; appear at interviews on time, properly groomed and sober; or remember to eat when they have been drinking incessantly. When CASPAR, a wet shelter for homeless men and women at 240 Albany Street on the MIT campus, sends out its van in subfreezing weather to pick up people who are sleeping outdoors, or when Cambridge does its annual homeless census each January, these are the people who run away or hide. These are the people who assault the staff at 240 Albany Street over and over, effectively barring themselves for life from the one shelter in Cambridge that will admit people who are drunk or high. These are the people who, on receiving a prescription for an anti-psychotic drug, either lose the prescription or, having filled it, sell the drugs on the gray market and use the proceeds to get high.

---

32. See generally Jencks' article, "The Homeless" and his book also titled *The Homeless*.

They are, in short, lousy clients. Any program that depends upon their cooperative behavior as clients will have great difficulty helping them.

Because of this, there is a subtle but very real incentive for social service providers to privilege well behaved clients over our congregants. Programs depend for their funding on success and, in this as in so many other areas, success is measured in numbers of clients served. Given a choice between spending ten hours with ten clients, all of whom will benefit from the service offered and be thankful for it, or spending ten hours with one client, surly and unappreciative, who loses forms, forgets meetings and, when he remembers to appear, is drunk or high, most social service providers will choose to serve those who clearly benefit from the service. And who can blame them? To secure ongoing funding, they must be both effective and efficient.

Responsible advocates have been calling for decades for forms of housing that are closely linked to the social services that the chronically homeless need to make sense of their lives. No one, if only for budgetary reasons, wants to recreate the extensive physical plant and expensive permanent public staffing that were the hallmarks of the pre-1970 mental health system. But the alternatives—like scattered site housing for former mental health patients—are still politically unthinkable, even though the social and economic cost of leaving people on the street is many times greater than the cost of providing supported housing.[33]

· · · · ·

Taking services outdoors is one way to address the inherent inefficiency of providing social services to chronically homeless people: Tuckerman's Ministry-at-large was about nothing if not taking services, material and spiritual, outdoors for those who could not or would not go indoors to obtain them. Taking services outside is not unheard of in Boston. Boston Health Care for the Homeless has offered medical care to chronically homeless men and women for more than twenty years by going outdoors, to the street and to shelters, where the homeless are to be found. Dr. Jim O'Connell, who founded Boston Health Care for the Homeless, said recently - at Fenway Park, where the Red Sox were collecting clean white socks for the homeless—that foot problems, especially in the winter, are the number one medical issue for homeless people, but that

---

33. Gladwell, "Million Dollar Murray," 96–107.

homeless people often believe that they have "more important things to do" than go to a hospital and have their foot problems treated. He meant that—from the point of view of a homeless person—getting to a shelter, getting to a meal, meeting a probation officer or making a court appearance as a material witness take enormous amounts of time and energy. There is not much left for a visit to an emergency room, especially if you will be asked to wait all day while more pressing medical problems are treated before yours. If homeless people can learn to live with the slow suicide of substance abuse, they can learn to live with the slower suicide of untreated chronic medical problems. So Boston Health Care for the Homeless goes outdoors to treat those problems.

Bridge Over Troubled Waters also takes medical care outdoors. Founded in the late sixties by a group of idealistic doctors and later named after the Simon and Garfunkel song, it served chronically homeless men and women in Boston who were able to find their way to the back yard of the King's Chapel parish house on Beacon Street, where the clinic had set up shop. Soon, Bridge Over Troubled Waters outgrew its clinic at King's Chapel. It bought a large van and parked it in Boston and in Harvard Square on different nights of the week in order to treat young people who had run away from home, who were living on the street or who were at risk for drug addiction, rape and violence, but who were distrustful or frightened of hospitals and clinics.

Even when medical care is taken outside to the patient, there are no assurances that the medical care will be effective. Prescribing drugs and managing their regimen are only two of the many forms of medical intervention that work well indoors but not outdoors. There is an active gray market on the street for scrip and for drugs. Given a choice between filling a prescription to treat a medical problem or selling the scrip to raise money for food, drugs or Listerine, homeless people often choose the short term fix, leaving a disease or infection untreated.

What is true for medical care is true for many other essential services and material goods. Starlight Ministries takes blankets and food outdoors in Porter Square on Wednesday nights. There are a handful of social workers from Tri State Mental Health who are outdoors on a fairly regular basis.

But these programs are expensive, hard to administer and difficult to fund. Taking services outdoors will always be a radical approach to the distribution of services to the homeless.

⋯⋯

For many of our congregants, what the Outdoor Church does is like hospice care. Substance abuse, mental derangement and the rigors of living outdoors all the time have placed them beyond the scope of services even if the services are brought out to them. Some people are too inebriated to eat; others are too frightened to seek the protection of a shelter even in the middle of winter; still others won't talk to anyone who looks or sounds like a person with authority, due to some real or imagined dreadful experience in a prison or hospital. For them, just as hospice care begins where medicine can go no further, we begin where conventional social programs and services can't help.

Serving chronically homeless men and women requires squandering human and material resources. But squandering human resources is a quintessentially Christian project. In the Christian view, every life is priceless. No amount of time, money, effort or resources can ever be worth more than that life. Any amount of time, money, effort or resources is worth investing in trying to save that life.

In this as in so much else, Tuckerman is our model. Having retired for reasons of health, he spent what health remained to him on a fourteen year ministry that was too challenging for men half his age. He gave his life to the poorest people he could find in Boston.

4

The Outdoor Church on the Cambridge Common

> We Christians are an army of defeated soldiers fighting for an invincible cause.[1]

THE OUTDOOR CHURCH HAD ITS FIRST PRAYER SERVICES ON THE Cambridge Common, across from Christ Church, whose membership once included Tories who fled Cambridge for Nova Scotia during the Revolutionary War. Holes from bullets fired by Revolutionary War soldiers are visible on its outer walls. Nearby, General Henry Knox delivered a train of artillery to George Washington in January, 1776, near the massive Civil War monument that commands the southern end of the Common. The monument is forty feet high; a generic Civil War soldier stands on a canopy that shelters a somber and reflective Abraham Lincoln. Lincoln looks out over people hurrying home from the seven nearby churches and Hispanic teenagers playing soccer on the fields at the northern end of the Common. A cobblestone apron surrounds the monument. There are simple benches made of unfinished granite slabs around the perimeter of the apron where homeless men and women gather to sleep or drink or have sex.

Our clergy always wear collars and crosses. We discovered early on that most people on the street couldn't believe that we were ordained clergy unless we wore a collar and a cross. The distinctive cross we all wear was designed by the Rev. Elizabeth Hall for Common Cathedral. It was originally carved from wood but, because pieces broke off so easily, it is now forged from brass. The cross is instantly recognizable everywhere in Cambridge and Boston, and as far away as San Francisco and British Columbia. Seeing the cross, people have stopped me on the

---

1. Casaldàliga, "Sermon," 81.

street in New York City to tell me that they have heard about Common Cathedral or the Outdoor Church.

It is unusual for United Church of Christ ministers to wear a collar. Joan Murray, who replaced Debbie as minister of Common Cathedral when Debbie began to travel the country to help other churches establish an outdoor presence, is the only other one I know. Many people on the street assume that I am a Roman Catholic priest. I long ago gave up trying to explain the difference; the explanation exhausted people's attention span and, in the end, it didn't seem to matter much. Now I wear a collar whenever I am doing anything as a minister. It is one of the many ways I have been shaped as a minister by my own church.

At first—especially before I was ordained—I was extremely self conscious standing on the Cambridge Common with a wooden cross perched on a metal kitchen cart beside me. I thought—rightly, as it turned out—that I would be mistaken for an earnest Mormon missionary or an evangelical. Occasionally, friends or acquaintances would wander past on their way to Harvard Square. Almost invariably, they didn't recognize me unless I called out to them. I had become invisible again. One friend, with whom I have shared the last five miles of one of his marathons and the last five miles of one of mine, jogged through the Common every Sunday at the same time that we were having our service. He never seemed to see me unless I made a point of intercepting him as he went by and he always seemed a little embarrassed to find me there. I was a little embarrassed, too. What *was* I doing out there?

My self consciousness was the symptom of a nagging uncertainty: how could I be a real minister if the Outdoor Church wasn't a real church?

Pat was a vocational deacon because her bishop had ordained her as such. She was a vocational deacon no matter where she was and no matter what she was doing. But my status as a minister was less certain. Historically, a congregational minister was called out of a gathered congregation to be its minister. The Cambridge Platform of Church Discipline (1648), the first concerted effort of Puritan ministers in America to codify their faith and its practice, held that a person became a minister only when called to a church's pulpit and ceased being a minister when he left it.[2] There could be churches without ministers, but

---

2. W. Walker, *Creeds and Platforms*, 217.

not a minister without a church. The Cambridge Platform made no provision for ministers of outdoor churches or ministries-at-large. In time, a number of factors undercut the simplicity of the initial congregational definition of minister. The Standing Order itself, the itinerant preachers of the Great Awakening, the proliferation of ministers in non-church occupations like teaching and, especially, the growing authority of the Unitarian Universalist Association, the United Church of Christ and many other denominations, led to the idea of ordained ministry as a permanent status, created and revocable only by the authority of the denomination itself.

I sought to assure myself that I was just like any other ordained minister. To be sure, the United Church of Christ was not likely to revoke my ordination because I had set out to establish an outdoor church; I was ordained with that project expressly in mind. But I felt the lack.

I was in the same boat as Tuckerman, who had not been ordained again when he began his Ministry-at-large. The issue emerged even more clearly at the ordination in 1834 of Charles F. Barnard and Frederick T. Gray, Tuckerman's associates. Their ordination was a positive and radical departure from the principles of the Cambridge Platform. In his ordination sermon, Tuckerman stated: "We are about to engage in the solemn act of separating two ministers of Christ to a department of service to which no others have in this manner been separated."[3] Theretofore, no ministers had ever been ordained by a non-church organization like the Benevolent Fraternity of Churches.[4] Conrad Wright held this to be a lamentable departure from established congregational principle:

> The familiar rites of ordination were indeed respected: sermon, prayer, charges, right hand of fellowship. But no one seems to have questioned the right of the executive committee of an administrative body to authorize an ordination. Nor was anyone prepared to provide a reinterpretation of congregation polity to give a plausible rationale for the departure. To this day, practical necessity has not been accompanied by theoretical justification or validation.[5]

---

3. Tuckerman, *Sermon (Barnard and Gray)*, 6.
4. Channing, "Appendix," *Ministry for the Poor*, 45.
5. Wright, *Congregational Polity*, 58–59.

Here was another important personal link between my ministry and Tuckerman's. His second ministry and my first were on shaky congregational ground. I was buoyed by the knowledge that no one had ever suggested that Tuckerman stopped being a minister when he started being a Minister-at-large. My collar had come to mean to me that I was a minister in every sense in which Tuckerman was.

The collar had also come to mean that I was a minister to a real church. But even as I continued to rationalize this—yes, our people were in fact gathered in Porter Square and on the Cambridge Common and, yes, they time and time again called me their minister—I began to gain confidence from my actual experience as a minister on the street, as Tuckerman gained confidence from his. The need to make symbolic public statements about my ministry and my church abated. Now, wearing a collar on the street emboldens me to offer to help people when I wouldn't intervene otherwise. The collar somehow explains to onlookers that this kind of intervention is just what to expect of clergy: I am only trying to help and I am not dangerous. Tuckerman may not have thought that he had established an outdoor church, but he certainly found being outdoors liberating. So had I. The collar and the cross both symbolize this freedom and enable it.

• • • • •

Just before 1:00 PM, we gather in our basement office at Harvard Epworth Church, on the Harvard Law School side of the Common, and sort through the sandwiches that the children of our supporting churches prepare for us on a rotating basis. We put them, together with some Juicy Juice boxes, snacks and toiletries, in a pink plastic bin that already contains copies of our order of service and everything we will need for communion. We push the cart across Mass Avenue, past sunbathers and clusters of kids playing the guitar and old men reading on the park benches. When we reach the cobblestones that surround the Lincoln monument, we cover the cart with the white linen cloth and pin it down against the wind that sweeps across the soccer fields. We are ready for our prayer service.

• • • • •

By now, some of our regular congregants have been attending for years. Ernie was one of the very first. I first met Ernie in Boston, more than seven years ago. Ernie used to live on the street, but now he has a room in Chelsea. His face is round and pasty, and his gray eyes squint through very thick tortoise shell glasses. He is always unshaven. He is self conscious about being nearly bald and wears a heavy woolen cap, even in the heat of July and August.

Ernie lives on Social Security disability benefits, but he also conducts an active can return business that he says earns him $15,000 to $16,000 a year. He is completely unembarrassed about scrounging for cans. As he shuffles up to our prayer service from the Harvard Square MBTA station, he stops at every trash bin along the way to check for cans while people shout at him to stop dawdling. He carries a large black plastic bag full of cans and has many more tucked away in the three or four shirts he wears for warmth. With his coat puffed out with cans he looks like Tweedledee or Tweedledum preparing for battle.

Among the homeless people who came to Common Cathedral, Ernie was reputed to be—without any evidence whatsoever—a child molester. Anyone could get a rise out of Ernie by accusing him of abusing children, and almost everyone did. Every Sunday Ernie would approach the Brewer Fountain dragging a noisy plastic bag and immediately get into a shouting match with the first person who called him a child molester. If every human being has at least one God-given gift, Ernie's is the ability to ignite an uproar whenever he gets within five feet of another person.

Now Ernie joins us on the Cambridge Common. When we started our service, in June, 2003, as many as fifteen or twenty homeless men and women attended. Then a rash of arrests on or near the Common—according to the Cambridge police, homeless people were doing drugs, drinking, having sex and using the Common as a bathroom—made homeless people very wary of the Common, and attendance became erratic. Sometimes only two or three homeless people showed up, sometimes ten or twelve, depending on the weather or on the number of volunteers we had that week. Some people drifted up to Porter Square. Then, the police withdrew, the complaints abated and homeless men and women returned to the Common. Now, just as the seasons come and go, homeless people live on the Common and attend our services, the Cambridge police roust them after an abutting resident complains, our numbers fall off, time goes by and homeless men and women slowly return to the Common and attend our services.

Ernie has never missed one of our services, even though he has to come in from Chelsea on Sunday morning to join us, except for Thanksgiving, Christmas and Easter, when he goes down to New London to join his sister and his nieces for the holidays. Ernie has never let me forget a Sunday when more than two feet of snow fell in the Boston area and I stayed at home, certain that no one would try to reach the Common with so much snow on the ground. I was wrong. Ernie did, and he spent an hour and a half in the parish hall of Christ Church waiting for us to appear. Ernie usually joins us just after the reading of the gospel, which one of us reads to him again after the service is over. Ernie can't read but he is Bible-literate, and recognizes almost all of the Scripture readings. He likes to comment on the second reading in progress by staying two or three verses ahead, as if to show that he has been there before and doesn't need to be reminded.

When he is collecting cans or taking them to the distribution center, Ernie is without inhibitions. When he sees cans in the bottom of a barrel but can't reach them, he simply knocks over the barrel and grabs the cans that have rolled out. In all the time I have known Ernie, I am still taken aback by his apparent lack of self consciousness about collecting cans. I admire his willingness to persevere at the cost of his personal dignity. If he didn't, he could never make his way in the world. As it is, he can indulge in endless contempt for homeless people who don't have a job or an apartment.

Ernie has a serious prostate problem and needs to go to the bathroom often. Ideally, he would always be within a short distance of a public restroom, but there aren't many and Ernie is sometimes forced to relieve himself wherever he can. He once got into a terrible fight with the assistant Sunday sexton at Christ Church across the street, which keeps its bathrooms open for homeless people to use, because Ernie was in great discomfort and the sexton—himself homeless—wouldn't let him in the building to use the bathroom. Characteristically, Ernie refuses to see a urologist about his condition. Instead, he constantly asks us to bring out extra large underwear or extra large pajamas, and reminds us every Sunday if there is an unfilled order pending. He favors red plaid.

We never ask about people's histories, as fascinating as they always are. In time, most people tell us big chunks of it anyway—the stories of abuse, of abandonment, of neglect—without us having to interrogate them. Ernie told us that his mother placed him in the Paul Dever School for Retarded Boys for the convenience of the Brockton School system, which didn't want to be bothered with a bright but deeply disturbed boy who needed lots of special attention. Now, whenever he has a run in with someone on the street, he calls me over to sit next to him, leans toward me confidentially and says at the top of his lungs: "Jed! That guy, I know him! He was at Dever!" In Ernie's telling, half of the chronically homeless population in Boston attended the Dever School. His years at Dever left this intelligent, humorous and caring man utterly unfit for a normal life.

Others come up to the Common from Harvard Square, often for a sandwich but sometimes for prayer as well. Some have been with us from the beginning. Mason, who used to be a short order chef, badly wants to gain a better understanding of the Bible; and, although he treats us as authorities, he is far more familiar with Scripture than we are. Mason is a large, balding brown-eyed man in his mid-thirties, always perspiring, with a bright, cheerful and energetic manner. He has a soft, gentle voice and elegant manners. Mason laughs when he is serious, so you have to be careful not to join in a joke that inevitably turns out not to be a joke. He does not appear to be a substance abuser or to have severe mental problems, but that is not unusual. Mason shines during the discussions that follow the Gospel reading. He always announces that he is completely confused by the reading, and then immediately launches into an exegesis that would do most seminarians proud. Mason is convinced that something very, very good is just about to happen to him—for example, he believes that he will find a winning $1,000,000 lottery ticket—and, every few weeks or so, he shows up deeply despondent that it hasn't happened yet. But Mason's troubles run deeper than that. He also believes that, while he was living in a trailer park in Orlando, he was overheard talking to his shoe about some monstrous evil he had perpetrated on a young woman. He maintains that word of this evil—the "buzz" on the street—has followed him from Orlando to Cambridge. He is convinced that this is not an accident, but, rather, that he has been called to suffer and be redeemed in public, outdoors, as an example and an inspiration to other troubled homeless men. Mason has befriended Ernie, and, in good weather, the two of them will sit on the granite benches in the Common together, eating their sandwiches, long after we have left for Harvard Square.

Ernie, in turn, and much to our surprise, became solicitous of Wendy, a young woman with a round, flat pale face and blue eyes who was with us regularly until she simply stopped coming after a year. Wendy radiates barely controlled rage and can be intimidating when she begins to shout at herself. Like many homeless people, Wendy dresses in many layers of clothes rather than carry them. Even in summer, she wears three or four heavy gray woolen skirts at a time, which emphasizes her bulk. She used to attend services at Christ Church, use the restrooms there to attend to her personal grooming and then come across the street with us afterward for our outdoor service. Wendy worries about denominational issues. She is an Episcopalian, and has been troubled from the beginning that we are non-denominational, and that clergy other than Episcopal priests and deacons administer the sacraments at our prayer services. Nothing—not divinity school, not ordination, not a collar, not argument—has persuaded Wendy that I, ordained by the United Church of Christ, should be permitted to lead a ministry of the word and of the sacrament. When anyone other than the rector of Christ Church presides at our prayer service, she circles the Civil War monument or sits on a nearby granite bench, glowering and muttering to herself, until the service is done and she can have a sandwich with us.

Wendy, like Mason and Ernie, is Bible literate, but, where Mason finds something to share with us in Bible stories, Wendy can only find proof that God is punishing her. The whole world evidences this discipline. She is extremely quick to take umbrage. Wendy has moments of lucidity in which she can describe her present life—living in a women's shelter in East Cambridge—and how she plans to go back to school and become a model—but even then her conviction that God is punishing her darkens her every hope. Far more often—perhaps it is when she stops taking her medications—Wendy, either in a conspiratorial whisper or at the top of her lungs, inveighs against all those people and institutions she thinks stand between her and her reconciliation with the God who judges her so severely—the church, its priests and ministers, the government, passersby. Sometimes, when she is so upset, she leaves our prayer service and finds her way to Harvard Square, where she stands in the middle of Massachusetts Avenue and screams at the startled drivers. Often as not, the Cambridge police pick her up in a matter of minutes and commit her to Cambridge City Hospital or McLean Hospital. Back on her medications, Wendy is released to the street within a few days, where she repeats the same cycle of loss of control and involuntary commitment over and over again. Sometimes, Ernie tries to help her by telling her that shouting just makes the police come more quickly, but, whenever he does, she snarls at him to mind his own business.

Then Wendy stopped coming altogether. Ernie sees her occasionally at meals programs around Cambridge and Boston, but he refuses to talk to her any more. Ernie can be surprising empathetic and he knows that Wendy's behavior doesn't have anything to do with him. But, like all of us, he has his limits.

Clergy from nearby Cambridge churches sometimes lead our services; students from many different churches attend as well. Otherwise, I, Pat Zifcak, an Episcopal vocational deacon or Jean Chapman, a Baptist minister, lead prayers and administer communion. After the service is finished, we have a meal with everyone who has attended the service. Tuna fish salad and egg salad are the universal favorites, followed by ham and cheese, liverwurst and boloney and cheese. Ernie hates cheese. Sometimes we forget to remind the children from one of our supporting churches who are making sandwiches that week to make a variety of sandwiches, and we only get ham and cheese or turkey and cheese. Ernie invariably takes his sandwich apart and throws the cheese on the cobblestones. This upsets Mason—he thinks it shows a lack of gratitude. Others become nervous that the police will appear at any moment to run them off the Common for littering, but Ernie is indifferent to their criticism. Christ Church being a wealthy church, we often have the leftovers from their catered events, and then, instead of sandwiches, we get hors d'oeuvres and sliced meat and gourmet sandwiches, complete with toothpicks with colored cellophane tassels, and slices of very elegant pies and cakes. Ernie awaits the day when we will appear again, as we did one glorious September afternoon, with individually wrapped roast beef and pastrami and tongue sandwiches that looked like they had—because they actually did—come from a very expensive delicatessen.

Our liturgy is based loosely on the Book of Common Prayer. We use the same liturgical prayers over and over again, to increase the sense of continuity and constancy that we want people to feel when they are with us. At first, we simply printed lots of copies of the order of service, but, after a few rain storms in which the ink ran so badly that we couldn't read the words, we put them in plastic sleeves.

The homeless people who attend our service on the Cambridge Common recognize traditional forms of prayer and worship and respond powerfully to them. They are deeply invested in very specific ideas about God, about judgment and forgiveness, about sin and salvation and about communion. For many homeless people, religion and all its manifestations—ministers, churches, liturgies—evoke all of their disappointment in themselves and their anxiety about their future. Many people refuse to take communion from us because they have been drinking the night before, or were abusive, or were abused, or took communion the week before, or because they are unworthy. And so people deny themselves a place in the loving community they so desperately need.

・・・・・

Pat and I first met in Bob Tobin's office at Christ Church Cambridge, one gloomy February afternoon in 2003. Bob had been rector of Christ Church Cambridge for seventeen years when I met him. He was a short, intense man, with penetrating eyes behind wire rimmed glasses, always wearing a collar and a tweed coat. He was quite bald and not a young man, but being bald didn't make him look any older. He bounced on the balls of his feet. He had made Christ Church an unusually welcoming place for the chronically homeless men and women in Harvard Square. The doors opened at 7:00 AM every day. People could come in and have a cup of coffee from the large urn that the sexton set up in the hallway leading to the parish offices. They could use the restrooms to wash up and sit on the benches in the hallway for a while to get out of inclement weather. Not everybody was happy with this radical welcome, especially mothers of very young children, who would discover used needles in the tot lot just to the right of the entrance to the parish hall. Accordingly, the church set some limits: no weapons; no drinking on the premises; no drug deals in the bathroom.

There are (I learned belatedly) two kinds of deacons in the Episcopal Church: all candidates for priesthood are deacons for six or so months before being ordained as priests; but vocational deacons are committed to doing the work of the church out in the world as a final vocation. Pat sat across the room in front of Bob's desk, hands folded demurely in her lap. She was tall and angular, with a round composed face and a tonsure of brown hair. Pat was a careful and thoughtful listener and a keen judge of character. She exuded a swimmer's clean athleticism and, in fact, she coached swimming and lacrosse at the Park School, a private elementary school in Brookline, a suburb of Boston. Pat sounded like she had been a deacon for a lifetime but she had been ordained only three years before me. Ordination followed years of discernment, with the obligatory disbelieving and astonished family and the dedication and energy of the newly converted. Pat had gotten her MDiv at Andover Newton; she had clearly learned a lot more theology there than I did at the Harvard Divinity School, and spoke with a quiet and well deserved authority on all matters ecclesial that would have done most priests proud. She left Christ Church soon after Bob retired. Deacons serve without compensation at the discretion of their bishop and aren't supposed to stay long in one place. Pat had already stayed at Christ Church beyond her allotted three years. In leaving, she also gave up her position as head of religious education at Christ Church. But she quickly became the head of the Boston Diocese's diaconal training program. And she was a grandmother. And she had a sense of humor. And she knew where to find the pastries and cakes that were left over from Christ Church's innumerable and superbly catered parties and receptions. Here was a vocational deacon of many parts.

Bob was one of the directors of Common Cathedral and was intimately familiar with the workings of Debbie's outdoor church. They had worked together for a long while and both had summer homes in Maine. I first met Bob through Common Cathedral when I was just starting my second year at the Harvard Divinity School and he knew that I wanted to do something like Common Cathedral in Cambridge.

Bob was just about to retire from Christ Church and he wanted to wrap up as much as he could before he left. For six or seven years, he had been trying to get the Harvard Square Clergy Association to sponsor an outdoor church in Cambridge like Common Cathedral. The Harvard Square Clergy Association met once a month in the library at Christ Church. There was coffee and muffins as large as pumpkins. The chocolate chip muffins were especially good. Many of the churches were enthusiastic—some of them were among our first supporting churches and their clergy played a role in our first few years—so there was no lack of interest, but Bob couldn't get them to commit to a concrete program. There were discussions about an appropriate liturgy, and administrative issues, and fundraising, yet somehow nothing ever happened.

Unwilling to retire without redeeming all those hours lunching with the Harvard Square Clergy Association and impatient to extend the reach of Christ Church's ministry to the chronically homeless men and women of Cambridge, Bob decided to push ahead on his own. He had already suggested to Pat that he wanted a clerical presence outdoors—it was part of her job description at Christ Church. In response, Pat had begun a service of Compline, the last Office of the day in the Episcopal Church, immediately following the free meal served at Christ Church on Thursday nights. Compline took place outdoors just in front of the doors to the parish hall when the weather was good and just inside the doors when it wasn't. The Thursday night prayer service continued a long while after we began our prayer services on the Cambridge Common; a different group of people—some, at Christ Church, not homeless, but forced to choose among shelter, food and clothes—appeared at both.

Coincidentally, I had been thinking about doing something in Cambridge like Common Cathedral. Debbie was encouraging. At her suggestion, I called Bob. I met with him one gloomy afternoon in February. He asked if I would be willing to meet with him and Pat to talk about an outdoor church. We met the very next day, just before the Thursday night meal. Bob talked about his plans and his frustrations with the Harvard Square Clergy Association. We talked about practical details. Bob said we could use storage space at Christ Church and one of the kitchen carts for an altar, Pat's children's group would make twenty or so sandwiches every Sunday and I would prepare an order of service.

With that, we began. Did Bob sense that the missing piece was the one or two people who would commit first and ask questions later? Looking back, neither Pat nor I can remember any time at which either of us said "I need to think about this," or "Since—after all—I'm proposing to spend Sunday afternoon away from my family, it might be considerate if I checked in with them," or "Is this what I was ordained to do?" We didn't do much planning—we just did it. This was either testimony to the power of our call or a reflection on how little practical sense we had gleaned from our preparation for ministry. Pat and I met again in May and, on a drizzly July 27, we were out on the Cambridge Common for the first time.

I wouldn't be ordained for another year and a half; Pat had only been ordained two years before. It took a while to sort out who was going to lead the service and who was going to administer communion. Pat could only administer a deacon's Eucharist and I wasn't ordained, so we asked Bob and then a succession of Episcopal priests and Congregational ministers to lead our services. This fell off after a while. But, in good congregational fashion, we agreed that Pat would do the liturgy of the word and I would do the liturgy of the sacrament: a bold ecclesial statement, but counter-intuitive, given our respective denominations. But we had decided right off—with Bob's experience with the Harvard Square Clergy Association before us—that we would not argue about denominational distinctions. We would not allow denominational rules to stand between our church—which existed, after all, to reach those who could not enter conventional churches—and the people we wanted to serve. We have since been joined by Methodist, Unitarian, Lutheran, Baptist, Roman Catholic and Presbyterian clergy, and denominationalism has never been an issue for us.

· · · · ·

Like everyone else, we struggle with the question of whether to give money to someone who is panhandling. On one hand, the answer to the question, "Can you spare a quarter?" is always "yes," that is, we can surely afford to give at least that much to someone who is hungry. And stopping (in order not to appear callous) and saying, "I won't give you any money, but let's have a conversation," is both self-aggrandizing and patronizing. On the other hand, how do we know where the money is going? Will the homeless person to whom we have just given the quarter go around the corner to get a sandwich or get a bottle of wine? On one of those rare occasions that I have given money to someone on the street, I passed a guy with a Starbucks cup standing in front of the Harvard Coop, dropped some change in the cup—and heard a splash: it was just some guy drinking a cup of coffee. I was mortified.

Now, I carry McDonald's gift coupons that can be redeemed for a dollar's worth of coffee or food and hand them out, or—if I don't have any coupons—I tell a person that I will get him food or a subway pass or whatever he might otherwise have spent the money on, other than drugs or alcohol. That, at least, makes the question one of how much effort I am prepared to make to help someone (Will I walk them down to the subway station and use my transit card to put them on the train?

Will I go across town to buy a blanket?) and not one of whether I am being asked to feed a habit.

Most of the time, it doesn't take a lot of effort to help. How much time does it take to make or buy a sandwich? How much time does it take to walk someone to a train station, especially if I am on the way there myself? If I can get past the internal moral monologue, I am more likely to encounter and make some connection with another human being.

In the end, this works because it promises to relieve the inevitable discomfort we feel when we encounter a beggar. When I use it in a sermon or a speech, the Starbucks joke never fails to get a laugh, but it is a nervous laugh: my audience is relieved to learn from a moral authority that it is all right to be made uncomfortable by a beggar and that there are acceptable ways of dealing with it.

The disgust that many feel when they encounter begging has a long history. Some, like Thomas Malthus, have been unabashedly direct about it:

> Even in the relief of common beggars we shall find that we are more frequently influenced by the desire of getting rid of the importunities of a disgusting object than by the pleasure of relieving it. We wish that it had not fallen in our way, rather than rejoice in the opportunity given us of assisting a fellow-creature. We feel a painful emotion at a sight of so much apparent misery; but the pittance we give does not relieve it. We know that it is totally inadequate to produce any essential effect.[6]

The principles of market-driven economics, raised up to philosophy, either transform begging into another, albeit pernicious, form of economic activity or treat it as the rationalization for disgust: "A man who is born into a world," wrote Malthus, "... if the society do [sic] not want his labour, has no claim of right to the smallest portion of food, and, in fact, has no business to be where he is."[7] Begging disrupts the natural order of things: what should be hidden in shame is, of necessity, made public. It promotes the radical notion that people ought to embrace the unhappiness of others outside their immediate family and are bound to do something about it.

---

6. Malthus, *Works*, 3:366.
7. Ibid., 697–98.

For people more willing to allow their personal compassion to moderate societal principles of economic exchange, disgust is coupled with guilt. Malthus, however cruel he may sound to modern ears, is not altogether short of the mark. In a society, like ours, that is based on equal exchange, begging is necessarily a disruptive and disturbing act. Christian economics offers an alternative. Its roots lie far deeper than capitalism; its principles are coincident with the birth of Christianity itself: "And all who believed were together and had all things in common; and they sold their possessions and goods and distributed them to all, as any had need." (Acts 3:44–45.) Tuckerman's advocacy for a "just wage" for female workers and his assertion that the poor have a right to support from the rich seem to suggest a willingness to see Christian economics as the basis for personal charitable activity, if not a structural alternative to a contract-based economics. Tuckerman, unwavering in his opposition to the public provision of financial support to the poor, points to a possible approach: the private cultivation of hope, mercy and humility by people and institutions of faith will promote a Christian economics that makes giving to beggars an act of grace rather than guilt.[8]

Henry, who lost the tips of his fingers to frostbite a few years ago when he passed out in front of the Unitarian Church in Harvard Square, is among the very few homeless men who know me and who will nonetheless sometimes ask for money to get a drink in order to suppress withdrawal symptoms or to avoid a seizure. Henry knows that I will tell him that I will get him anything other than a drink, but he asks anyway, partly on the off chance that I will surprise him but mainly, I think, to tell me that he is feeling miserable and very frightened that he will have a seizure. Some community organizers and social workers carry nips of vodka with them in the event that they encounter someone who is on the verge of a seizure. They say that giving a person a little alcohol when they are at risk of a seizure will prevent a more serious, perhaps fatal, convulsion later, while withholding the alcohol won't make it any more likely that the person will give up drinking or drink less.

I can't bring myself to do this. It is one thing to give money to a homeless man. If there is a risk, it is the same risk inherent in making a gift of money to any person. It is another to hand someone a bottle;

---

8. Johnson, *Fear of Beggars*, 215.

the possibility of becoming inadvertently complicit in substance abuse is now intentional and certain. And, in the end, I don't think Henry or anyone else wants me to do it. We hope that the homeless people we serve will come to believe that we care about them as a parent might, if the parent were paying loving attention. Drug addicts are prepared to steal from their parents, but they don't want the parent's approval of their habit. The word would get around quickly that a minister was walking around Harvard Square and Central Square giving out drinks. Our ministry would be irrevocably compromised. But I am not certain I would be quite so sure if I were a social worker or a doctor.

· · · · ·

Shortly after Mason stopped attending our prayer service on the Common because of "theological differences," Howard appeared. He has been with us ever since, except for a few weeks when he was in Mount Auburn Hospital. Howard is an older man, slight and somewhat hunched, reticent and gentle, with carefully combed hair and a meticulously trimmed salt and pepper handle bar moustache and very pale blue, hooded eyes. We share a passion for sweets. In the winter, Howard wears two or three woolen scarves that he wraps around his neck and face, hiding everything except his eyes. He carries everything he owns with him in three or four carefully packed knapsacks that he has modified to make bearing so much weight a little easier: thick foam rubber straps to protect his shoulders; cord and twine in place of plastic snaps that long ago fell off; tightly rolled rubberized sleeping pads in place of top flaps. Howard speaks very softly but in carefully crafted sentences. He reads our Scripture lesson each Sunday. Ernie—who rarely sits more than three feet away—yells at him to speak up (and then nods off during Howard's reading.)

Howard takes exegesis very seriously. His interpretations are not based on a long standing familiarity with the Bible but, instead, on a commonsense response to what he has just read to us. He seems to have no agenda, no preconceived idea of what Scripture holds for him; whatever tribulations he has suffered indoors and out have not yet crowded out a reasonable and thoughtful response to the text.

What little Howard has shared with us about his background is of a piece with his quiet intelligence. He attended Harvard (he said) and used to work for a bank in its data processing department. He is also trained as an architect and works from time to time as a carpenter and construction worker. We have never seen him drunk or show any signs of drug use; he is, when he is with us, always sober and cogent. Occasionally, he can be persistent in presenting an idea or a thought, but—even if his tenacity is a sign of an underlying obstinacy—it is hard to see a crippling psychological disorder in so mild a behavior. Howard is the paradigm of the homeless person in whom you can't see any reason or cause for his homelessness and yet who is clearly unable to do anything to help himself.

Howard usually arrives just before 1:00 on the Common. One day, I arrived early also, dragging our cart through the March ice and slush that still covered the brick walks. As we sat on the concrete bench at the far side of the Civil War statue, Howard began to tell me about the stained glass windows at Trinity Church in Boston. Here, in the early 1870's, John LaFarge virtually reinvented the art and craft of stained glass windows, using opalescent glass to create entirely new visual effects: "I used almost every variety of glass that could serve," LaFarge wrote. "... I began to represent the effects of light and modulations of shadow by using the streaked glass, the glass of several colors blended, and glass wrinkled into forms, as well as glass cut into shapes or blown into forms." But Howard dismissed LaFarge out of hand as "sloppy" and "undisciplined." He favored the less well known windows designed by Edward Burne-Jones and installed by the William Morris Studios, otherwise famous for their wallpapers. "Cleaner lines," said Howard, "better drawing ... more tasteful use of color and shape ... elegant in its modesty." The opposition of Burne-Jones and the William Morris Studios—"fixture makers," said Howard, responsible for woodwork and lighting as well as the stained glass windows—on one hand, and the church officials and architects who retained responsibility for the overall design of Trinity on the other, gave rise to a running battle over the design and installation of the stained glass windows that continued beyond the completion of the church. But at this point Ernie arrived, dragging his plastic bag of redeemable cans behind him. Howard shrunk deeper into his shoulders and waited for the service to begin.

What happened to this man? Why is he outdoors? He accepts our sandwiches and juice, and nothing else. We are planning to get him a new, ergonomically designed backpack; the one he uses is literally falling to pieces. If we knew what would get him off the street, we would give him *that*, too.

• • • • •

Of all our volunteers and interns, Helene was with us the longest. She was a slight, perfectly proportioned woman in her late twenties or early thirties with classically beautiful Vietnamese features. Helene had luxurious black hair that fell just below her shoulders. Ernie was entranced by it. He went through a period where he sat next to her on the granite benches on the Common and wanted to touch it but Helene would sharply discourage him—perhaps a little too sharply—and Ernie didn't press. Helene was intensely secretive about almost everything about her life. She said that she had been born in Vietnam but raised in Paris, that she had been at Harvard and that she had been homeless for a while. It all seemed a little implausible, but Butch, a homeless man who sold *Spare Change* at the corner of Church Street and Brattle Street, recognized her the first time he saw her as a fellow guest at the Holy Family shelter in Dorchester. She loved to bring unusual treats for us to give out as snacks with the sandwiches and juice—chocolate covered Vietnamese jellies, unusual cakes, elaborately iced cookies—because, she said, homeless people see unusual food as a sign that someone cares enough to give some thought to the food they are giving out.

Ernie became very attached to Helene. He asks questions that other people don't ask because they are too well bred to ask them—How much money do you have? How big is your house? What do you do when you go home?—but people are often willing to answer his questions no matter how unexpected they are. Scott Campbell, the senior minister at Harvard Epworth Methodist Church, who comes out once a month to lead our service, had gone through a dreadful period in which he and his wife Lynn endured one family tragedy after another, including the death of their daughter because of drugs, which left them to raise their two grandchildren in their father's absence. Scott mentioned it once during a discussion about the Lectionary text for the day, when he was leading our service, and Ernie asked him question after question about his daughter and how did it happen and what did Scott do and what about the grandchildren—which Scott answered directly and without hesitation. In his fashion, Ernie showed a concern for Scott at a very difficult time which the rest of us, fearing to overstep some boundary of good taste, hesitated to express.

Helene's obsession with her privacy was like catnip to Ernie, who is surprisingly sensitive to people around him if he is not fighting with them. The more she refused to answer his questions, the more fun he had asking them. It was clear to everyone except Helene that Ernie was toying with her: an early lesson in just how complex were the people in our church and how complicated our relations to them could become. When Helene decided to rejoin her family in California, he asked after her for months. Typically, she hadn't told us she was going until her last day with us and she didn't give us much detail when she did, so we didn't have much to offer Ernie after she left.

• • • • •

The Cambridge Common was where we first sensed the powerful community ties that bind groups of homeless men and women together, often to the detriment of its members, and how hard it is to break away from such a group in order to stop drinking or drugging or get an apartment.

Early on, before the police sweeps, Billy was with us every Sunday. Billy's head was shaved before it became fashionable to shave one's head. His scalp was covered with scars and infected abrasions, the marks of endless assaults on the street. Billy is a small, slightly built man with enormous brown eyes that are always wide open. He is a little slow and always seems to be staring out at the world in mild confusion. Younger men prey on Billy, beating him up whether he has anything worth stealing or not. He is like a moth drawn to violence's flame. In order to feel like he belongs, he hovers at the edge of groups of angry, loud young men and mouths off to gain a place among them. Their contempt for him incites them to violence. They wait for him to get so drunk that he passes out in front of them, and then kick him in the head and rib cage until they get bored or distracted. Before he got an apartment, Billy was often so drunk that he would pass out in the middle of our service, roll off the granite slabs around the edge of the Common's brick apron and hit his head on the bricks. Sometimes he would fall asleep, wake up suddenly and stagger toward Christ Church to use the bathroom that the church then kept open for homeless men and women to use during the day. I would watch him try to cross Garden Street with my heart in my mouth. I was sure he would trip and hit his head on the sidewalk.

After a year or so, Billy qualified for subsidized housing and, much to his own astonishment, he stopped drinking completely. He was a man transformed: his eyes were clear, he had some color in his cheeks and he could walk without staggering. He was still a little vague but very pleased and proud of what he had managed to accomplish.

But Billy couldn't stay away from his old friends. For people who have been on the street for a long while and who then get an apartment, it is very hard to leave the only community in which you are understood and welcomed. Some people don't use the apartment and continue to live on the street, just to stay close to their friends. Others invite their friends to stay with them indoors, usually in violation of their lease. Invariably, the apartment is trashed and the lease is terminated. Billy did both. He spent most of his time on the street; but when he was in his apartment, he invited his friends in with him. When he invited Doug and Fran in, his life unraveled.

Doug and Fran have been together for so long as I have been a minister in Cambridge. Doug is a young, open faced man with broad shoulders and strong hands. He is quiet, phlegmatic, endlessly forgiving of Fran's outrages. Fran is very short and stocky, with an oval face and spiky, pitch-black hair, well groomed for someone who has been barred from 240 Albany Street for life and who spends more time in the Massachusetts Correctional Institute in Framingham than outside. She is pretty and, when sober, charming and flirtatious; but when she is drinking or using heroin, she is loud, volatile and very violent. Billy was charmed by Fran and invited them both into his apartment. They drank a lot, ripped the wall paper and broke a lot of windows. It was in the middle of winter but the landlord refused to replace them.

A few weeks after Billy had invited Doug and Fran into his apartment, they got into a fight and Fran stabbed Doug in the chest. He recovered quickly, but refused to press charges. He told the police that they had been fighting and he had fallen down and cut himself on some glass. Fran was released after a few days in the Middlesex County jail. (Spending a lot of time with Fran is a high risk proposition. A year or so later, she stabbed Doug again, opening a gash that ran from his left nipple to his waist. He refused to go to the emergency room at Cambridge City Hospital to have it treated and the wound became infected. He wandered around for months applying over-the-counter antibiotics to the wound, a big stain across the front of his shirt where the antibiotic cream had soaked through.) The next day, Billy's landlord terminated the lease, alleging that Billy had encouraged violence on the premises. Cambridge Somerville Legal Services couldn't keep Billy in the apartment. He was back on the street. He was so shocked to have lost his apartment that he began to drink again. We see him now in Central Square, usually sitting in front of the Salvation Army. His eyes are dull and unfocussed, his face and scalp and hands covered with lacerations and abrasions. When I ask him if he would like a sandwich, he says, "Give me everything you've got. I need everything. Sandwiches, juice, socks, just give me whatever you've got. I don't have anything." He sounds utterly defeated.

Homeless people, like everyone else, have circles of friends and enemies within which they live most of their lives. The ties that bind may be loyalty or violence or habit or substance abuse or any combination of these. The communities undergirded by these ties—however fluid or changing because of illness, incarceration or death—are powerful. They are often the only meaningful attachment that a homeless person has to another human, excluding service providers. But these communities are also very dangerous and, for all the brave talk about watching someone else's back and always being there when a fight breaks out or the police arrive, they are no more reliable than any other part of living on the street.

• • • • •

Pat and I wanted the Outdoor Church to serve an area large enough to encompass a significant number of chronically homeless men and women but small enough that we could quickly reach most of the people we wanted to help. Cambridge, as it turned out, was just the right size. We could cover most of it on foot—with some help from the T—in one day. We estimated that there were roughly a hundred and twenty chronically homeless people on the streets of Cambridge at any one time. We thought we would be able to reach them and minister to them with the help of some volunteers and interns. Soon enough, we were encountering eighty to one hundred homeless people every week. We will see twenty or so people in Porter Square and another ten on the Common, and the rest as we walk through Harvard Square and Central Square. Not always the same people—at any given time, a third or so of our people are in prison, in a hospital or in a detox program—but usually the same number of people. Attendance changes with the weather, with the day of the month—if it is toward the end of the month, people will have gone through their Social Security disability checks and will be looking for something to eat—and with the time of day, but we are pretty sure now that we are ministering to most of the chronically homeless men and women in Cambridge.

Because of the geographic limits we had imposed on ourselves, we decided to think in terms of the richness of the experience of belonging to our church, rather than the number of people who were attending our services. We would try to provide each of our congregants with an experience of church that was as close as we could make it to the church experience of members of First Church Cambridge or Christ Church Cambridge. That effort—which we are now sure will continue for so long as the Outdoor Church itself exists—has been full of shocks, disconcerting discoveries and surprises. Pastoral visiting—visiting any of our people who finds herself in a hospital, in jail, in a mental institution or in prison, voluntarily or not—soon became a time consuming but extremely gratifying and rewarding effort. As the more violent among our members are sentenced to ever longer terms, we have become persuaded that we will never see them again if we don't visit them in prison. Our other pastoral services are also shaped by our congregants; we don't do confirmation classes or weddings, but we do many, many memorial services for people who have died on our watch.

We also wanted to give people as rich a liturgical experience as we could provide. We celebrate every church holiday with our congregants in a memorable way—with free Loew's theatre tickets or home made brownies or Dunkin' Donuts gift certificates—so that no one will feel forgotten as people rushed past during a holiday season laden with brightly wrapped presents and shopping bags. Church children sewed altar cloths in appropriate parament colors that allow us to acknowledge the different church seasons; we use Advent candles in Porter Square, although someone has to stand close by to keep them lit in the sleet and wind of early December. What in another church is tradition we recreate in constancy: summer and winter, one Sunday after another, we hold our prayer services in the same places, follow the same liturgy, sing the same songs and walk the same routes through Harvard Square and Central Square at the same times.

This ministry is not for everyone. Many of our interactions with homeless men and women are one on one, with people that we have seen and come to know over three or four or five years. This is very different than, say, a meals program, in which a table and a plate are always between the volunteer and the homeless person moving through the line. Encounters with chronically homeless people, Sunday after Sunday, are emotionally and physically draining.

Perhaps because of the unusual intensity of our work, clergy, interns and volunteers select themselves, as Pat and I did. We have yet to make a "personnel" decision. Some people show up once or twice, and never return. Others show up again and again and again. They are the ones who will join us as clergy or interns or volunteers. Like the handful of young associates who clustered around Tuckerman in the early years of his Ministry-at-large, our interns and volunteers are not in training for a vocational life on the street, however much they joke about acquiring a skill set that features how to make egg salad sandwiches and sort through contributed clothes. But the ministry is as transforming of our staff as it is of our congregants. It is a source of enormous pride to us that our tiny church sends forth two or three ordinands every year to be evangelists in the very best sense of the word.

· · · · ·

Some believe that Tuckerman felt it necessary to trim his sails in the face of the conservatism of his financial supporters.[9] Among his own contemporaries, there was nothing but praise and admiration for his ministry and his commitment to it. But whether praised or criticized, Tuckerman's work was assessed in terms of its social efficacy, not its theology. Tuckerman may sometimes have wished that someone, other than Channing, was interested in the theology that informed his ministry. I know I would welcome more discussions with people outside our church about the theology of *our* ministry.

---

9. Daniel Howe believes that Tuckerman may have felt compelled to emphasize "middle-class self-interest in order to secure financial support for his activities." Howe, *Unitarian Conscience*, 243. And see Griffin in "Religious Benevolence as Social Control, 1820–1865"; Schlesinger, Jr., *Age of Jackson*, 273; and Bremner, *American Philanthropy*, 60: "The only commodity [that Tuckerman] dared offer [to the poor] was advice." Others have been more sympathetic. McColgan, for example, found Tuckerman's religious motivations compelling and praiseworthy. McColgan, *Tuckerman*, xiii.

Most people respect our evident commitment to the homeless, and so it is unusual that anyone criticizes what we do. Some of the criticism we receive comes from people—including clergy—who provide social services to the homeless. They sometimes feel that we are not doing anything to end or even ameliorate the homelessness of the people we encounter on the streets of Cambridge. But we are a church, not a social service agency. We, like Tuckerman, did not set out to end homelessness or even, strictly speaking, to improve the material lot of those to whom we minister. We seek to restore and enhance the spiritual lives of those who for any reason cannot go inside a church building. Theologically speaking, we try to assure our people that we love them regardless of whether they get "better" or not. We will not love them the less if they don't stop drinking or don't stop beating up other homeless people or don't find housing or don't show up for an interview with the Social Security Administration. However rare it is—we can count the number of people on the fingers of one hand—we are always overjoyed to see one of our people get off the street and stay off the street. But we will love them just as much if they never get off the street or never try to get off the street. Our congregants are not our clients or our guests or our beneficiaries. They are fellow members of our church, in which we are bound to them by covenant.

It is the workings of that covenant—and not vows, formal professions of faith, membership rolls or confirmation classes—that makes us a church. Of course, throughout our five years of outdoor service, many of our people have attended our outdoor services in Porter Square or on the Cambridge Common. (Like most churches, we are not unduly bothered if people don't show up every Sunday. We don't take attendance, as we assure our congregants when they arrive late for our services or stay away for weeks at a time.) But whether they come to us in Porter Square or on the Common, or whether we go to them in Harvard Square and Central Square, our people know and welcome us as clergy, rarely failing to ask for a blessing or communion. We are a church gathered in our congregants' explicit or implicit acknowledgment of our ecclesial relation to them. Moreover, we and they are gathered together in the sharing of a Eucharistic meal (whether formally, as in communion, or in the simple sharing of a sandwich) which we understand to be—and our congregants experience as—a converting ordinance, which awakens them to a recognition and acceptance of membership in our church. We delight in the ways in which people express their affiliation with the Outdoor Church. "Here is my minister," a homeless defendant will say to her public defender when I arrive in court to provide a character witness, or "this is a church, pal! watch where you're going!" when a commuter inadvertently walks through our midst in Porter Square. The covenant that binds us together may be implicit, but it is no less strong for that.

Sometimes, more conservative people of faith offer a theological critique of our church and its mission. They are concerned that we are not bringing people to a personal relationship with Jesus, or impressing upon them their need to repent of their dreadful lives and seek their salvation, or teaching them about theology or Scripture or their faith. I find their criticism bracing, although such people rarely stay around to talk about it after unburdening themselves of their point of view. I would love to spar about universal salvation with someone from a Reformed church or from Calvin College, because, although I don't agree with much of their theology, I know that their faith has led some of them to go outdoors and provide sandwiches and blankets to the homeless just as compellingly as my faith has led me to be the pastor of the Outdoor Church.

Not everyone is entranced by our work. As in all churches, not every project generates universal interest or gains universal support. I know that the Outdoor Church lives at the edge of most people's willingness to spend the material and spiritual resources that caring for the homeless requires, but I have not forgotten that, not much more than a decade ago, this entire ministry—the idea of ministry itself—would have been inconceivable to me. This is one of the most gratifying things we do: to be with our interns, the clergy and lay people in our associated churches, our volunteers and our supporters as they explore life as people of faith. This is the balm for much of the pain we see on the street.

5

The Outdoor Church in Porter Square

> He went among the poor to serve the purposes of no sect, but to breathe into them the spirit and hopes of Jesus Christ.[1]

A YEAR OR SO AFTER WE BEGAN OUR PRAYER SERVICE ON THE CAMbridge Common, we started a prayer service in Porter Square at nine o'clock on Sunday mornings. We gather next to the MBTA Station, across from the Porter Square Shopping Center and right under the red steel mobile sculpture called "Homage to the Wind," with its constantly twirling amoeba-shaped fins.

Lots of people come up to Porter Square early Sunday morning from the wet shelter at 240 Albany Street. Evan, who was with us in Porter Square until he stopped drinking and went into a program, works there evenings. The shelter's building is a low slung cinder block affair on Albany Street, just around the corner from MIT's main campus. For years, it was the only building in use on that stretch of Albany Street—the area around it looked like Dresden after World War II. Now, MIT's ceaseless redevelopment of their corner of Cambridge has reached the end of Albany Street, and the shelter is now dwarfed by new dormitories and new laboratories.

240 Albany Street has been caring for alcoholic homeless men and women for more than twenty years. It is a shelter for alcoholics and substance abusers, the only place in Cambridge that will shelter men and women who are drunk or using drugs. It has a van that picks up people who are too immobilized by drink or drugs to find their way back although, recently, funding cutbacks have limited the van service to weekdays. When the temperature drops below twenty degrees, 240

---

1. Carpenter, *Memoirs*, 120.

Albany Street will take in as many people as it can until it runs out of floor space. Jean and I try to stop by 240 Albany Street every other Thursday night to see people we may have missed on Sunday, and to check up on others who only know us through our visits there. During the summer, people drift in during the evening, or don't come in at all. The men and women who are there will still be awake when we arrive, finishing dinner or watching the Red Sox or smoking outdoors on the enclosed patio behind the dining area. When it is colder and the days are shorter, more people will stay inside.

Because it welcomes people who are drunk or using, 240 Albany Street is where most of our people go indoors if they go in at all. (When they don't, they sleep in ATM booths, behind City Hall, down by the Charles River, in the basement entrance to the Tannery in Harvard Square, in the garden behind St. James's Church—any place that is out of the cold and where a policeman isn't likely to roust them early in the morning.) Guests can come in to 240 Albany Street any time but once you leave, you can't come back until the next night. Some people will bury a bottle outside—guests can't bring liquor in either—catch a few hours sleep and go back out again early in the morning and dig up the bottle. But Rick says it is too complicated for him to buy a bottle and bury it; he wants the assurance of having a bottle right at hand, even if he has to stay outside.

Our church members are always getting barred from 240 Albany Street for a night or a week or even a year. The worst infraction is putting hands on a staff member, but fighting with other guests is almost as bad. It is harsh to be barred in the middle of February, and the shelter will take in people who have been barred on a night-by-night basis when the temperature drops below twenty degrees.

· · · · ·

After a few months, we realized why homeless people were congregating in Porter Square on Sunday mornings. There is a CVS drugstore right across the street, and you can get gallon jugs of Listerine there at any time of day or night. There are many more liquor stores in Central Square than Harvard Square or Porter Square, but they don't open until noon. Guests at 240 Albany Street who forget to bury a bottle nearby before they go indoors will wake up very early and find their way to

Porter Square and the CVS. Then they will hang around the Porter Square MBTA station until mid-day.

When the temperature drops well below freezing or it is raining or when the wind starts blowing our communion wafers around the Square, we will take refuge inside the T Station. (It is often a close call whether we should go inside or not; many homeless people don't like to be in small enclosed spaces with people who are drinking Listerine.) People sit on the green florist's display from which an old Chinese couple sell cut flowers during the week. On Sunday, it works as bleachers. Most people sit on the stands and the rest gather around the cart. During the week, people sleep on it, when they are not across the street at the White Hen Pantry convenience store trying to nurse a cup of coffee through the early morning.

When we are outdoors we actually look like a church. A low granite wall makes a semicircle where Somerville Avenue and Mass Avenue intersect. People sit on the wall holding our laminated orders of service, following along with the prayers or just dozing. Men and women whom we see here, early in the morning, we will see again in Central Square later in the day, much the worse for wear but still pleased to see us.

・・・・・

Porter Square was a likely place to extend our reach. I had recently been ordained at North Prospect Church, just a hundred yards from Porter Square. The preceding year, I and Tom Lenhart, another lawyer from Washington, D.C. just about my age, and Kevin Smith from the West Coast, fresh from a stint as the head of staff for the Governor of Oregon, had all been interns together at North Prospect. Tom and Kevin were a year behind me at Harvard and they were both serving as student ministers at North Prospect. Late in the fall of 2004, the three of us took a cart and some socks and juice and sandwiches and a nondescript wooden cross that broke after three Sundays and began a service in Porter Square. It was a long cold winter. As a church project, it was a failure. Only a few North Prospect parishioners came out with us, and even they didn't stay beyond one or two Sundays. But Kevin and Tom and I were able to keep it going until people began to hear about us. We had a slow start. It took a while for homeless people to get comfortable with three guys who looked and sounded as if they had dropped into Porter Square from a parallel universe. Our first congregants were quiet and appreciative; we weren't as challenged emotionally and theologically as we would be a year later. After graduation in the spring of 2005, Kevin went out to the West Coast with his wife (herself a Unitarian minister) to become senior minister at Alamaden Valley United Church of Christ in San Jose, California, and Tom was called to the pulpit at First Church Congregational in Chappaqua, New York. But by that time, Jean Chapman had appeared.

We had been in Porter Square for almost a year when Jean showed up. Jean had just graduated from the Boston University School of Theology. She was a member of Old Cambridge Baptist Church—one of the churches in the Harvard Square Clergy Association—and she heard about the Outdoor Church in Porter Square from the chair of OCBC's social outreach committee, which had reviewed—and then rejected—our application for funding. Jean was intrigued. She had worked at a homeless shelter in Cambridge, where she did "go-fer" work, and discovered that she was very comfortable with people on the street. After a flurry of e-mails, Jean joined Pat and me at Christ Church for Compline. I asked if she could help out in Porter Square. She said yes. She remembers my saying, "This is auspicious," but what I *meant* was, "This is nigh unto miraculous," because up to then I had no idea how I was going to replace Tom and Kevin.

Jean has a perfectly round face, haloed with gray hair. Her small blue eyes gleam above full, rosy cheeks. She looks like Tenniel's White Queen, like everybody's mother. This is a blessing in a community where most people can't remember, or don't want to remember, their mothers. Jean is quick to hug, something I can't and shouldn't do. She favors prayer and healing through the laying on of hands. She has a warmth of spirit that draws on both a deep spirituality and an impulse toward social work: she is currently seeking her MSW at Boston University.

Just beneath Jean's amiable and benign appearance lurk a incisive and analytic mind, a confidence of moral judgment and—best of all for me, all too hesitant to act in a time of crisis—an ability to fling herself into the middle of things in order to be physically as well as emotionally present for people who need her.

Shortly after Jean joined us in Porter Square, Shaggy, very, very drunk, staggered into the middle of our service to say with tears in his eyes how happy he was that Vickie, his partner, had been released from Framingham State Prison for Women and was with him again. Even as

Shaggy was sharing his jubilation with us, Vickie was in the lower level of the T Station, directly underneath us, where Shaggy had just left her after beating her almost unconscious. The B&M Commuter Rail stops in Porter Square. The tracks run under Mass Avenue and under a portion of the T site, running southeast toward North Station in Boston. An underground pedestrian walkway runs parallel to the B&M tracks, connecting the Porter Square T station with a small steel girdered bridge on the opposite side of Mass Avenue. Shortly, we heard a commotion across the street. A crowd had gathered, an ambulance pulled up and we could hear patrol car sirens in all directions. (It is no longer possible for us to hear a police or fire engine siren without immediately thinking that they are there to pick up one of our people.) A young woman had seen Vickie struggling to crawl up the metal steps on her hands and knees, and called 911 on her cell phone. Astonishingly, Shaggy announced he was going to "help out" and began to weave his way through traffic to the other side of the street. He was arrested immediately. Jean ran to the other side of the street and recognized Vickie. She persuaded the EMTs and the police to let her ride with Vickie in the ambulance, and spent the rest of the day at Cambridge City Hospital vainly trying, together with the resident on duty, to persuade Vickie to go home to Maynard or at least go into a shelter for battered women. Not surprisingly, Vickie refused to even consider it. The police brought assault charges against Shaggy but Vickie wouldn't cooperate as a witness and the police had to drop the charges. Jean says, with amazement, when she stops to think about how she found her way up to Porter Square, "All I was looking for was a way to minister . . ."

The Porter Square T station has four levels: the first, at street level, where we worship, is little more than a glass box with doors leading out to the street. Escalators lead down to the second level, where the turnstiles and Charlie Card machines are and where homeless men hawk copies of *Metro Boston*. Once inside the turnstiles, a bank of escalators leads down to the inbound T tracks to Boston and the south shore and then, further down, to the outbound tracks headed for Alewife. The T requires that buskers—if they are inside the turnstiles—apply for permits. The issue is contentious, and led to a law suit in Federal District Court. But as a church, we are entitled to worship inside or outside the turnstiles without first asking for or obtaining permission, as long as we don't threaten the safety of the T's passengers and personnel.

For the most part, the T police and station managers have acknowledged our right to have our services on their property and in their station, and only ask us not to block the doors. Sometimes, one of our members falls asleep on the thick gray outdoor carpet in front of the one of the doors and the T hears about it from irate commuters. We try to anticipate their concern and get him sitting up on the florist's display before someone thinks to call the police. One station manager—a young woman with short, spiky blond hair and a perpetually sour expression—was disturbed by our service. She would take me aside and tell me how much she admired what we were doing, but "regulations" required that we leave, and hadn't we seen the "No Trespassing" sign outdoors? There wasn't any sign and there weren't any regulations. No matter. The station manager would stand about thirty feet away, on the other side of the station, glower at us for ten or fifteen minutes and then ostentatiously use her cell phone to call in the T detectives. This always annoyed the on-duty T detective, who was required to respond to the call. No matter how many times he had been there before, he would ask for my identification, look at my driver's license and wrestle with the proper spelling of my first name. Everyone at church thought it was hilarious that I—a lawyer—should have to explain myself to the same cops who harassed them during the week. Finally, I sent an email to the T's legal department, asking for clarification of their policy. The next Sunday, the T's head of community relations and the commander of MBTA police for our district—each unaware of the other and both off duty—came down to visit us. They were friendly and sympathetic and the station manager was assigned to another station. My reputation on the street was established forever.

Patrick has been sleeping in the Porter Square Station for as long as we have been holding prayer services there. Patrick is thin and slouches. His snow white hair hangs over his face and nearly covers his wide blue eyes. He has a dreamy and detached manner but can work himself into a rage in seconds. He can be stubborn and provoking. When he is panhandling, he is too confrontational. In Massachusetts, it is legal to ask passersby for money so long as you don't physically impede their progress, but Patrick gets in front of people as they walk through the T Station and won't get out of the way when they try to avoid him. Commuters who are emerging from the station at the end of a working day call in to complain. The Cambridge police jail him for the night, give him a meal and release him in the morning.

Patrick can also be endearing. When he talks with me, he makes eye contact and holds it—that is unusual for someone who drinks as much as Patrick. Patrick is the only homeless man in Cambridge who calls me by my full first name, "Jedediah." He reminds me of the Confederate General Harry Heth, who was famous, in a way, for being the first general shot at the Battle of Gettysburg. He survived only because a haberdasher from whom he had bought a hat the day before had stuffed cardboard in the brim to make the hat fit. Heth was the only Confederate general who called General Robert E. Lee, his classmate at West Point, by his first name. Even Lee's wife called him "General." Patrick is always delighted when I tell him about Harry Heth. He has a musical laugh.

Now, Patrick sits in a corner of the Porter Square T Station all day and drinks Listerine. Sometimes he simply passes out. If he is not blocking an entrance, the T police, who have known him for a long while, will leave him alone. Patrick used to be a lawyer. He says he used to be Clerk of the Probate Court in Malden, a much coveted position among local attorneys. Most state reps would rather be a clerk of courts—the pay is better and there is much more job security. But Patrick couldn't control his drinking.

(Patrick's steep descent into homelessness isn't extraordinary. Among our congregants are lawyers, school teachers, a commercial fisherman, an antique dealer and members of many other professions and occupations. Not all of our people were born to poverty, abuse and neglect. Many led apparently successful lives and supported apparently successful marriages and families, only have substance abuse destroy it all. We are always shocked by how great the distance that some of our people have fallen and how complete the destruction of their lives.)

Patrick has been drinking too heavily for too long to get off the street, much less return to his family or his work. He understands that he is irrevocably damaged. He never talks about going into a program or finding housing. Do the T police know that Patrick was once a Clerk in Malden? It is hard to believe that they don't. In Cambridge, all the T police are politicians. If they do know, it doesn't matter any more. "Jedediah," he rasps, when a pair of undercover detectives come up the elevator from the lower level, "these bastards have got nothing better to do than to harass an old man." The detectives smile and move on. Patrick takes another swig of Listerine.

Like any large institution, the T's enforcement of its own regulations on the ground is often inconsistent and unpredictable. We have always served a meal to our people in Porter Square on T property and, if the weather is inclement, inside the station itself, but the T has barred Hope Church, an evangelical church just down Beech Street from St. James's, from serving a hot meal to homeless men and women on Wednesday evenings in Pigeon Park, just a few steps east of the station but still on T property. Sporadic police enforcement is a serious matter for the members of our church. Many have spent time in prison, are awaiting trial or are violating parole. A few years before, undercover T police staked out our services. They had figured out that some of the people who attended our services were likely to have warrants outstanding and that this was a convenient place to find them. They would stand at the periphery of our service, waiting for us to finish, or watch the Dunkin's Donuts at the corner of the Porter Square Shopping Center through high powered binoculars. After a few weeks of this, our attendance plummeted. We urged the undercover police we could identify not to arrest people immediately before or after our services and they backed off. It hasn't happened in a long while.

T personnel can be extraordinarily sympathetic. Homeless people know which station managers will allow them to stay in the T's tunnels, out of the way of trains, when being outdoors means frostbite. But the first person I saw kick a homeless person was a T official. We had just finished a service inside the station in Porter Square. It was well below freezing outside. Feathers of frost had formed on the windows wherever people had been standing during the service. One of the T's animal rescue vans pulled up. Benjie, Patrick's friend and drinking companion, was sprawled against a glass wall, smoking a cigarette whenever he wasn't nodding off. He was well away from any entrance where he might have created a safety hazard. A young blond woman in a T uniform got out of the van and came into the station—she had been called to rescue a dog that had fallen onto the tracks. She saw Benjie, leaned over him and asked him to get rid of the cigarette. Benjie didn't respond; he was too drunk. The woman straightened up and kicked the cigarette out of his hand. Fran, who was eating a bagel next to me, yelped. I went over to the young woman and asked her to check with us before kicking one of our congregants. She denied that she had kicked anyone. I repeated what I had said; she repeated what she had said. We did that two or three more times. Then she said, "And I didn't see you anyway," although the station is only two hundred feet square and I was wearing a bright red winter coat. Then she said, "And if you care about this guy so much, why didn't you call the police?" I was speechless. Call the police? I would sooner kick him myself. She walked away. Benjie was listening to all this and thought it was a great joke.

· · · · ·

Whenever the T detectives arrived, I would become apprehensive that Mike O'Grady, who had joined us in Porter Square shortly after Jean began to lead our services, would try to provoke a confrontation with them. It was easy to forget, as I was worrying about Mike getting himself arrested, that Mike had had plenty of experience getting arrested and knew far better than me what he was doing. Mike is a Jesuit brother from Chicago, in Boston to further his formation in a life of spirituality. He took seriously the Jesuits' special regard for those at the margins of society, and dedicated himself to caring for homeless men and women who are sick, who are hospitalized or who are recuperating from a serious hospitalization. He has warm grey eyes and a toothy grin, tucked behind a beard that seems to ebb and flow in size and color on a weekly basis. After much prayer and thought, Mike decided not to seek ordination as a priest, believing that it could only complicate his call to care for the homeless. (In that unselfconscious willingness to forego the "honor" of priesthood, he echoes Pat's commitment to the vocational diaconate.) Mike is fully present when he is with homeless people—it is a great gift. As part of his formation in St. Louis, Mike spent years nursing homeless men and creating a prayer life for them. While he was part of the Claver Jesuit Community in the South Cumminsville area of Cincinnati, he was arrested and spent some time in prison for protesting in front of the School of the Americas. He reminds me of a group of young Jesuits and much older nuns with whom I demonstrated against the War in Vietnam in 1970 by sitting in the middle of Cambridge Street in front of the Federal Building in Foley Square and refusing to move. Sitting with the Jesuits on the asphalt, I watched a line of Boston police, helmeted and booted, very slowly riding their motorcycles down Cambridge Street toward the nuns, who were sitting together and singing. I imagined the emotional conflict and distress that each policeman must have felt, threatening to run down nuns, and thought about the Jesuits' and the nuns' certainty of call, their peaceful acceptance of the palpable risks we faced and their utterly centered and convicted lives, little imagining that, more than thirty years later, I would be joining another Jesuit in a similar witness.

Mike was especially good with Irving. Irving was the first to have a memorial service in Porter Square. He died in the Porter Square T station, after rolling off the green wooden stand in his sleep and hitting his head on the edge of a granite curb. Irving was a porcine older man—he was built like a Belgian draft horse—with thinning, unkempt white hair and puffy red cheeks. His eyes were always mere slits, whether he was smiling and looking avuncular or whether he was snarling at someone who was making fun of him. He slept on the cement benches at the entrance to the commuter rail station, or around the corner, opposite the Chicago Uno Grill, in all seasons and weather. Irving stored all of his belongings in shopping carts from the Porter Square Shopping Center. He tried to keep them near him at all times, to prevent other homeless men from stealing from him. He could have as many as four or five shopping carts lined up next to the concrete benches.

Irving spoke very, very softly, forcing you to lean in toward him to understand anything he was saying. Irving obsessed about his feet and his legs, which were badly swollen, discolored and scabrous. He refused to see a doctor. He was convinced that if we could provide him with knee high white socks without elastic at the top, his legs would get better. Irving could barely walk, even supported by one of his carts. He would usually appear just as the prayer service ended, apologizing for having overslept. Irving had no interest in the service itself. If he came up before the service had ended, he would slump on the granite wall and doze until it was time for the meal. He loved egg salad sandwiches, the only kind that Jean made for Porter Square. He had a number of recipes for egg salad and—as with most things—was adamant about the way that egg salad ought to be prepared. Irving would never let food get by him if he could help it. He would take as many sandwiches as he could and as many juice boxes as we had, simply asking for one more every time someone gave him one.

Irving was especially fond of doughnuts. Before every service in Porter Square, Mike would buy a box of twelve assorted doughnuts and an insulated box holding ten cups of coffee from the Dunkin' Donuts at the edge of the Porter Square Shopping Center. We counted on Irving to deal with any leftover doughnuts and coffee and clean up the used napkins, empty sugar packets and little plastic cups of milk that people dropped or threw away. He would wrap up anything that was left over in newspaper and store it in one of his shopping carts. Shaggy used to tease Irving unmercifully about the doughnuts and called him "Doughnut Man," which enraged Irving. But Irving could barely stand, much less threaten someone half his age like Shaggy.

Despite appearances, Irving had some money in a bank account, though rarely on his person; younger homeless men periodically rolled him, knowing he could barely walk. The money was income from a trust fund established for him or by him before he became too deranged to manage his own affairs. He would get annual reports, dividend statements and other corporate mailings and, knowing that I was a lawyer, would ask me to explain a takeover announcement or some arcane language in a footnote to a financial statement.

Irving was very insistent that we attend to him, especially when he was in one of his manic periods and talking about the demons and devils who preyed on the young women he wanted to protect. He, like many homeless people, had mastered the art of never completing a sentence, knowing that most people wait for the end of a sentence to end a conversation and walk away. It took a long time for me to get used to walking away from Irving when he was in mid-thought.

In his way, Irving was one of the most dangerous people in Porter Square, even though he was virtually immobile. We learned, well after he joined us, that he was a registered sex offender. He nurtured vicious, destructive fantasies about women in which his former wife and his daughters were confusedly marked either as the seductive temptation in a Satanic plot to ensnare men, or as the chaste victims of a Satanic plot to ensnare women. His diatribes in the presence of men were horrific—full of foul sexual allusions and grotesque stories about hypnosis, temptation and seduction—but the things he said to women were worse. Irving often mistook our younger interns for his daughters, telling them that he wanted to protect them against the dangers of the street and offending them with vile sexual innuendo when they approached him. The only volunteer who ever walked away from our church was a young woman, a member of St. James's, who had faithfully attended our services in Porter Square for more than a year. One Sunday, she simply wasn't there. We didn't find out until many months later that she had been so upset and revolted after listening to Irving that she vowed to never return to Porter Square. It took many more months before she told me what had had so disturbed her.

Virginia, a slender homeless woman in her thirties, was the last woman to be drawn into Irving's orbit before he died. She had long lustrous sandy hair and, in winter, wore a floor-length padded scarlet coat that was visible from blocks away. She slept on the metal bridge that spanned the commuter rail tracks. Virginia was pretty, with regular features and large brown eyes. She wore enormous sun glasses which made her look like Holly Golightly. She wanted an audience with the Pope. Virginia was especially drawn to Mike, because, being a Jesuit, he could help her get to the Vatican. Irving bought her waterproof winter boots and other useful but expensive presents, all of which she professed to disdain. Virginia probably supported herself by selling herself to men, homeless or not, who passed through Porter Square. One Christmas, she disappeared. Irving developed a convoluted fantasy about a young man who had hypnotized Virginia and lured her away from his protection, embellished with Kabalistic symbolism and complicated theories about sin, punishment and redemption. Months after she had gone, Irving continued to talk about her as if she were just across the street or visiting her sister in Washington, D.C. Toward the end, it was all he would talk about.

When Irving fell off the wooden bleachers and hit his head on the corner of a concrete abutment, we had a memorial service for him. We used the same order of service we always use, with a text from Wisdom of Solomon—"But the souls of the righteous are in the hand of God, and there shall no torment touch them" (Wis 3:1)—but most people in Porter Square disliked Irving intensely and could barely wait until the service was over to have coffee and doughnuts. We never learned what happened to Irving's trust fund; perhaps it is cached somewhere in the Department of Revenue as abandoned property, waiting for an enterprising relative to retrieve it. We never heard from Irving's family or learned where he was buried or if he had a funeral. He was the first, but by no means the last, of the homeless men and women we were bound to love no matter how much we disliked them.

● ● ● ● ●

At first, on the Cambridge Common and then later, in Porter Square, we used a version of the order of service for Morning Prayer that Common Cathedral uses in Boston. Debbie had edited the order of service down to its most essential elements but without radically changing the language; she wanted to make sure that the language was familiar but also accessible. The service had Taize prayers, which we often use, and songs, which we rarely use. For our services, I shortened the order of service even more, thinking that people would get impatient and walk away rather than wait for the sandwiches and socks, and then rushed through the entire service. But ten minutes this way or that didn't matter that much to people who were going to be sitting in Porter Square or Central Square for the rest of the day anyway. The service stretched out and relaxed. Mardi Moran, who owns Tags Hardware in the Porter Square Shopping Center, laminated thirty or so copies of the people's version of the order of service and a few copies of the minister's version. Laminating the orders of service made them impervious to rain, snow, sleet, grape juice, shampoo and coffee. We are still using them, although most people have the order of service memorized by now.

● ● ● ● ●

In Porter Square—especially when we are inside the station because the weather is especially bad—the space in which we gather to worship together becomes a sacred space to everyone there. Something—the intensity of our engagement with one another, the powerful sense of community, the Holy Spirit—makes that expanse of concrete, that patch of gray, gritty outdoor carpet a church.

The feeling is palpable. It is especially evident when we are inside the station and a commuter starts to walk through the space where we are worshipping. There is always a collective frisson of astonishment: why, you might as well ride a bicycle down the aisle of a conventional church during a sermon, or jump across the communion rail during the administration of the Lord's Supper. Sometimes the less inhibited among our congregants, like Jeannie, complain to the offending passerby: "Hey, there's a church service going on here!" The commuter is mystified and sometimes stops to see what Jeannie is talking about.

It is evident, also, in the way that our members enforce rules of behavior once the service is underway. Our only formal rule is, don't carry a weapon in church. But there are other, informal rules: don't talk loudly and turn your back on the altar while a service is in progress; don't harass visitors from other churches or hit them up for money; be careful of children; don't use violent or blasphemous language; don't drink openly or smoke when we are inside the station; treat your clergy gently and with respect.

Homeless people treat us gently no matter where we are. Most people know that I am a lawyer and that most of us are over sixty; we are not likely to be offended or shocked by profanity. But our people like to think of us as needing protection from the harshness of their lives. In fact, we never see the kind of violence that puts our people in the hospital or in prison or bars them from 240 Albany Street for a month or a year. We never see people using drugs. We never see the beatings, assaults or other violence, like homeless men putting razors between their fingers and slapping other homeless men around, that the Cambridge police see all the time. It is important to our people that they set us apart from the abuse and degradation that they live with on the street every day.

It is not that we, as individuals, are special—it is the ministry that is special. People treasure the Outdoor Church. They want it to be as far removed from the horrors of the street as they can put it. And so do we: whatever else it is, the Outdoor Church is, for its members, an hour of peace, relative safety and community that is almost impossible to find anywhere else. But there is also a sweetness to this protection from reality: people don't want to see us hurt and this is one of the very few ways they can do something about it. Homeless people don't have many ways to tell us that they love what we do: this is one of them.

•••••

Not all of our church members are Christian or even religious. Lynn is Jewish. Like so many people on the street, she is Bible literate and very proud of her Jewish upbringing. Lynn has been living in Porter Square for years; she was there when we appeared with our cart and grape juice for the first time. Lynn has enormous, bulging gray eyes and stringy gray hair. In every season but winter, she wears no shoes or socks, although, apart from calluses, her feet are well cared for. She has a shopping cart filled with her belongings—extra coats, important papers, Dunkin' Donuts bags. It never leaves her side. She sleeps on the bench at the bus stop on the Somerville Avenue side of the T station, her shopping cart pulled up next to her head so that she will feel the difference if someone tries to take it. Irving complained bitterly about having his carts stolen, or things stolen from his cart, while he was sleeping; Lynn, although she takes fewer precautions against theft than Irving, rarely complains about missing any of her possessions. You couldn't miss it if she did; when she is in full voice, you can hear her across the Porter Square Shopping Center.

Lynn stoutly maintains that she is blind and carries a white walking stick with a red tip. No one takes this seriously, since she makes eye contact when she speaks to you, reads the newspaper every morning in Porter Square and has no trouble following along with our order of service. Lynn also says that she suffers from cellulitis, diabetes, vitamin deficiencies, neuropathy, asthma and many other ailments and diseases, many of which have been caused or aggravated by the drugs that she is given every time she is involuntarily committed to a Department of Mental Health facility.

Lynn believes that she is the owner of two buildings on Mt. Vernon Street, just off Mass Avenue, that are now divided into very expensive condominiums. It may be that she lived there as a child, before her father died. She believes that the buildings are being rehabilitated and, when the work is done, she will be able to move back in. From time to time, she goes over to check on the workmen's progress and gets upset with the quality of their work. Lynn is deeply puzzled by the presence of strangers in her buildings—the owners of the condominiums—by political signs that appear in the windows and by the unfamiliar names on the mail boxes. She *likes* Obama, she says, but isn't it a violation of her first amendment rights that someone else has put an "Obama for President" sign in her window? Once, when she worked her way into the vestibule to inspect some new carpeting, a resident called the Cambridge Police, who sent an officer up to investigate. Lynn didn't hear him come up behind her and, when he spoke to her, she was startled, spun around and kicked him. She was arrested for assaulting a police officer, committed to Bridgewater for a thirty-day observation and then to the Lindemann Center in Boston. A court appointed attorney, specially trained to represent people who have been involuntarily committed to a state mental institution, represented Lynn, and I attended the hearings as her minister. The assault charges were ultimately dropped, but it took months for Lynn to get out of Lindemann. She was vehement that the condominiums were her property and that she would defend it against any trespasser. That persuaded the doctors at Lindemann and the district court judge who reviewed her case that she was a threat to others and should remain incarcerated. Finally, the antipsychotic drugs that Lindemann gave her over her violent objections—those drugs were what caused her diabetes, she has been asserting ever since—began to take effect. Lindemann finally released her after six months, on the condition that she stay in one of its own shelters, go into counseling and continue to take the antipsychotic drugs. Within weeks, Lynn was back in Porter Square, living outdoors and not taking her medication. She had lost weight and she sounded clear headed—that was the effect of the antipsychotic drugs—but within days the effect had worn off and she sounded as deranged as ever.

This is a predictable and familiar cycle. Wendy, when she wasn't taking her medications, would stand in the middle of Mass Avenue in Harvard Square and scream at the drivers of the passing cars, until the police would come and commit her involuntarily—"pink slip" her, as the police say, for the color of the form they have to fill out—to a hospital or mental institution. There, she would be given some medication—after four or five times, all the hospitals in the area knew exactly what combination of anti-psychotics worked best for her—and held for four days. In Massachusetts, a person who has been involuntarily committed for four days is entitled to a hearing and representation by an attorney. But, by then, the drugs had taken effect and Wendy was no longer delusional. Since she wasn't, she was no longer a risk to herself or to others, and she had to be released with a prescription for her medications in hand. Once on the street, Wendy would lose the prescription or sell it to another homeless person. In any event, she wasn't taking her medications.

Like many people, homeless or not, Wendy believed that, once she felt better, she was "cured" and didn't need to take any drugs. Taking drugs meant you were mentally ill; not taking drugs meant you were sane. No one wants to think that they are insane. So Wendy wouldn't take her medications and, within weeks or even days, she would be back in the middle of the street screaming at passing busses.

Lynn was caught up in the same regulatory loop. Her hearings at the Lindemann Center were dreadful. Neither the judge nor Lynn's treating physicians wanted to hold her, but she was adamant in her insistence that she would do it all over again if someone trespassed on her property. There were no realistic alternatives; it was only because Lynn finally consented to living in a Massachusetts Mental Health Department shelter that she was released. Lindemann knew, and Lynn knew, that she would only stay there for a day or two, but there was no better choice.

Unlike Wendy, Lynn rarely gets in trouble with the police. She believes that she is a Cambridge police officer on special assignment, charged with keeping the peace in Porter Square and helping homeless people in difficulty. Lynn takes her job as a Cambridge police officer very seriously. She can cite statistics proving that Porter Square is a safer, quieter place since she was assigned to keep order there. After Patrick complained that the mayonnaise in our egg salad sandwiches would go bad if they sat in the sun, we got a cooler and a Freez Pak and kept our sandwiches in the cooler until the prayer service was over. Once, in the confusion that always follows the end of a service, when we are handing around sandwiches and doughnuts, I left the cooler in Porter Square. Lynn found it and gave it to a policewoman a few days later with a note: "For Jed Mannis Sunday Street Church returned to Cambridge Police by Mrs. Lynn Greene Gold Badge 1854." When I got to the Lost Property Department on the third floor of the police station in Central Square, the police woman on duty knew who I was, knew who Lynn was and knew exactly where the cooler was. "She's a lovely lady," said the police woman. "I see her every day when I take the T in to work. But she should wash more often."

Lynn badly wants the City of Cambridge to acknowledge that she is married. She thinks that if she can get the City of Cambridge to confirm her marital status, she will be that much closer to recovering her buildings. She says that she is married to Ed, who has worked for years "on the Blue Line." Lynn feels warmly toward Ed; he is her defense against the drug dealers and prowlers who pass through Porter Square every evening: "You're not my boyfriend! I'm married. I don't need a boyfriend," she yells at them, loudly enough to attract a lot of attention, and they keep their distance. ("It's the drinking," says Lynn. "That's why they're all criminals."). She has showed the City Clerk Christmas cards that she signed for herself and for Ed and a plastic card she received from the Republican National Committee thanking her for her interest in John McCain's presidential campaign, but the City Clerk remains unmoved. After yet another rebuff at City Hall, she wrote out a description of her marriage to Ed, and asked me to bless it. I gave Lynn what I hoped she would understand to be a non-Christian blessing. Lynn said, "No, no, you have to write it down or the City Clerk won't acknowledge it." I wrote down, "I have blessed Lynn Greene's marriage." "No," said Lynn, "you have to sign it as Reverend Mannis." So I did.

Lynn was very, very pleased. I don't think she ever took the blessed description of her marriage down to City Hall—perhaps she sensed that the City Clerk would reject this too, and preferred to leave the fantasy intact. But she always has it with her. One Christmas, just after a service indoors at Porter Square, Lynn handed me a Christmas card which played "Rudolph the Red Nosed Reindeer" when you pressed Rudolph's nose and a bank check for $10. She had signed the check in her name and in Ed's name and written across the front: "This is for the Outdoor Church of Rev. Jedediah Mannis who has blessed my marriage." "Spend it wisely," she said gravely. "We could use another plastic bin," I suggested. "That's good," she said. "Very practical."

I wake her up every Sunday morning when I arrive in Porter Square, so that she has time to wash up and not miss the sandwiches and coffee. Lynn always declines communion but recites all those parts of the order of service that she thinks are "Old Testament" rather than "New Testament." She tells me that she tries to persuade other homeless people to attend. "It's the same God," she says. "We're all in it together. And you get socks and shampoo and coffee and doughnuts and sandwiches. How can you beat that?"

• • • • •

We have been blessed with a run of extraordinary interns and volunteers. We are a field education site for the Harvard Divinity School. Students from any of the eleven schools that make up the Boston Theological Institute can do an internship with us. We get most of our students and volunteers from the Harvard Divinity School, Boston University School of Theology, the Episcopal Divinity School and the Weston Jesuit School of Theology. They are usually in their mid-twenties, although Sylvia Weston, who was seeking ordination as a vocational deacon in the Episcopal Church when she interned with us, is in her sixties, a former warden at St. James's and the parent of five adult children. Our interns share a willingness to engage the world directly and unselfconsciously. I can't recognize myself in them; when I was in my twenties, I was more worried about my fast pitch softball league batting average than about homelessness. Working with our interns is the brightest and most promising part of our ministry.

And, they are like family. People on the street see Pat and me as an old married couple and our interns and volunteers as our daughters. This is the only way some men can make sense of us as a group. It doesn't matter how many interns we have with us or what ages they are. Pat and I have had as many as four interns and volunteers with us in Central Square, all in their mid twenties, all of different ethnicities, and some people thought all of them were our daughters. Domesticity doesn't stop some of the more drunken young men from hitting on our interns, who in turn have become experienced in fending off unwelcome advances without giving offense. It helps, a little, for a man to be present; it is one of those gender realities that we're forced to acknowledge, however grudgingly.

Our interns' promise is underscored by the people from Hope Church who plant themselves at both entrances to the Porter Square T Station and hand out granola bars and calling cards. Hope Church, which is just up the street from St. James's, is associated with a large fundamentalist church based in Dallas. Throughout the year, but mainly in the spring, the Dallas church sends up gaggles of interns, always young adults in their twenties, to learn about evangelism in a religious environment that is nothing like Dallas. They are uniformly fresh faced, friendly and cheerful, not always dressed for the season but prepared to stand out in an April drizzle or May heat wave to hand out their granola bars. The people who attend our services love the granola bars—they don't get anything so brightly wrapped from us—but simply ignore the rest of the package.

Although the Hope Church interns stand at the entrance to the T Station when they give out their granola bars, Jean and I seem not to register on their radar screen. Nonetheless, we always invite them to join us. Until recently, they have always refused. But Irene, one of our more outgoing interns, once persuaded three of them to become part of our circle. Brad and Shaggy had been at one another for a number of days and were a few yards off to the side of the T station, trading insults. Shaggy had been taking Percocet and drinking Listerine for weeks. When he is sober or just drunk, he is abusive, but the combination of Percocet and Listerine had made him impotent and incontinent. Brad was riding him, taking his hat and throwing it into the middle of Somerville Avenue, and Shaggy was reduced to screaming at him in frustration. One of the Hope Church people—a young man with a round, open face and broad shoulders—began to push Shaggy away from Brad, thinking, perhaps, that a fight was about to start. Irene had to talk him out of his rescue mission. The young man backed off, but he and the others soon left and never returned.

Maybe it is culture. Maybe it is style. We're simply not evangelical in the same way. It is not that we are not saving souls; but our ministry isn't grounded in the conviction that we need to get there before God does.

• • • • •

Mardi Moran got interested in homeless people because a few homeless men and women were panhandling in front of Dunkin' Donuts and some of the other stores in the Porter Square Shopping Center. Mardi and her husband, Si, own Tag's Hardware, one of the businesses in the shopping center. She heard about the Outdoor Church from Michael Povey, the Rector at St. James's, which is two blocks to the west, and came out to see what had so excited Michael. Mardi and Si have been involved in Cambridge politics for a long, long while. When the City redesigned the intersection of Somerville Avenue and Mass Avenue to cut down on the number of bus and pedestrian accidents, it carved out a small park, just in front of the CVS, and dedicated it to Si. Mardi looks a little like Jean—blond hair swept back in a page boy, wide smile—but a little taller and a little slimmer, with much larger gray eyes. Jean bounces; Mardi glides. She has been endlessly generous to us, contributing metal carts, laminating orders of service, buying coffee and donuts—and equally supportive of the homeless men and women in Porter Square. She allows them to store things at Tag's, collect mail there and use the bathrooms. Some people take advantage—they shoplift small items, like key chains, that Mardi would otherwise be happy to give to them—and she has had to ban one or two, but—banned or no—homeless people in Porter Square love her because her generosity is obviously genuine.

Mardi is often grieved by the betrayals that are always a part of being with homeless men and women. Brad and his girl friend, Louise, Shaggy and Vickie and a number of other homeless people use the backyard of St. James's to sleep, party, drink, use drugs, and generally carry on. It annoys and angers the sexton at St. James's, who has to pick up their used needles and dirty toilet paper. But the noise annoys and angers nearby residents even more. While Brad was awaiting trial on a charge of assaulting a police officer, Mardi attempted to mediate an agreement between him and the church, but Brad sneered at her efforts to help him and embarrassed her in front of other homeless people and representatives of the church. This hurt Mardi deeply. She has great faith in the essential goodness of the people she is trying to help. When they act poorly, she feels foolish and exploited.

Mardi has worked hard to promote federal, state and municipal programs that will alleviate, if not end, homelessness. Together with Jean and Evan, she attends meetings of the Cambridge Continuum of Care—an umbrella organization for Cambridge social service groups committed to helping homeless people—goes often to conferences and symposia on homelessness in Cambridge and has played an important role in the formulation of ten year plans to end homelessness in Cambridge and Somerville. All of this effort has achieved important results: our new governor, Deval Patrick, recently signed a housing bond authorization for $1.25 billion for a five-year plan to fight homelessness: $500 million is committed to the rehabilitation of existing public housing and the remainder to six regional pilot homeless prevention networks "with $10 million [each] in state-approved aid to re-house families and provide them with economic stability by 2013."[2] But I am doubtful that much of this will benefit the emotionally unstable and substance dependent homeless men and women in our church.

• • • • •

Different people have found different ways of participating in our work, beyond writing a check. Carl MacDonald of the City Mission Society of Boston, a ministry of the United Church of Christ, regularly refers youth groups to us. Women at our supporting churches collect clean white socks for us, or make sandwiches, or assemble bags of toiletries. Priests

---

2. Kantor and Wolchover, "One Roof at a Time."

and ministers from Ecclesia Ministries' "Come and See" weekend, a three day symposium for churches that are considering starting some kind of outdoor worship for homeless men and women, come up to watch and kick the tires. Mike and Ann Scott come down from Kennebunk, Maine, every month or so, loaded with sandwiches and socks, and walk around Harvard Square with us. A group of Buddhist students from the Zen Peacemakers Center in Montague, Massachusetts, who had been sleeping outdoors and begging on the streets of Boston to gain an understanding of what it must be like to be chronically homeless, joined us one beautiful late spring day in Porter Square. We depend upon the imagination of those who would like to help us, even if they find the idea of a direct encounter with a homeless person too frightening or too revolting.

• • • • •

Porter Square is where many different communities of homeless men and women meet. Homeless people call Central Square "Mental Square" because so many mentally ill men and women cluster there, but Porter Square bids fair to surpass it. Unlike Central Square, which is home to Homestart, a housing agency, CASCAP, a non profit that serves as representative payee for many disabled homeless men and women, the Cambridge Multi-Service Center and many other social service organizations, there aren't any services for homeless people in Porter Square. But it does have many public spaces that are far from residential neighborhoods and relatively private, like Pigeon Park, in which homeless people can sleep, fight or have sex with less worry about being rousted or arrested.

Porter Square is also where the Outdoor Church overlaps these communities and intersects them, if only for an hour or so every Sunday morning. Most people arrive and congregate in groups: Fran, Doug and Vic from Inman Square; Eugene and Patrick from 240 Albany Street; Brad, Louise, Shaggy and Vickie from Porter Square itself. Some are loners, like Irving and Ed, while they were still alive. Some do better than others. A group of young adults, mostly men and looking very fit, join us from time to time during the summer. They are part of a program run by Harvard students under the auspices of the Philips-Brooks House. It is a job training program for people who have just secured subsidized housing in Cambridge. These people won't be with us for long; they are just passing through.

• • • • •

Barb is one of the group from Inman Square. Fran says that Barb is her daughter, but she probably means that she loves her as if she were a daughter. In fact, Fran has two daughters, whom she never sees; we don't know where they are. Barb is a young woman, probably in her mid-twenties, with a heart shaped face, hooded green eyes, very high cheekbones, a bee-sting mouth and no color in her cheeks. Barb attracts men and women both—sex, for the men, and a maternal impulse in the women. She whines incessantly and is difficult to like.

We had been going through a transitional time in Porter Square. The job training people from St. James's had been showing up for a few weeks. Three or four very serious older men were now with us. They were in different stages of recovery and needed to talk about their substance abuse and how they had overcome it and how they were maintaining. Kyle was in this group. He had heard about us from the director of a detox program in Central Square. Kyle is a very short man with a florid face, saggy jowls and clear aviator glasses. He wears cut off T shirts, khaki shorts, white wool socks and running shorts. It is precisely the wrong outfit for Kyle. He has very thin thighs and slender hips, with an enormous stomach hanging over them. He isn't obese—everything else is in proportion—but his stomach is simply huge. Every Sunday, Kyle listens carefully to the Scripture and then uses it as a platform to talk about how he has successfully confronted his substance abuse. He had been a very successful contractor, he said, with a large house in Wakefield, cars and a beautiful wife. He bought antique cars and repaired them; he dabbled in commodities futures; he collected stamps. But he began to drink and he lost it all. Faith has saved him, he says, and has given him the strength to fight back. Now, he doesn't have any money and he lives in a shelter, but he is a free man, and for this he thanks God.

There were three or four men at Porter Square then who shared this kind of experience—not as articulate as Kyle, but sober and focused—and they heard Kyle's testimonies as their own. We had never had a group like this in Porter Square—sinners saved by God's grace and praising him loudly—and it was tempting to bask in the glow that

Kyle and his friends radiated. But while Kyle was testifying, Doug and Fran, Brad and Louise, Jeannie, Shaggy and Vickie and, from time to time, Barb, would create an enormous racket just at the periphery of our worship circle. Brad would play his boom box or Fran would sashay up to Doug and Vic as they sat worshipping, turn her back on Jean as she was conducting the service and start a shouting match with Vic. Jean worried for three or four weeks about whether she would be able to keep the service under control. Finally, she decided to trust that the liturgy itself, buttressed by all those worshipers who were fully engaged in the service, would sustain a sacred space that even Fran and the others would finally respect. And, in time, they did.

But before that, Barb appeared one fall Sunday when the balance between the sanctity of the morning service and the level of distracting activity seemed especially uncertain. She contented herself with sitting apart from the prayer service and flirting with all the nearby men. When I offered her communion, she neither refused nor accepted it, but simply didn't acknowledge my presence. Then, she changed her mind, accepted a wafer and little plastic cup of grape juice from Jean, drank the juice, walked over to the cart and tossed the used cup into the bowl of consecrated but undistributed wafers.

I was astounded. Apart from the intentional insult, I was nonplussed at the ease with which Barb had desecrated the sacramental symbols that meant so much to the other people there. She might just as well have urinated on the altar.

As I stood there, trying to think of what to do, I sensed Ken standing beside me. Ken is one of the men from the St. James's job training program. He is enormous—maybe a full head taller than me, and over 250 pounds—a linebacker, at least, if not a tight end or a defensive tackle—with a bald, bullet head and a smooth, unlined, earnest face. "Should I just throw them away?" he asked. Thinking of Pat (who would have had a heart attack had she been there) I said, "Since the wafers have already been consecrated, we can't just throw them away. We should eat them all ourselves. How do you feel about eating eighteen stale wafers?" Ken was game for anything that would restore the integrity of the sacrament in which he had just participated. He took the bowl of wafers and ate all eighteen, one at a time, picking up each tiny, stale whole wheat wafer between his Kielbasa-sized thumb and forefinger and taking two or three dainty bites of each until he had finished them. "Thanks," I said when he had finished them all. "Thank *you*," he said. "Now it's right."

In this, as in so much, we are just like any other church. We have our tensions and our struggles, our factions and our dissidents, our pouters and sulkers, our coalitions and our power struggles. Week by week, we pray that the church will not just survive it all, but make sense of the desire of most of our congregants to worship together under the most trying circumstances. We do as well as anyone else.

• • • • •

Every now and then, something serendipitous happens that could not be more wonderful had we scripted it in advance. A youth group from First Church in Weston, one of the three or four remaining Christian Unitarian churches in the Boston area, joined us for a second time; they had come out to be with us a year before, and the kids and their parents had been deeply touched by their visit. It was a dank, late winter day—a cold intermittent drizzle had left everyone wet and cranky—and some twenty or so homeless people and visitors from Weston were huddled together inside the T station, their body heat causing the windows to fog over. In response to our Scripture reading, Jeannie told us about the night before, when Vic had beaten her very badly in a motel room they had rented for just that purpose and how frightened she was that she wouldn't survive the next beating. One of the girls from Weston began, "I can relate to that, because . . ." and burst into tears. Jeannie stumbled over and hugged her. The group's adult leader stepped forward to intervene, but the girl persisted, through her tears and sobbing, in her story. Afterward, Jeannie couldn't get over it. "That girl from Weston, with all that money and all those advantages, she was actually *listening* to me!" she said. She was still talking about it weeks later.

• • • • •

After nearly five years, we now see ninety to one hundred chronically homeless people every Sunday—pretty much most of the homeless people who are outdoors in Cambridge on a regular basis. These are the people we want to serve. We hand out bright red wristbands with our name and telephone number on them, so that our church members—and the social workers, nurses, chaplains and others who care for them—have a number to call in an emergency. We make court appearances for our people, and serve as character witnesses. When a church member is in a mental health facility, a prison or a hospital, we visit regularly. We, like any other church, want to be a constant pastoral presence in the lives of our congregants.

We work as a team, of necessity; no one person could remain fully open to the pain and suffering we see all the time without continuous support. Each of us—myself, Pat, Jean, Mike—has our own characteristic way of keeping enough distance between ourselves and what we see and hear so that we aren't overwhelmed. Pat listens more intently, speaks less; Jean smiles and waits, waits for resolution or relief; Mike retreats into a deep spirituality in which everything in front of him is completely subsumed. I become ironic. Irony plays well on the street. Homeless men and women are only too glad to clown around with someone they trust. Ernie, for instance, has a dry sense of humor that belies all those years in the Paul Dever School for Boys. He has a gift for spontaneous repartee that easily competes with the conversation I hear at most cocktail parties. Others are just as funny in their own way. How is Dave today? "Fair to partly cloudy." Has Dan heard anything about the biopsy of his stomach? "Can't do a biopsy if they can't find his stomach, and he hasn't seen that since he started drinking and put on all this weight." Where are Lynn's dentures? "Someone punched me, I dropped them and the guy ran off with them. And they're 'One size fits all!' I'll never see them again."

I know I'm exhausted when I can't stop kidding around. I try to catch my breath, stay focused, listen carefully and not respond too quickly. Sometimes that works. Sometimes I just step back and let Pat and the interns take up the slack, and content myself with scrounging for juice boxes at the bottom of the coolers.

Most of the time, our people make it easy for me. (As Oscar Romero, Archbishop of San Salvador, loved to say, "With this people it is not difficult to be a good pastor."[3]) Estelle comes to Porter Square for the opportunity to go to church and for the sense of community. Now, she walks with the aid of a walker, which she got brand new from Medicaid. She is a tiny woman, well spoken with a soft voice, straight gray hair and bright pink circles on her cheeks. Estelle was homeless once. Her son, Franklin, who lives with her and may be slightly retarded, became very

---

3. Sobrino, *No Salvation Outside the Poor*, 92.

sick a few years ago and she didn't keep up with the medical bills. In the face of so many difficult financial decisions, Estelle couldn't hold all the pieces together and lost her apartment. Ironically, she lost Franklin, too—she had to give him up to the Department of Youth Services—but with the help of a sympathetic DYS social worker she got him back again and her apartment too. Now and again, she brings Franklin with her to Porter Square. Franklin is a gentle young man, with a smooth, unmarked vacant face, short brown hair just going gray and wide open brown eyes. He always looks surprised. One Sunday morning, Franklin brought a box of sticky buns with him. It was clear that he had paid for them himself. He gave me the box with great quiet pride. When the service was over, I handed around the buns. I tried one myself; they were bone dry. Most of the people who had taken them surreptitiously wrapped them in napkins and stuck them in their pocket. Franklin didn't notice people stuffing the buns in their pockets. He was beaming. I thanked him profusely for his generosity and forethought. He beamed some more. The next week, Estelle told Jean that it was one of the best days of Franklin's life.

Shortly after I became a grandfather for the first time, Estelle appeared in Porter Square with a small Whole Foods shopping bag that had been designed—Estelle told me—by Sheryl Crow. Inside was a card addressed to "Grandfather Jed" and a little bag with a miniscule chain across the front and clothes pins holding up little cut-outs of children's clothing. Inside the bag was a tiny blue hooded sweatshirt with a pink lining, and "89" stitched in a floral pattern across the front, with "Baby Gap" underneath. Estelle wrote on the card attached, "Welcome to the world, Baby Nina!" The sweatshirt was new. Lord knows where Estelle had found the money to buy a present for my granddaughter. But she had remembered and taken the time to shop for it.

Estelle is one of a very small handful of people who refuse communion. We talked about its various meanings one morning, before the service began, but communion reminded her too strongly of an unhappy Roman Catholic childhood and she just didn't want to do it. I told her that some people don't take communion but receive a blessing instead, wanting to reaffirm their place in the community but without reference to a specific liturgical practice. Oh, she said, I didn't know that. Jean or I could offer you a blessing during communion, if you like,

I said. I would, Estelle said. Because this *is* my church now, and Franklin's. Yes it is, Estelle, I say silently. We are blessed together.

6

The Outdoor Church in Harvard Square

> We are there bringing together parents and children, the young and old, the greatly exposed and the greatly suffering, and even those who have long been skeptics and unbelievers, as well as inconsiderate and reckless; and are connecting them in the bonds of Christian faith, consolation, encouragement, affection, and desire and effort for self-improvement.[1]

PORTER SQUARE MAY BE WHERE WE LOOK MOST LIKE A CHURCH, BUT Harvard Square and Central Square are where we look most like the Ministry-at-large.

Attendance at our prayer service on the Cambridge Common fell off in the second year. Pat and I decided to take our extra sandwiches into Harvard Square. When we started walking around Harvard Square, we were carrying no more than fifteen or twenty sandwiches in a shopping bag. We were soon hauling more sandwiches, socks and juice than we could stuff into bags or even cram into knapsacks. Michael Povey, then the Rector at St. James's, gave us two Wheelie Coolers. We put ice in the bottom but the ice kept melting and everything got wet, so we bought some Freez Paks and put them in the bottom instead. We put the sandwiches in the coolers to refrigerate them and the juice boxes in the coolers because they were too heavy to carry. Then Rebecca gave us two more Coolers, much fancier than the first pair, with pockets and adjustable handles. The handles were a little too short; when you pulled the cooler behind you it would catch on the heel of your foot and you'd drop the cooler. Even so, the interns preferred the new coolers, despite the running jokes.

---

1. Tuckerman, *Principles and Results*, 150.

We don't have enough space to store clothes but, if someone requests something special—size 34 pants, women's underwear, a warm coat—we will make an effort to get it and bring it out with us the next week. Invariably, the first time we bring out a new coat or a shirt, the person who asked for it won't be there. It takes three or four times at least; and, if the person has disappeared altogether, we just give it to anyone who notices that we have been carrying it around with us for a few weeks and asks if they can have it.

If Christ Church has recently had a catered event, they give us whatever deserts were left over. For a few years, Harvard had plate sized, individually wrapped oatmeal cookies made up for commencement and class reunions; we'd still be handing them out long after summer school had started. We also carry fruit and snacks—not apples, because so many people on the street don't have any good teeth, or any teeth at all, but, instead, oranges, tangerines, grapes and, especially, bananas. Everything we hand out, other than oranges and bananas, is wrapped in plastic or in a plastic bag.

Whenever we see someone who looks homeless, we stop, introduce ourselves and offer a sandwich or some socks. This calls for some judgment. If we offer a sandwich to someone who looks homeless, but isn't, we risk giving offense; but if we hesitate to offer a sandwich to someone because he doesn't look homeless, and he is, we have missed an opportunity to minister. There are some helpful indicators—shoes, cuffs, a bottle, how many bags a person has, how she sits on a bench—but, even after all these years, we make mistakes.

Rebecca was our first volunteer. She came out to the Common one Sunday with Scott Campbell. Rebecca was an intern at Harvard Epworth then and had just graduated from the BU School of Theology. She came from a small town in Wisconsin and, from time to time, her family would visit, catching up with us in Harvard Square or in Central Square. Her mother and father would stand a little apart from us as we gave out juice and sandwiches, amazed that their daughter had found her way to such a madcap enterprise.

At first, Rebecca was intensely shy and didn't say much. She has a round, wide, open face with soft brown eyes and a musical voice. Everything about her was modest and subdued. It took a few weeks before I realized that she was coming back again and again. It was the same on the street. At first, homeless people hardly knew she was there.

But she gained a quiet confidence as we went along and people began to notice her. Some of the men in Central Square thought she was our daughter. Then they hit on her, even though she was wearing a wedding ring and even though Pat and I were standing right next to her, as much, it seemed, because it was somehow expected of them than that they thought that Rebecca would do anything other than gently decline. Rebecca was nonplussed the first time it happened. She thought her wedding ring set up an invisible defense perimeter, but no one paid it any mind.

As people got comfortable with Rebecca and she with them, her genuine and warm affection for the homeless people we encountered began to emerge. Rebecca speaks French and Spanish fluently—Pat and I speak neither—and she was wonderful with the Hispanic men that we encountered in Central Square. There was something about parsing a different language—what is the word for egg salad? what is the word for hand warmers?—that gave Rebecca a way to relate to Hispanic men. She was with us for three years. When she and her husband left Cambridge, people asked after her for months and months.

Rebecca and our other interns and volunteers are one of the very few things that ever change from year to year in our ministry. We are obsessive about consistency and continuity. The lives of homeless people being as fractured and unpredictable as they are, we want to be as predictable and routine in our timing, offerings and locations as we possibly can. From the beginning, we have stayed with the same routes in Harvard Square and Central Square and tried to follow them every Sunday at more or less the same time, so that people can rely on us for a sandwich or some company. In time, people did.

We try to have a range of sandwiches—egg salad, tuna salad, roast beef, ham and cheese, bologna and cheese—instead of just peanut butter and jelly. Helene said that homeless people resent always getting peanut butter and jelly because it requires so little preparation and attention, so we try to mix it up. Then there are the exotics: liverwurst, ham loaf, roast beef and something I had never heard of before, Fluffernutter, a combination of Marshmallow spread and peanut butter, and even ice cream, Korean cakes and Vietnamese noodles. Rebecca prepared sushi, cheesecake and all sorts of cakes and cookies, which we regularly carried around Harvard Square and Central Square. After watching Ernie dismantle his sandwiches and throw the cheese away, I told him we would come out with lobster salad sandwiches one day, and it became, as so much with Ernie, a running joke. Then we actually did it. Helene and Rebecca made the lobster salad and we put it in small hot dog buns and wrapped them in plastic sandwich bags. Ernie was astonished, and took three. The lobster salad sandwiches were all gone before we reached Harvard Square.

• • • • •

In Harvard Square, we start at the granite memorial gate at the eastern end of the Cambridge Common, where the anti-war demonstrators hold up their "Get Out of Iraq" signs and wave to the irritated drivers on Mass Avenue who are already confused and distracted by the hairpin turn onto Garden Street.

Across the street, Neil walks among the cars on Garden Street with a hand printed cardboard sign, asking for money. He is a tall thin man with thick wavy black hair and a deeply lined face. His partner, Gladys, sits on the shaded benches nearby, resting her legs. She has stringy brown hair and a doughy face. Her legs are red and swollen to the size and shape of fire hydrants. She has been in and out of Cambridge City Hospital for years with a variety of circulatory ailments. Neil drinks constantly but most heavily when Gladys is in the hospital. Like many people on the street, he asks for more of everything because there's nothing to be lost by asking. We hesitate only when we don't think we'll have enough sandwiches to get through Central Square.

It is hot work here in any season except winter. By the time we reach Harvard Square, the sun has been beating down on the asphalt for hours, and heat radiating from the road is worse than the direct sunlight. Some homeless men and women wear everything they own— they are understandably apprehensive that their clothes will be stolen in a shelter as they sleep, or they don't have any place to store their belongings—and for them the heat is especially onerous. It is hard, too, because drivers entering and leaving Harvard Square are already worked up over the seemingly random stop and go traffic in the Square, and don't want to engage any one or anything that distracts them from their driving. Here, they are even more abusive than passersby on the nearby sidewalk.

Other than the Common itself, Harvard Square is the least chaotic place we will be in all day. Homeless people are in better shape here.

It is early in the afternoon and there are no liquor stores and very few shelters in Harvard Square. The shelters in the vicinity of Harvard Square are hard to get into. The shelter in the basement of First Church Congregational, for instance, wants only people with referrals who have a reasonable chance of getting a job and an apartment. Most of our people can't meet such a high standard.

The drug dealers won't be out in force until the evening. Harvard's proximity provides a kind of ballast for the various communities of people, especially young runaways, who hang around the Square in the summer. The Harvard Police are a calming influence, too. Harvard owns a lot of open space around the Square, like the outdoor café in front of Au Bon Pain, and their police, though nearly invisible, are very much present.

The Harvard Square Business Association tries to keep Harvard Square orderly for the benefit of its member businesses. It has succeeded in suppressing most public drunkenness in Harvard Square and redirecting it to Central Square and Porter Square. But Harvard students are a presence, too. During the winter, they run an emergency shelter in the basement of University Lutheran Church, one block toward the Charles River from the Square, and in the summer, they operated a program at St. James's church for homeless people who need help getting a job. They engage homeless men and women in wonderfully surprising ways. One spring, a Polish exchange student interviewed Myron, a very articulate homeless man who panhandles all over Harvard Square and developed an economic model for maximizing proceeds from panhandling. At her direction, Myron learned to panhandle in front of the CVS drugstore, where customers make small purchases and invariably receive change, and not in front of Abercrombie & Fitch, where everything is paid for by credit card. (Myron took the student's attention to mean that he had become a part of the Harvard University community, and attended as many commencement parties, picnics and receptions as he could.) The students are a very sympathetic counterweight to the Harvard Square Business Association.

Vera usually sets up her glass harmonica in front of the Unitarian Church. She is a short, charmingly open and innocent woman who sits on a metal folding chair and plays the glass harmonica outdoors during the summer. She dips her fingers in a little dish of water to get a constant tone from the harmonica's nested glass plates, but she also bites her finger nails and the ends of her fingers are always white and wrinkled and gnawed. It's dangerous work—she keeps boxes of band-aids close at hand because she cuts her fingers so often on the glass. Parents with children are drawn to Vera and her exotic musical instrument; the parents get to choose a song and the children get to turn the handle of the glass harmonica. Vera is always surprised when we offer her a sandwich and invariably offers to play "Amazing Grace" if someone will turn the harmonica's handle. "Here's a religious song," she says brightly when we appear. Apparently, other than "Die Himmel erzählen die Ehre Gottes" from Haydn's *The Creation*, it's the only one that she knows.

If we stop to talk to Vera, Stan, who has been camped on the benches on front of the CVS waiting for us, will amble over and join us. He is a gentle, soft-spoken pale faced man who works part time at Mt. Auburn Hospital as an orderly. He is heavy set and wears very tight T shirts that exaggerate his obesity. Stan has brilliant white hair and jowls that hang from his face like slabs of meat. He always looks woebegone and mournful. His very pale blue eyes are perpetually teary. Stan also gets Social Security disability benefits and has a small room in a three-decker in Alston but he is often uncertain and confused. Other street people wait for the third of the month, when Social Security checks are mailed out, and roll him a day or two later. What little he has left he drinks. Stan is slightly retarded but he doesn't like to think of himself that way. When people on the street call him retarded, as they often do, he yells at them that he takes care of retarded people all day and he knows what retarded people look like. For a long while, he refused to consider moving into a subsidized congregate housing facility because he thought that all the other people there were retarded. As we come up, Stan rushes over to complain that we are late again, he's just about to leave, he didn't want to miss us. He shares recent developments with us—"I got an increase in my benefits this week" or "Arthur (a social worker from 240 Albany Street) says I need to talk to a lawyer"—as if only we can fully appreciate their importance.

We walk past CVS, stopping to talk to the homeless men who are opening the door for customers in hopes of getting a tip, and up to the Harvard Coop's covered arcade, where people can sleep at night if they're not violent or doing drugs. Lisa—a sweet, deranged older woman whose hair hangs down her back in one enormous dreadlock, even after cutting it last year—sleeps on the low granite walls that surround the trees here. Lisa is terrorized by authority figures or anyone who seems to be an authority figure. Others on the street think that something horrible happened to her during an involuntary commitment, from which she has never fully recovered. Lisa carries a school notebook in which she writes desperate messages: "I've been hurt badly"—"I'm very frightened"—"I'm sick and need help"—which she holds in front of her almost as an afterthought or on which she sleeps. She never asks for money but, when offered boots or clothes, invariably finds some reason why they're inadequate: wrong size, wrong manufacturer, wrong brand, wrong color.

Lisa wants to go home. People on the street tell us that, once a month or so, family members in a long black Limousine with tinted windows pull up in front of the Coop and whisk Lisa away for a bath and a meal, but we have never seen it happen. Lisa's family is in North Carolina, and that's where she wants to go, but she thinks that North Carolina is a fifteen or twenty minute drive from Harvard Square. Rebecca worked at Traveler's Aid. They will pay for one half of a bus ticket to North Carolina if Lisa can give them the telephone number of someone at the other end of the trip. Lisa gets angry with Pat when Pat tries to explain this, and insists that Pat give her the cab fare for the ride home.

Lisa is not good at taking care of herself. She used to share a space in front of the Tannery with other homeless people, until they began to get lice from her and insisted that she leave. A hole-in-the-wall luncheonette on Church Street gave her food at midday and allowed her to sit at one of the tables, writing in her notebook. One summer, a customer noticed her lice and complained to the City Health Department. Health officers threatened to close the little restaurant unless they stopped serving Lisa. With that, Lisa stopped eating and began to soil herself. A social worker, after many anguished days of indecision, finally had her committed. Lisa was incarcerated in a locked ward at Lemuel Shattuck Hospital, a psychiatric hospital at the edge of Franklin Park in Roxbury. When Pat and I went to visit, we couldn't locate her at first. Different floors at Lemuel Shattuck are managed by different state agencies, and there is no central registration information at the front desk. After trying four or five wards, we found her in Nine North. Lisa looked much thinner without her street clothes. The orderlies had washed her and cut her hair. Her large light blue eyes glowed and she looked almost elegant.

Lisa didn't want to leave her room, didn't recognize either of us when an orderly persuaded her to come out in the hall and didn't want to talk with us. She seemed exactly the same, but no one would tell us whether she was take medications and it didn't occur to me to ask her to sign a disclosure form right on the spot. After a few minutes, she told us that she had to go to a meeting, just as supper trays were being rolled in on huge metal carts.

In the end, like Lynn, Lisa will be released to an unlocked Department of Mental Health facility. After a few days, she will walk out and return to the Square.

We cut past Out of Town News and through the Pit, where summer school students, summer school student hangers-on and young people passing through gather in elaborate Goth hairdos and studded leather jackets and boots. I am never comfortable giving sandwiches to the young people passing through the Square because they make no effort to hide their contempt for older people who they think can so easily be gulled into helping them. Neither Pat nor anyone else feels this way. We continue across Holyoke Street and into the open area in front of Au Bon Pain, past the tourists, gawkers, graduate students and visitors drinking iced coffee at the metal tables just off the street and watching all of Harvard Square walk by. For decades, Murray Turnbull, a chess master and a 52-year-old Harvard dropout who has been making a perilous living playing blitz chess at the first table, was the only player out there. He is famous for the broad brimmed straw hat that protects his florid face from the sun and for defeating the entire Harvard chess team in one match. Now, whenever it is not too wet to set up the pieces and a clock, the other tables are taken by noisy Russians, waiting for someone to play for two or three dollars.

Nelson is a pretty good chess player, too. Like a number of people we encounter on the streets, Nelson has an apartment but his orientation is toward the street. He likes to sit in Holyoke Center. He has been playing chess and checkers in Harvard Square for as long as we have been outdoors. He is almost completely bald, with a few wisps of thinning salt and pepper hair combed back behind his ears. Nelson sounds sour and grumpy all the time, as if he has just woken up. His smile is a grimace—the corners of his mouth turn down instead of up—and his brown, squinty eyes shift rapidly from side to side, although he is one of the most open and direct people we know on the street. In dead of winter, Nelson goes to San Diego where he has some family for a few weeks of sun. In the summer, he goes to Suffolk Downs for Eddie Andelman's Hot Dog Safari, where he can eat all the hot dogs, kielbasa, sausages and ice cream he can keep down for $10 dollars. It is too good a deal to resist.

Nelson is very fragile emotionally. One summer, it rained torrentially every Sunday afternoon at 4:00 PM or so for six or seven weeks, more like Florida than Massachusetts. Late in August, we were caught in a downpour with our coolers and knapsacks and shopping bags and took refuge in the covered arcade that runs through the Holyoke Center office building. Nelson found us there and stood with us, watching the tourists scurry for cover and the students who were already completely drenched running up and down the sidewalk splashing in the biggest puddles. The thunder was phenomenally loud, following right on the heels of the lightening. It poured for an hour and a half, and we decided to simply turn around—no one would be waiting outdoors in Central Square on a day like that—and leave our sandwiches at Christ Church, where the people attending the weekly AA meeting could make use of them.

Nelson was extremely anxious. He shook violently and paced up and down the arcade, wringing his hands. He told us about a time when he was in second grade and a tremendous thunder storm forced the school to close. All of the other kids' parents came to pick them up, but Nelson's mother couldn't be reached and none of the other parents would take him home. Nelson was left standing in front of the school, drenched and terrified by the lightening. Then he told the story to us again. We gave him some more sandwiches, and he told us the story a third time. He was just as agitated at the end of the third telling as he had been before he started the first one.

Usually, Nelson sets up shop at one of the stone inlaid chess tables that stand in a row in front of Au Bon Pain. Nelson doesn't keep his chess set out on the table. Instead, he reads his sports book and waits for passersby to somehow intuit that he is a chess player, too. Nelson reads sports books exclusively: baseball books for the baseball season, football books for the football season and basketball books for the basketball season. He is a voracious reader; we have never seen him with the same book two weeks in a row. All of our interns and most of our volunteers have stopped off to play chess or checkers with Nelson as we walk past

Holyoke Center, thinking that he will enjoy the company. Not one of them—not even Christina, one of Pat's students from Park School, with her father coaching her—has ever beaten him. Nelson gives them free lessons. After the lessons, he gallantly escorts them to the entrance to the Harvard Square T station, where we are waiting.

Nelson has been complaining about another chess player for years, a much younger man, pale and cranky who, as Nelson sees it, lures young boys and girls into a game and then takes their money when they lose. He can't understand how we can offer this man a sandwich and juice when he is such a despicable person. We leave it to the interns to try to make sense of acts of Christian charity.

Like many people who spend a lot of time outdoors, Nelson doesn't want to look as though he has been waiting for us, but, if we are late, we will find him standing at the edge of the terrace, looking anxiously up and down the street. "You're late," he complains and sulks for a bit, until one of the interns offers to stay and play a few games with him.

Nelson has become very attached to these weekly chess games with our interns. After she graduated from the Harvard Divinity School and before she was to begin teaching at St. Paul's School, Irene joined us in Harvard Square and Central Square as a volunteer. Irene has large, deep brown eyes from which she always seems to be looking up at you. She is tall, with a very slight stoop and a diffident manner that masks a very determined and positive character. Unlike all of our other volunteers, Irene didn't want to play chess or checkers with Nelson. She was firm about it. She said she'd learn more from spending the time walking around Harvard Square with the rest of us. And, perhaps, being such a competitive person, she didn't relish the idea of losing.

It took a long while for Nelson to get over it. We would show up in Holyoke Center, offer Nelson a sandwich, and Nelson would immediately start complaining about Irene's unwillingness to stay and play chess. "Why doesn't she want to play?" "I could give her a lesson." "It's only a few minutes." "Why doesn't she like me?" Months after Irene had left for New Hampshire, Nelson was still asking after her. Nelson's need to keep the games going and his dread that they might end had become disturbing: we had been understood to make a promise that we couldn't redeem.

James stands in front of the Harvard Bookstore, just around the corner from the Grolier Poetry Book Shop. Both are on the ground floor of an apartment building at 8 Plimpton Street, where I used to live with my wife in two small rooms overlooking the very spot where James now stands. It is disconcerting to juxtapose two parts of my life so distant in time and focus. James is a tall, wide-shouldered black man, probably in his thirties, with a round, smooth face. He seems young and healthy, but he stares listlessly at the sidewalk, empty Starbucks cup hanging at his side. He says nothing and does nothing. James seems to have no instinct for self-preservation. Mass Avenue is a wind tunnel in the winter and there isn't much sunlight at that corner, but James stands there regardless, as if he were chained to the lamppost.

When we first met him, James' face showed no expression whatsoever. We would say hello, offer him a sandwich, pause and then head down Plimpton Street. After a year, he would accept a sandwich and some juice, still not showing any emotion or even an acknowledgement of our presence, and then walk away. A few minutes later, as we turned onto Mt. Auburn Street and began walking back toward the Square, we would find him crouched in the doorway to Montvale Hall, cramming the sandwich into his mouth. We would smile and walk on, sensing that we had impinged on his privacy. Then James began to take the sandwich and juice and ask for "Holy Food": communion. We had no idea how he knew that we were offering it—he was stationed blocks away from anyone to whom we usually offer communion—but we were delighted to have another way to engage him. We still find him staring out across Mass Avenue when we approach him but when he sees us coming, he smiles broadly and asks if we have any of that "Holy Food." We talk about the weather, about what sandwiches we have that day, about our snacks, about how cold it is on this corner. James grins, his eyes flicker from side to side as if abashed, and we try to give him enough room.

Now, communion is part of a routine by which James invites us into a small part of his life. First, he asks for the "Holy Food." Then he asks us for a sandwich and waits for us to offer him egg salad, which we know—and he knows we know—is his favorite. Then he asks for some juice. Then he asks if he can have another egg salad sandwich. Then he asks for another juice to wash down the second egg sandwich. He always refuses socks and toiletries.

No one else on the street takes such obvious delight in sharing communion with us. If we could, we would circle the block and offer him communion again and again. But, by now, he has taken his sandwiches around the corner and found some place more private than the entryway to Montvale Hall to eat them.

From there, we walk down to Mt. Auburn Street, across JFK Boulevard and over to Brattle Square. There are buskers all around Harvard Square, even in winter, but Brattle Square, just a few steps to the west, has more performance space. Mimes, performance artists, jugglers, magicians, singers and string quartets all perform there. If we stop, we are drawn into a magician's act or a juggler's patter. The most elegant performers are the motionless mimes. Usually women, they are painted silver or gold or red, and stand completely motionless and silent until you put a dollar in the hat or the box in front of them. Then they sing arias from popular operas or tell jokes or stories. Then they fall silent and motionless again, until someone else offers them a dollar. We've tried this with sandwiches, and it works. One summer, it seemed that every mime was singing Puccini.

This kind of activity frames the world in which our church and its members live; it is all of a piece. But there are other activities and events that make our people invisible. Twice a year, the Harvard Square Business Association sponsors a street fair in Harvard Square. The streets leading into the Square are closed and tents line the streets, filled with T shirts and costume jewelry and CD's and food—endless amounts of food. From year to year, it is always the same: the same T shirts, the same fast food, the same jewelry, as if these fairs are franchises of one mother-of-all-street-fairs, like Wendy's or Dunkin's Donuts. Our people disappear. Some go down to the river, some go to Central Square or Porter Square, some hide. The press of the crowds and the noise—especially when the featured band is playing on a grandstand set up in front of the Out of Town News—are simply overwhelming.

In the past, commencement and class reunions at Harvard University also cleared the streets of homeless people. No one would acknowledge a formal policy to rid Harvard Square of homeless people when Harvard's graduates return for class reunions—but come commencement, Harvard Square looked like it had been vacuumed. We couldn't find anybody. By the time we caught up with our people at 240 Albany Street or the following Sunday, they had forgotten to complain. When I graduated from the Harvard Divinity School in 2004, the Outdoor Church had already been in Harvard Square for nearly a year. It was deeply disturbing to find that members of my church had been banished from Harvard Square for my psychological comfort. It cast a slight pall on my graduation. Recently, this policy has been relaxed; homeless people can stay in Harvard Square during commencement if they don't drink openly or panhandle too aggressively.

Brattle Square is home to Deacon Blue, a son of ministers, a sixties radical, a puppeteer and the most fascinating man in Boston according to a scientific survey conducted by WBCN. Blue is an island of peace in the middle of performance chaos. He has a political puppet show that features three puppets costumed as demented versions of Uncle Sam—two of which can be worked by kids in the audience—songs, jokes, a charming patter about the depredations of our government and a gentle good nature that is always calming. Blue knows nearly everyone in Brattle Square. If we hang around while Blue is doing his show, we will end up in it.

A block away, at the corner of Brattle Street and Church Street, is where Butch used to sell *Spare Change,* the newspaper for homeless people. We always saw Butch at the corner of Church and Brattle Streets, where Sage's specialty grocery store used to be. It was our last stop before we left Harvard Square and took the T down to Central Square. Butch was a short, black man, with a puffy face, yellow eyes and short, snow white hair. Individual tightly curled hairs sprouted from his face and neck and cheeks. He sold *Spare Change* sitting on an upturned plastic milk crate. Harvard students and Cambridge residents liked to talk with Butch. He was interested in everything and had an opinion about everything. He would look up and ask, "What do you think about Iraq?" or "What do you think about the welfare reform?" and, without pausing, launch into his own lengthy and usually well conceived opinion.

Butch used to sit on the board of directors of *Spare Change*. He quit when the board cut back on the size and number of papers the street vendors could sell rather than adopt a systematic fund raising campaign. He saw himself as championing the interests of the street vendors. Once he decided that the board wasn't supporting the vendors, he wouldn't go back. In any event, selling papers was as much a way to be outside and be with people as a way to earn money. He had another source of income—probably Social Security disability benefits—and had his own place. When the weather was dreadful, Butch would stay in, but rarely for more than one weekend at a time. If we missed him one week, we knew we would see him the next.

Butch grew up in western Pennsylvania. He was a varsity swimmer in high school—unusual in that era for a black kid, and especially where he grew up. Surprising, too, because Butch was so short. He followed collegiate and Olympic swimming closely. He knew more than I did about the great Yale swimming teams of the late '50's and early '60's—Don Schollander, Mike Austin and the other Yale swimmers who made up most of the 1964 US Olympic swimming team—and about swimmers throughout the Ivy League and then, later, at Indiana, USC and Stanford.

The only family member he ever mentioned was his grandmother, whom he revered. She was a Baptist. Butch said she could preach better than any itinerant he ever heard anywhere. It must have been in his genes, because he could lead a prayer better than any of us. Butch could see us coming as soon as we left Brattle Square. He would set down his pile of *Spare Change* next to his crate, get to his feet and greet us long before we got to his corner. He liked things to be in the same order every Sunday: first communion, then sandwiches, then juice and desert, underwear or socks or gloves, then prayer, then conversation, until we would manage to pull away. When we were praying, we would stand in a circle, just to the side of the sidewalk across from the Brattle Theatre. Shoppers would stream by us, apparently oblivious to us. I was always conscious of how different our hands looked when we were praying with Butch: old, young, black, white, wrinkled, smooth.

Rebecca and Tracy, a volunteer from St. James's, liked Butch because he was so approachable: he was articulate, not obviously unstable or addicted and not angry. For his part, he was impressed that they were learning about faith on the street. Butch liked to take communion from Tracy and Rebecca and wanted them to lead our prayers, but soon he was leading all the prayers. He could remember their concerns from week to week and always built them into his prayers. It was a reminder of how aware of us our people were, whether they could express it, like Butch, or not.

A few summers after we met Butch, he had stomach surgery and, after that, he seemed to suffer from one ailment after another. He was very vague about his medical condition. A year later, he was scheduled to have a colonoscopy at Mt. Auburn Hospital, but he said he couldn't afford the emetics he was supposed to take before the test. We offered to buy the medicine for him, if he would tell us what the doctor had recommended. Butch put off giving us the information week after week. We began to push him a little bit—something we tried never to do, making an exception for him because we liked him so much—but it didn't make any difference. Then, in July, we didn't see him at his corner any more. I telephoned *Spare Change*, but they didn't know anything either. I called all the local hospitals but no one would acknowledge that he was a patient or had recently been a patient. Months went by. Then, one sleeting Thursday evening in late January, as I was walking through the Square, I heard that Butch had died in his apartment of a heart attack. His sister, not hearing from him, came up from Pennsylvania and persuaded the Cambridge police to let her into his apartment and they found him there. *Spare Change* had run a picture of Butch on its back page. I took a copy up to Christ Church, where Pat was helping to prepare and serve the Thursday night meal, to show her. As I walked up there, I was thinking of myself and hoping that her grief would somehow make my own more bearable. It didn't.

Every year, a little piece of Cambridge real estate becomes a virtual resting place for one or two of our people who have died on the street, as if the city were an enormous cemetery, with invisible gravestones scattered along the ways and behind the buildings where our people gather to drink and huddle against the cold. We still walk past the corner at Church and Brattle on the way to the T, but quickly. That was Butch's corner—he owned it.

7

The Outdoor Church in Central Square

> Do not neglect to show hospitality to strangers, for thereby some have entertained angels unawares. Remember those who are in prison, as though in prison with them; and those who are ill-treated, since you also are in the body. (Heb 13:2–3)

WE TAKE THE REDLINE ONE STOP TOWARD BOSTON TO REACH CENTRAL Square. We emerge from the underground station into a roughly triangular, brick paved park called the Carl Barron Plaza.

Central Square is very different than Harvard Square, although stores like the Gap are starting to appear there. Harvard Square goes further upscale every time we walk through it. Shoe stores replace hole-in-the-wall burger joints. Bank ATM machines replace delis. Franchises replace mom and pops. But Central Square is gritty and distinctly down-scale. Trash stays in the gutters longer and police prowl cars and patrolmen on foot are a constant presence. Where Harvard Square has Au Bon Pain, Central Square has discount clothing stores; where Harvard Square has Cardullo's, Central Square has McDonald's. There is much more subsidized housing near Central Square than Harvard Square, many more liquor stores, which will have been open for three or four hours before we arrive, and many more homeless shelters. The police will tolerate public drunkenness in Central Square, but not in Harvard Square. The MIT and Harvard students who don't want or can't afford to live on campus find apartments to share here. The Cambridge housing market is always tight because of its universities and colleges; Central Square is one of the few places in Cambridge where students, retirees on Social Security and other economically marginal people can find a place to rent.

Central Square is where we see most of the people to whom we minister. We see them toward the end of our day, when we are tired, and toward the end of their day, when they have been drinking for a few hours. Harvard Square, with its edgy shoe stores and trendy restaurants, might as well be in a different city. Here, the dirt and the despair can be overwhelming.

•••••

As we emerge from the subway, we find a large crowd of homeless men and women sitting or sleeping on the slatted wood benches in the plaza. They will soon be joined by people further down Mass Avenue who have been waiting for us to appear. As many as ten or twelve people may gather to ask for sandwiches or socks while others, not wanting to compromise their dignity, wait for us to approach them. This will happen three or four times as we walk through Central Square, depending on the weather and the time of day. Some people are afraid that we will leave before they get something to eat, and press us to give them something right away. Some believe that getting a free sandwich or juice—even after five years—must be a scam, and want the benefit of it before it gets closed down. Most are just desperately hungry.

It is very easy, especially for the interns, to feel pressured into just handing out sandwiches without interacting with the people who are receiving them. The interns don't want to give offense and don't want people to be disappointed. And we, like others who offer food to the poor, are tempted to use numbers to assure ourselves that we are doing a good job: if we hand out one hundred sandwiches, it is a more successful day than if we hand out only eighty sandwiches. Resisting this—remembering that we are a church and not a mobile food dispensary, taking the time to talk with people before, or as, they take a sandwich—requires some self-discipline, often more than we can muster. It is easier for me and Pat—we have known some people for four or five years, and have lots to talk about. It is harder for the interns, who are usually just getting used to the drill.

Jocelyn is usually part of this first group. She keeps an eye out for us and comes striding up as soon as we appear. Jocelyn is slight but seemingly sure of herself, easily in her fifties, with large round gray eyes and scraggly grey shoulder length hair that she now dyes pitch black. She cocks her head and smiles slyly. Jocelyn enjoys clothes, but it is her makeup that catches the eye. It is all over the place—lipstick on one side of her mouth, powder on her chin and her jacket, rouge under one eye and next to the other—but she has taken pains with it, like her clothes, and her appearance is important to her.

Jocelyn always asks for one more of everything we have already given her, whether the week before or right then and there. Our interns, who have carefully labeled and organized the sandwiches by type—tuna salad, peanut butter and jelly, egg salad—have little patience with Jocelyn when she paws through the coolers and the bags of clothes, looking for something she wants or some color she likes. One of them fantasized for weeks about slamming the lid of one of the coolers down on Jocelyn's hand the next time she reached into it.

Often, like other homeless people, Jocelyn says she wants another sandwich or another juice for someone else, usually Dean, her occasional boyfriend. We used to see Dean with her a lot. He is a tall, silent man, with small squinting eyes and a square face. Whether Dean was standing next to her or across the street or out of sight, Jocelyn asked for one more for him, as if he were unable to speak. He seemed a little embarrassed by Jocelyn's assertiveness and shrunk into himself the more she urged him to take a pair of socks or a sandwich. We saw Dean more and more infrequently, until he disappeared altogether.

Jocelyn never takes it amiss when someone finally says say "no." She just keeps asking for whatever she can see we are carrying until we won't give her any more. Then, the next week, we will start all over again. Aggressiveness works on the street. Even if we were offended, there is little risk—we couldn't possibly treat Jocelyn more poorly than most passersby do. Shame is a losing strategy outdoors. Some people can't shake it, but it helps if you can.

We soon became convinced that Jocelyn was fencing the crosses and the clothes. We give everything away, so there is no need for anyone to buy anything that we are carrying. If someone does, it means they have never heard of us, or they don't want to or can't wait for us. It is one of the many measures of the limitations of our ministry.

There are some who believe that giving a homeless person more than one sandwich, or one serving of a hot meal, or one pair of socks, is morally suspect. They feel that it encourages moral laxness and disrespect for the meal and for the server of the meal. It suggests Tuckerman's distinction between the deserving poor and undeserving paupers and implies that more than one sandwich will make the homeless person dependent and interfere with his moral improvement. I think not. The sandwiches cannot be fenced or sold. They have no value to anyone other than the person standing in front of us. There are some, like Jocelyn, who will take something just because it is offered, but usually people will take only what they can eat then or later in the day, since taking food into shelters is usually prohibited. We are not in the business of calibrating a moral response to people's hunger and we are certainly not in the business of encouraging people to take as much food as they think they need and then passing judgment on their lack of self-control.

Jocelyn takes communion every week. It is hard to tell whether it is just one more thing to ask for, or whether she values it as a religious practice. When Dean is around, she tells him to take communion. At first, he would, thinking that he couldn't get a sandwich unless he did, but, in time, he realized that we would give him the sandwich anyway and begin edging away when Jocelyn asked for communion.

From Carl Barron Plaza we walk down Mass Avenue toward MIT. The City of Cambridge has placed wooden benches on both sides of Mass Avenue, from Lafayette Square up to City Hall. The benches are usually placed at right angles to the street facing one another, to encourage groups of people to sit and talk. Homeless men and women gather at the benches, sit, gossip, drink and sleep, until 240 Albany Street, which is just a few blocks further down, opens for the evening or until it is time to start worrying about where else to stay for the night. In the summer, the north side of Mass Avenue, which is in direct sunlight, is usually too hot for comfortable socializing, and people congregate on the south side, which is in the shade. In the winter, it is the other way around. We see large groups of people in Central Square because of the benches. There aren't any benches in Harvard Square.

In the summer, people gather in groups up and down Mass Avenue. In the winter, they will go into Wendy's or McDonald's or any of the many discount stores in Central Square, buy a cup of coffee and nurse it for as long as they can. As we walk by Wendy's and Burger King, we peer into the windows to see if any of our people are inside. If they are, we will go inside and offer a sandwich or some juice. Management never seems to mind, perhaps because they know that our people aren't going to buy much anyway. If there is a large group of people, we will ask them to come outside for a moment, so we don't tempt the management to kick everybody out.

Joe was one of the people who used to stay in Wendy's during the winter. Although, like Butch, Joe sold *Spare Change* in Harvard Square, we associated him with Central Square, where he lived. Joe died of a heart attack in his girl friend's apartment. She spent the next two or three weeks on the street complaining about it. This was ironic, because Joe couldn't stop talking about his "girl problems." His girl wouldn't talk to him, his girl talked too much when he just wanted to sleep, his girl was "crazy about sex," his girl hated sex.

Joe was an enormous black man, built like a tight end and looking just as fit, even after living on the street. Joe had a droopy, hang dog expression whether he was sober or drunk. He had a big jaw and small sad brown eyes. Joe sold *Spare Change* in front of the Cambridge Savings Bank ATM machine in Harvard Square, next to the main entrance to the T. It is a popular location for people who sell *Spare Change* and most of the salespeople are aggressive and well-known. Joe, despite his size, seemed to shrink into the sidewalk. He was always depressed. He would put his unsold newspapers on his upturned plastic milk crate and sit on them, head in his hands. I don't know if he ever sold an issue of *Spare Change* to anyone but me. At the end of the day, Joe would drift down to Central Square and begin drinking. It was difficult to understand him in any event—he spoke very softly and forced you to lean into to him to make out what he was saying—but, when he was drinking, it was almost impossible to make out what he was trying to say.

Joe liked to help us hand out sandwiches in Central Square. As soon as Joe spotted us in Central Square, he would announce that his "friends" had arrived with lots of sandwiches. Our interns would have been just as happy if he didn't—they were usually under a lot of pressure from people who wanted sandwiches, all at the same time, as soon as we emerged from the T Station. Joe took a propriety interest in our ministry. If it looked as if we were going to have a lot of sandwiches left over at the end of the day—this was before we starting leaving our extra sandwiches for the people who attended the AA meeting at Christ Church—Joe would take them all and assure us that he was going to give them out to people on the street we had missed as we made our rounds. There was no reason not to believe him—if we had enough we would give out as many as anyone wanted anyway. It made Joe proud to think that he was helping out, he told us, and it got his mind off his girl problems, at least for the moment.

Joe was a man of great and quiet dignity, which his drinking did not diminish. Like many people in Central Square, he would stay warm in the winter by buying a cup of coffee at Wendy's or MacDonald's and sitting quietly at one of the small plastic tables. One Sunday in March, we spotted Joe in Wendy's, a cup of coffee in front of him. He had been drinking and he had fallen asleep sitting up in the warmth of the store. Mucus was running out of his nose. I didn't want to wake him, so I left some sandwiches and juice on the table for him. A part of me wanted to clean him up—I was self-conscious and embarrassed for him. But that was for me to sort out. As for Joe, his dignity was intact.

• • • • •

Central Square has street fairs, too. We usually miss the fair itself but meet people coming back to Central Square after it is over. The street fairs in Harvard Square are packed with college and prep school students; they are enormous outdoor mixers with tents full of fashionable T-shirts and exotic snacks. In Central Square, the fairs have a distinctly Brazilian Mardi Gras flavor. Excited, chattering Latino women old enough to be grandmothers and young enough to be in primary school wear fabulous and—for America—wonderfully suggestive costumes in brilliant oranges, blues, greens and yellows. The costumes are covered with brightly dyed feathers and the women carry enormous feathered fans, some as tall as they are. Up close, the costumes are frayed and soiled. They are probably rented.

We continue on to the park behind the fire station. This is an immaculately groomed park with filigreed metal chairs and a circular granite bench surrounding a fastidiously landscaped island. It belongs to MIT, which carefully maintains and patrols it. For a while, we could always count on meeting two couples here, Pamela and Jake, and Gwen and Cal.

Pamela is a self-possessed woman in her thirties, with lustrous brown hair and enormous blue eyes, one of which is weak and looks away. She is perfectly groomed and meticulous with her dress. When she was outdoors, it was impossible to understand why she was homeless, because she is so charming and intelligent and well-spoken. She stayed at 240 Albany Street, which meant that she was having trouble with drinking. As time went on, Jean and I would see her there, having dinner, quietly drunk and feeling sorry for herself. She was at odds with her family, she said. But who wasn't? She was too good for all this, she said. But there she was. Her boyfriend, Jake, was devoted to her. He had a plump face with tiny little eyes embedded in it, a rounded unarticulated body and unruly thin brown hair. He kept good care of himself, because Pamela insisted on it. Every time we saw them together in the park, they seemed to be just finishing an argument, in which Jake was always the loser. The reasons for each argument were different, but Jake's face always said, What can you do? His passivity and endless devotion to Pamela made him very sympathetic. He was the more serious drinker. We would see him terribly drunk, sometimes out cold, on the benches in front of the Salvation Army when Pamela wasn't around.

When Pamela got an apartment, Jake moved in with her. We never saw her again, but Jake was soon back in front of the Salvation Army, drinking heavily. "I love her and I respect her," he told me, "but she's so distant and so cold, I ask her, why even bother to make love when you're so detached?" Pamela had finally left the street and, nicely but firmly, was leaving it all, including Jake, behind her. It was a devastating blow.

Jake was one of those people, like Steve and Billy, who couldn't protect themselves outdoors and who wouldn't stop mouthing off even when they were so drunk that they couldn't defend themselves against a third-grader. Three days after Jake told us that Pamela had got an apartment, we heard that he had been mugged by three young men near McDonald's. At 240 Albany Street, there were rumors that both his legs were broken, that the three men were returning Iraqi veterans, that they were skinheads, that they were dealers, that the police had picked them up immediately and they couldn't make bail. But the next Sunday, Joey grabbed my arm and pulled me into a doorway right next to Wendy's. He said he was in serious trouble. He already had a warrant out for felonious assault, and now a uniformed officer he knew told him that the detectives assigned to Jake's case thought he was one of the three men who had assaulted Jake. He didn't deny he had been there, but after the other two guys had kicked Jake's head around for a few minutes and scraped his face on the sidewalk, he told them to knock it off and beat it. Maybe, maybe not. The officer told Joey that he would go with him to talk to the detectives. What should he do? This sounded a lot like a good cop bad cop routine. Wait and see what the police do, I said. If they pick you up, the public defender can talk to them, if they still want to talk. If not, you're OK. And get rid of the warrants. I need a blessing, Joey said. Pray for me, now.

I can do this—pray for someone whom I am persuaded has put one of my other congregants in the hospital—only if I can completely suppress all the dreadful things about him that I have heard and seen and know. If I don't, I can't do it. And since we are called to minister to the abuser as well as the abused, I have to do it. But it doesn't save me from wanting to throw up on the sidewalk.

That evening, Pat and I went into Boston to visit Jake at Beth Israel Deaconess. As we expected—it had been at least three days—Jake had been discharged to the streets. Maybe Pamela would take him in until he was a little stronger.

Gwen is just as intelligent, just as attractive and just as charming as Pamela, but she is also tough and mean, with a long string of felonies behind her. She is a huge woman, heavy throughout like a quarter horse, with a square face, a dark complexion and high cheekbones that make her look like a Native American Indian. Her voice rasps from years of heavy smoking. There has been a lot of violence in her past—she had two fingers broken and her nose was flattened—and some serious illnesses, including colon cancer. Her mother had died of colon cancer and she is sure that she will, too. When she is drinking she is loud, overly familiar and vulgar. Her partner, Cal, is seemingly indifferent to Gwen's powerful eroticism. He is a tall lanky man, always too close and too physical, always trying to drape himself over our young female interns, much to their annoyance and Gwen's very vocal disgust. Gwen's disapproval never discourages Cal; it may actually incite him. Gwen talks about marriage but she seems to be talking a place in a distant, foreign country that she might visit some day. In any event, Cal is completely and ostentatiously uninterested whenever she raises the subject.

A number of couples, like Pamela and Jake, and Gwen and Cal, talk to us about marriage but nothing ever happens. The reasons why people stayed together on the street—protection, sex, drugs, and alcohol—weren't the reasons why you would want to stay with someone for a long while. And the practical problems were formidable. Even Pamela and Jake were no exception; no sooner had Pamela put the street behind her than she put Jake behind her too.

The park behind the fire station is a little beyond where the benches stop. From there, we cross the street and head back toward Central Square. Hispanics, all men, seem to have staked out this part of Central Square. As a group, they are defensive and withdrawn. When they are drinking heavily, their suspicions and their anger, taken together with the language problem, make talking with them difficult and frustrating. Often, one very drunken guy would try to serve as a translator for one or two other equally drunken guys, which made things even more confusing. Almost all of our interns can speak Spanish—some are fluent in three or four languages—and this helps us make some sense of our encounters with people from the Islands, from Puerto Rico, or from Haiti, Guatemala and other Central and South American countries. Some of the men are in America to earn money for their families and send it back home—perhaps that is why we rarely see any Hispanic women. These were guys with jobs, unlike most other homeless men and women, and Sunday was a day off, when they could sit with their friends in good weather and drink. But even with friends, they long for home.

Walking east, we reach Prospect Street. As if we are crossing a national boundary, the people we now encounter are radically different: quieter, less abrasive, sweeter, kinder, more loyal if not less abusive to women. Dave is here, sitting on an overturned plastic milk carton in front of the bank that pays him a few dollars to sweep the front steps, with Rick and—while she was still alive—Wanda.

Rick and Wanda had been together outdoors for a long while. Rick is tall and emaciated. His hands tremble constantly and his head shakes gently from side to side. He has a long, pale face and sorrowful brown eyes. Every now and then we can persuade him to take a sandwich but, more often, he will only take some juice. As Lisa is Pat's weakness, Rick is mine. I can barely accept that he is committing suicide in front of me, probably faster than either he or I imagine. I have to consciously restrain myself from trying yet again to persuade him to do something to save his life. Rick teases me by telling me that he likes me well enough but it is Pat who has stolen his heart. He is a great favorite with the interns, with whom he flirts outrageously. He is no angel, of course. The people who live in apartments over the bank used to call in all the time to complain that he was assaulting Wanda. Dave said that Rick was just trying to prevent Wanda from hurting herself but he kept winking at me as he told me this. Most likely, Rick was abusive and trying to help her at the same time.

For me, this is the hardest place to be each Sunday. As a group, Rick, Dave, Wayne and Charlie are among the most compelling people we see outdoors. To be with them all at the same time, as we often are at this point in Central Square, knowing, as they do, that they are as likely to die this winter as not, is heart-wrenching. Despite Rick's endless clowning, irony has no place here. It is all too immediate. Even Rick knows that. I lose a piece of myself every time we leave them.

The restaurants are more fashionable east of Central Square—as if even the most tenuous proximity to Harvard Square pulls everything upscale—and many have put tables and chairs out on the sidewalk where patrons can eat and drink outdoors as if they were in a Paris café.

This is where Claire holds court, in the shelter of the entrance to a convenience store in winter or sitting on the benches in front of the store in summer. She is short and very stocky, with mousy shoulder length brown hair and deeply tanned skin from being outdoors all the time. Like many people who live on the street, she seems to be wearing all the clothes she owns—layer on layer of brown, heavy misshapen sweaters and raincoats and winter coats. It makes her look like a huge dumpling. In all this brown, Claire's eyes glitter like diamonds. They are very light blue, round like buttons and always wide open. When she smiles, her whole face crinkles and warms. In the summer, she sits on her bench, both feet tucked under her like an eight year old girl in crinolines at a school dance. There, Claire attracts lots of men, heavy drinkers and unpredictable. There is something about her indifference that encourages them to act out in her presence. They sit on the bench facing hers, and talk to themselves, or fall off the bench or sing loudly or stand on the bench and declaim. Claire occasionally tells them to behave, but otherwise pays them no mind.

For years, Claire would retreat to the rear of the convenience store when she saw us coming. After a while, she would stand in front of the convenience store, but not acknowledge us when we asked her if she wanted a sandwich or some juice. Then, she would respond, but coldly, and only to say that she didn't want anything. Then, still remote, she would listen to the variety of sandwiches we had that day, and reject them all. Then, she would ask for a peanut butter and jelly sandwich; for so long as Claire would only take peanut butter and jelly, our interns would fiercely protect the last peanut butter and jelly sandwich from the mob of drunken Hispanics on the other side of Prospect Street, so that there would be one left for her. Then, she would consider any sandwich. And, finally, Claire began to talk with us.

When she did, we discovered that Claire is a strikingly intelligent and well read woman. She can talk confidently about banking and World War I and stem cell research and the coming Presidential primaries. Claire was, if not caring, then at least polite. She began to inquire about our health and coo sympathetically if we looked tired (as we almost always did by the time we reached her) and to ask after our former interns. And we discovered that, if we let her talk long enough, a furious paranoia would emerge, in which banking and World War I and stem cell research and the coming Presidential primaries were all evidence of a malign conspiracy to oppress and punish the weakest among us: women, the poor, the homeless, the disabled. Like many paranoids who have trouble getting people to listen to them for more than a few minutes, Claire, when in a rage, would spew out her fear and her anger in one never-ending sentence, sensing that if she paused for breath we would seize the opportunity to walk away.

But this is increasingly rare. We have found a comfortable place—always making sure that we have saved at least one peanut butter and jelly sandwich—where Claire can care for us as we stagger through the last few hundred yards of our ministry without frightening us or herself.

Now we are just a few steps from City Hall. We cross the street and head back toward the T. This part of Central Square is full of bookstores and upscale restaurants; there are few homeless people to be found here. We stop, now and again, to look at one of the television sets perched over an open air bar to see how the Red Sox or the Celtics or the Patriots are doing—recently, quite well—and soon we are back where we started. There is a small group of benches here, not configured as attractively as Carl Barron Plaza, which is right across the street, but still a place where, now, a friendly group of Hispanic men gather to play cards.

Until recently, Wayne and Charlie were a fixture here. Wayne had no teeth and his face had collapsed inward. He had small, beady eyes but he was a sweet and self deprecating man. He always wore a jacket and tie, although he took his shoes off when he was sitting down. Every Sunday, he would quiz us on his favorite prayer:

> God, thank you for this wonderful day
> And thank you for an even more wonderful tomorrow.

Wayne never took offense that I couldn't remember his poem from week to week. He delighted in repeating the prayer over and over as proof that he was a person of abiding faith, even if he never went to church.

Charlie was Wayne's constant companion. Charlie was every bit as short as Wayne. He has thinning blond hair that he wears very, very short. He has widely spaced gray eyes and an enormous bulbous red nose. Wayne was funny, but Charlie is hilarious. He dresses impeccably, astonishingly, since he lives behind a dumpster at the rear of City Hall. He has a very dry sense of humor that endears him to us.

Wayne and Charlie camped on one of the benches facing Mass Avenue. Wayne kept all of his belongings in a Star Market shopping cart. He was so small and the shopping cart piled so high with stuff that when he was sitting down on the bench with the cart in front of him we couldn't see him and had to walk around behind the bench to see if he was there and awake. Unlike most homeless people with shopping carts that overflow with anything that might be of value later, Wayne's belongings were folded carefully or packed away and covered with a waterproof sheet of clear plastic. Wayne and Charlie were usually the last people we saw at the end of the day in Central Square.

A long time went by when we didn't see Wayne or Charlie. We aren't surprised when people appear or disappear without warning or explanation. Very few of them use email or the postal service to keep us informed of their movements. But then, one Sunday, Charlie appeared by himself. He was deeply distraught. We had never seen him so disheveled. Charlie said that Wayne had died. He said that Wayne had complained of stomach pain, but refused to go to the hospital. He was going to be stoic about it. He began to vomit blood. He wouldn't eat or drink. Charlie pleaded with him to go to the hospital but Wayne wouldn't budge. Finally, Charlie took matters into his own hands, walked around the corner and told the police that Wayne was next to the dumpster behind the Cambridge Savings Bank and that he was dying. The police knew Charlie and let him ride in the ambulance next to Wayne, but by the time the police had got Wayne out from behind the dumpster and over to Cambridge City Hospital he was dead.

For months, Charlie was devastated by Wayne's death. He drank more heavily than usual. He complained of chest pains and when he went to Mt. Auburn Hospital the doctors thought they saw white spots that could have been tumors. When we saw him, Charlie would point to his heart and say, "There's still a big hole here."

Next time we saw Charlie, Pat and I were talking to Dave in front of the Cambridge Savings Bank. It was raining and we were trying to persuade Dave to head down to 240 Albany Street a little earlier than usual. Charlie took me aside and asked if I would talk to his mother. I thought he wanted me to drive him to his mother's place. But it was Mother's Day, and his mother and brother had come in from Chelsea, rousted him from behind the dumpster and taken him across the street to Au Bon Pain for a meal. They were waiting there. Would I come over and meet them?

Charlie's mother was short, like Charlie, with a lined brown face and sharp brown eyes. Her hair was pulled back in a severe bun. She wore no makeup and looked like a no-nonsense woman. Her visit was a Mother's Day present to Charlie and she was going to be with Charlie come hell or high water. "You can't stop me when I've got the bit in my teeth," she said. His brother was enormous, at least 300 pounds. He looked just like Charlie—cropped blond hair, gray eyes—despite being a foot taller and hundreds of pounds heavier. He wore khaki shorts, cut much too high; his thighs were like enormous white hams.

Charlie's mother was a little apprehensive about meeting me. The words came out in a rush: Charlie could come home any time, he was always welcome, his room was just the way it was when he left. Charlie put a hand on her arm, and she slowed down. "All he has to do is stop drinking," she said. Charlie gave me a look that said, "But we all know how likely *that* is." Charlie's brother was a little embarrassed to be seen as the brother of a homeless alcoholic, but his affection for Charlie overcame his self consciousness. I couldn't stay long—Pat and the interns had already moved down Mass Avenue—but Charlie's mother said she was glad that Charlie knew such a nice man and Charlie's brother almost crushed my hand when he shook it.

We are finished in Central Square but we are not finished with the day. We take the T back to Harvard Square, often joining men and boys with Red Sox or Celtics or Bruins shirts, caps and other paraphernalia, coming back from a home game. We emerge from the Harvard Square T station and take our leftover sandwiches up to Christ Church for the people who attend the AA meeting there. Then we take the empty coolers and knapsacks back to Harvard Epworth and leave them there for the following Sunday. After saying goodnight to the interns and volunteers, Pat and I catch up on anything that we missed during the afternoon. We are exhausted, but always privately pleased to see that our interns, who are thirty to forty years younger than us, are even more tired than we are. We both have long drives home. Pat will get a Chai from a nearby Starbucks to tide her over until she reaches Rhode Island. I will get a chocolate frappe at Emack & Bollio's in Porter Square, praying that I won't run into any homeless person I know while I am carrying it back to the car. In fact, it happens all the time and no one is perturbed except me.

Emotionally and physically, I am completely drained. I won't want to talk about anything that has happened that day when I get home—it will have to wait until Monday morning. We had decided that Jean would be the minister at Porter Square to free me to preach at other churches and, especially, not to be on the street all day, but Porter Square is my church. I want to be there when I am not preaching somewhere else. This is not good practice. Someday, Pat, Jean and I will have to acknowledge that grandparents in their sixties are not built for this. For the moment, though, there is no other place I want to be.

• • • • •

One year, Christmas Eve fell on a Sunday and so did more than a foot of snow. We managed to collect ourselves, have a service on the Cambridge Common and walk through Harvard Square, but by the time we got to Central Square it was very late, it had been dark for at least an hour and the snow had started again, driven almost horizontal by a steady, cutting wind. Traffic had virtually disappeared, and we dragged our coolers up and down the middle of Mass Avenue with more cross country skiers for company than transit busses. We could barely see the City of Cambridge's non-religious white Holiday Season lights stretched across the street. Somehow, word had trickled down from Harvard Square—probably borne by people trying to make their way back to 240 Albany Street—that we were out with movie tickets and Dunkin' Donuts cards, because there were nearly as many people still outdoors as there would have been in early spring before sundown. We were astonished that anyone was outdoors, and the people we encountered were astonished that we were out in a blizzard giving out movie tickets. It was a picture postcard New England Christmas, but with homeless people in it.

8

Covenant and Church

> Are these not also men? Do they not have rational souls? Do you not see this? Do you not feel it? How can you stay in such lethargic sleep?[1]

FOR JOSEPH TUCKERMAN, THE CALL TO EXTEND PHILANTHROPY TO THE poor as a theological imperative was the easy part. The hard part was getting people to acknowledge the covenant that bound rich and poor together in a church congregation and to foster and strengthen that covenant. Tuckerman eagerly promoted friendly visiting as a simple, effective way for the rich to engage the poor.[2] He was genuinely surprised when no other ministers, other than his assistants, showed any inclination to join him in his friendly visits to the poor.

For the Outdoor Church, endemic violence among our congregants, especially domestic abuse, so powerfully and continually threatens to violate that covenant that we despair for all who are engaged in it and for the survival of the church itself. It is very, very difficult to abhor the violence that engulfs homeless people like Shaggy and Vickie, or Brad and Louise, all of whom attend our Sunday morning prayer service in Porter Square, and still minister to both abuser and abused. It was to bring the church to not just the least but also the worst among us that we began the Outdoor Church in the first place.

We had decided early on that we wouldn't ask people about themselves. We weren't social workers and we weren't journalists. If a person wanted to share their past or their present with us, they would share

---

1. Sobrino, *No Salvation Outside the Poor*, 7, 85. In December of 1511 the Dominican Priest Antonio de Montesino preached an inflammatory sermon demanding fair treatment of the Indians and condemning the injustices of the Spanish colonial system.

2. *Joseph Tuckerman on the Elevation of the Poor*, 94–95.

it without any urging from us. And they did, but in very idiosyncratic ways. The stories we heard were unremitting narratives of abandonment, physical and emotional abuse, illness, unwanted pregnancies and neglect. The inevitable arc of those stories was from bad to worse to terrible. As we watched and witnessed, the stories almost always ended in violent death, lingering and painful disease or serious injury.

Vickie is small, slight and a deep mahogany from all of her years on the street. She has luminous grey eyes and hair that is almost always washed and curled. Her nose is broken and her lips are cracked and split. Vickie's passivity masks an unyielding obstinacy: no one can get her to do what she doesn't want to do—not Shaggy, her current boyfriend, not her husband, not Mardi, whom Vickie loves, and not her doctors, who tell her every time she is hospitalized that her pancreatitis will kill her if she takes another drink. We have interrupted our prayer service in Porter Square two or three times to call for an ambulance to take her to Cambridge City Hospital when the pain is too great for her to sit up. She only rarely complains. Vickie has a brilliant smile and—amazingly—most of her teeth. On those rare occasions when I press her to see a doctor about her stomach, she looks up into my face, opens her eyes even wider and grins ruefully at me, as if to suggest that some *other* Vickie has laid down the law and there is nothing that *this* Vickie can do about it. "But what can you do?" she says winningly, looking up into my face with her enormous gray eyes.

Vickie has a family in Maynard, a husband and two children, who would gladly take her back, no questions asked. The last time she saw her daughter, her daughter screamed, "Ma, what happened to you?" Vickie said she would "clean up her act" and get some new clothes and they made a date to have lunch, but Vickie was picked up on an outstanding warrant and never got there.

"What can you do?" was also Dolly's attitude toward the endless physical abuse to which Shaggy subjected her. Until Shaggy became too sick to assault her, Dolly would arrive in Porter Square on Sunday morning with black and yellow eyes, bruises around her mouth and shoulder and abrasions all over her face. There were times—as when Vickie, badly beaten, crawled up the steel steps on the other side of Mass Avenue while Shaggy, in tears, was telling us how overjoyed he was that she was out of prison and back with him—when we couldn't imagine how she managed to survive. Between her pancreatitis and Shaggy's abuse, we were never sure when Vickie didn't show up in Porter Square if she was in MCI Framingham, dead or simply oversleeping.

When Shaggy is not sober, he simply gives up on personal grooming. His shoulder length hair falls over his face in long dirty strings. He has high cheekbones, a sallow, pockmarked complexion and vague, evasive dark eyes that shift rapidly from side to side all the time, like a tic, whether he is lying or just asking for a pair of socks. He is arrogant, almost as stubborn as Vickie, and self-defeating. Shaggy likes to tell us that he doesn't need doctors or lawyers or anyone else to help him—particularly not us. In his telling, he is untouched by any of the horrors that visit people who live on the street.

But when he is sober—and that is almost always when Vickie is in prison—he washes his hair, pulls it back in a pony tail, shaves and washes his clothes. His eyes clear and he can make eye contact. Sober, Shaggy is expansive: he will take Vickie to Oregon to stay with his mother, he will get rid of his public defender and handle all his pending court cases by himself, he will stay sober without detox. See? he boasts, I'm sober now. It's all under control.

When Vickie is in prison, both Shaggy and Vickie stop drinking, she of necessity and he by choice. Then, once reunited, they both start drinking again. Once, anticipating some more time in prison for each of them, they decided to use drugs to wean themselves from alcohol. This wasn't a problem for Vickie; as soon as she reentered Framingham, she stopped drinking and using. But Shaggy started drinking on top of enough Percocet (if he could be believed) to fell an elephant. Living under the industrial sized air conditioner in Pigeon Park, a dank cluster of trees behind the Porter Square T Station, Shaggy began to go to pieces. He stopped eating, he became incontinent, he could barely walk and, by the time Vickie was released, he could barely stand up.

At this point, Brad and Louise became a more prominent part of Shaggy and Vickie's life. Brad and Louise have been a fixture in Porter Square from long before we began our prayer services on Sunday mornings. They sleep in the garden behind St. James's or behind the Stop and Shop supermarket in the Porter Square Shopping Center, and spend their days in Porter Square, reading the newspaper, drinking, talking with passersby and just hanging out. Brad is a dark young man who looks as though he works out every day. His arm and chest and shoulder muscles ripple when he moves his upper body. He has dark, piercing eyes, set well back in his head, and a shock of dark brown hair. He is very aware of his body and its appearance. When he is high, he can be frightening: loud, agitated, constantly on the move and unable to sit in one place for more than a few minutes. He has a cheap gray plastic boom box that he carries everywhere with him, including into our services, although he always turns it off when the service begins.

It is jolting to hear Brad talk about our weekly Scripture readings. We don't have sermons or homilies in our morning prayer service; instead, after Jean reads the Scripture passage for the week, anyone can comment or offer an opinion or say how they feel about it. Brad is a born theologian. He unerringly senses what a Scriptural passage is about and can describe it clearly and compellingly. He is a great favorite of visiting clergy. It is always a shock, because it seems—although it isn't—completely at variance with all the other things we know about him. This happens a lot on the street: we will learn something about a person to whom we minister that is totally unexpected but that, on reflection, isn't contradicted by anything we knew before: we just didn't anticipate it. This hasn't endeared Brad to us—he is violent, dishonest and endlessly self pitying regardless—but he is a cautionary reminder that everyone in front of us is some mother's son, rich in personal history and fully developed in character.

Louise is Brad's girl friend, small and seemingly delicate, with blue eyes set in a dough-colored face. She is blowzy and unfocussed when she is drinking. Louise tries to be attentive to her appearance. Friends do her hair for her with blond highlights and lots of curls. She has a fetching smile and when she is with us she seems to bathe in the warmth of the community. She thanks me or Jean over and over again for the socks, for the sandwiches or for the coffee, but she is really saying how glad she is to be in a safe and quiet place. When she isn't with us, Brad takes two of everything—sandwiches, juice boxes, socks and toiletry kits—because Louise is "sleeping in" or "feeling sick." When Brad is drinking, he is very violent. Lynn, who harbors an intense dislike for Brad, once told us that Brad had slammed Louise's head through the glass window of an ATM booth. When the T police arrived and arrested him, he claimed that she had tipped over backwards before he could catch her.

Brad has an explanation for the violence: he doesn't assault Louise; she assaults him. When Louise is drinking, he says, she gets out of control and attacks everyone within reach in Porter Square, Brad included.

What stands out from this narrative—which we hear over and over, because Louise is hospitalized or imprisoned frequently—is Brad's self-righteousness as he becomes persuaded by his own story. "Jesus," he whines, "She gets out of control and I've got to clean up the mess. Where's the justice? I've had it with 'Vic' and 'Tim'—I'm sick and tired of being the fall guy for someone who is always drunk and violent."

Yet it is likely that, despite Brad's dishonesty, Louise is as violent as he says. She has been arrested many more times than him for fighting. Once Fran found her lying on the sidewalk near the White Hen Pantry across Mass Avenue, after a fight with another woman, and took her into the restroom at the convenience store to wash away the blood and put some makeup on the bruises around her eyes. When violence frames every encounter, homeless men and women are more likely to be both aggressor and victim, and it is often hard to tell who is who in any given encounter. I immediately assumed that, as between Brad and Louise, Brad was always the aggressor because he is a man. Now, I have suspended judgment—as I should have all along—unable to discern in Brad's incongruous qualities a clear sign one way or the other.

Vickie had emerged from Framingham just as Louise was being involuntarily committed to Mt. Auburn Hospital for a psychiatric evaluation. This left Brad to his own devices and, seeing that Shaggy could barely move, much less assert or defend himself, he began to spend more time with Vickie, who seemed to enjoy the attention. Even when Shaggy is sober, he is no match for Brad, who outweighs him and is in much better shape. As it was, he would sit twenty or thirty feet away from Brad and Vickie and scream or cry or mope. Brad was cruel, making fun of Shaggy's incontinence, which, because he only had one pair of pants, forced him to waddle to keep his legs apart. He smelled terrible, and knew it. Vickie tried to help Shaggy, but he wouldn't stop drinking, he wouldn't stop taking the Percocet and he wouldn't go to a hospital.

Then Brad began to unravel. Just before Louise had been committed, she and Brad and Shaggy and Vickie and some others were using the garden behind St. James's as a campground. The neighbors complained. I suggested to Brad, who (with Louise) was out on bail for assaulting a police officer and had a long string of convictions for assaults with a deadly weapon, that his bail would be revoked if the neighbors continued to complain to the police. Brad had already reached the same conclusion. With Louise gone, he began to sleep behind the Stop and

Shop instead of in the garden behind St. James's. He became very subdued and couldn't stop talking about what would happen if the police pulled him off the street. He was still in better shape than Shaggy, but he was drinking more and his hands shook badly as he tried to tune his boom box.

• • • • •

Because Shaggy's mental and physical collapse seemed to have left him hardly able to walk, much less assault someone, we came to believe that Vickie was safe for so long as he was ill. We were wrong. A few months after the nightly disturbances in St. James's back garden had subsided, we heard from Brad that Shaggy had again badly beaten Vickie in the passageway connecting the T Station with the T tracks and that Vickie had once again managed to crawl along the passageway and up the stairs on the opposite side of Mass Avenue where a passerby saw her and called 911. Shaggy was being held at the Middlesex County jail pending trial. Brad said that Vickie wouldn't go to Cambridge City Hospital but that she was staying with his mother. Doug was in jail too; Fran, who had just got out of the hospital, said that he had gotten into a knife fight and cut the other guy. I looked around: Shaggy in jail, Louise in jail, Doug in jail, Vic in jail, Fran just out of the hospital, Jeannie out of sight and recovering from a beating, Vickie out of sight and recovering from a beating, Dixie in prison. This was our covenantal community.

• • • • •

Tuckerman came to the Ministry-at-large with conventional, academic ideas about religion and social policy, but his direct experience of ministering to the poor on the streets of Boston—what he saw and what he heard and what he could not and would not deny—transformed these ideas into a theology that was fundamentally Christian. Only a theology that raised up Christian duty to a form of discipleship could make theological sense of what Tuckerman encountered on the street.

Tuckerman's initial debt to Unitarian moral philosophy was discharged by his ability to see that Unitarian Christianity's emphasis on loving relations among men was reflected in his own visceral affection for the poor people he encountered in their homes and on the street. He discovered in himself an impulse that transformed the moral system developed at Harvard into a theology. He wrote:

> [T]he poorest and the most degraded of our race possesses the principles of a common nature with ourselves, and is equally with ourselves a child of God, and as our Father's child, is our brother ... [W]ho can thus comprehend his own soul, and thus feel his relation to his fellow man, and not feel his heart drawn in sympathy with human weakness, and ignorance, and want, and wretchedness, and sin?[3]

The very intensity of Tuckerman's experience seemed to evoke the traditional congregational idea of covenant theology. Covenant theology had its roots in the thinking of John Calvin. The covenant was between God and the individual. The covenant paired God's commitment to save his people with his people's commitment to obey God's commandments. There were variations on this understanding; Calvin himself saw the covenant as completely fulfilled in Christ's life, death and resurrection. For the Puritans who were Tuckerman's congregational forebears, baptism initiated the covenant, the Lord's Supper sustained it and the sanctification of the elect was required to fulfill it. To this covenant, the Puritans added a second: the covenant among those gathered together out of the world to form a church. This second covenant was one of the distinguishing marks of a congregational church. For the Puritans, the two covenants, taken together, framed the congregational church.

The concept of covenant resonated for Tuckerman because it had its roots in the Puritans' idea of the church and their desire to ensure its purity. From the beginning, the Puritans understood themselves to be called out of the debauched world of the Anglican Communion to ensure that the church would remain untouched by the world's depravity. Locating the power to discipline in each individual congregation would keep the church free of insufficiently committed Christians, unprepared and uneducated ministers and a distant and easily corrupted apostolic hierarchy. The sinew that held each congregation together was the strength of the agreement among its members to follow the congregational way—the purpose section, as it were, of a corporation's articles of organization.[4]

Given its importance, gathered churches invested substantial time and energy in the drafting and adoption of their ordinances. Some covenants were extensive texts and some were beautiful in their simplicity,

---

3. Gerando, *Visitor of the Poor*, xxii–xxiii.
4. Punchard, *View of Congregationalism*, 29.

brevity and clarity. The covenant of the church in Salem, Massachusetts, adopted in 1629, read: "We covenant with the Lord and one with another; and do bind ourselves in the presence of God, to walk together in all his ways, as he is pleased to reveal himself unto us in his Blessed word of truth."[5] A longer, but no less compelling, covenant was reaffirmed at Wellesley, England, in 1949: "We acknowledge Christ to be the sole Head of the Church. We believe that were He present among His people there is all that is essential to a Church. Thus each community of believers is the Catholic Church in essence and is empowered by Christ to govern its own life under the guidance of its Spirit."[6]

The covenant could be explicit, where there was a formal written covenant, or implicit, where the church was gathered without a verbal or written formal covenant.[7] In the end, it was the covenant, and not the minister or stained glass windows or the blessing of a bishop, that endowed a gathered church with substance and legitimacy.[8]

The Ministry-at-large was modeled on an idealized covenantal community. In theory, it consisted entirely in the covenantal relation between God and the poor and in the covenantal relation among the poor whom Tuckerman had gathered to his ministry. In fact, it existed in the substance and immediacy of his continuing encounters with the poor. Tuckerman would never have described as a church the community of poor people he regularly visited, but they were a church nevertheless—no less churched than his former parishioners in Chelsea. Among themselves and with him, the covenants required to institute a church were essentially fulfilled.

· · · · ·

Had we also idealized our relationship to our congregants? What was required to create the covenant that we believed was central to our church? Was it sufficient that our people were present at our services? Did they have to be awake, at least for some of the service? Did a person have to be sober enough to recognize that we were asking her to love God as

---

5. W. Walker, *Creeds and Platforms of Congregationalism*, 116.

6. Sell, *Saints*, 93–94. See Forsyth, *Church and the Sacraments*, chapter 3; and see John, *Congregationalism in an Ecumenical Age*.

7. Cummings, *Dictionary of Congregational Usages and Principles*, 130.

8. Ibid., 52.

God loved her, and to want to do so? Did a person have to acknowledge being a member of a church, however unusual and unfamiliar?

No more than in any other church. For us, the members of the Outdoor Church are those people who profess a faith in God and who have gathered together to hear God's word and to celebrate his sacraments. "Gathered" means: anyone to whom we minister. Like any other church, not all of our congregants need to attend church every Sunday or attend church all together in the same place—think of all the members of conventional churches who show up only for Christmas and Easter, or who go to church on Sunday morning, not to attend services, but to lead children's religious education classes or prepare refreshments for the welcome hour following worship. Any member of our church need only understand at some point in our ongoing relationship with them that they have encountered a minister and that, by an implication no more explicit than the early Congregational church covenants, they have joined a community of people of faith. We have yet to minister to a homeless person of faith who was not once sober enough to understand who we are and to appreciate the meaning of the invitation that we are extending to him.

· · · · ·

Tuckerman's Boston was like Tuckerman's Chelsea, that is, like the Boston of his father's generation: relatively homogenous in religious outlook, church organization and class structure. "There," he wrote about Chelsea, "the rich and the poor, or, in other words, those who had some capital and those who had none, met on terms of equality before the church door on Sunday, interchanged expressions of friendly greeting and separated to pass into their own pews or into free galleries, without the slightest feeling, in either case, that distinction of condition was thus implied between them."[9] Tuckerman always retained a sense that in the Boston of 1820, as in the Massachusetts Bay Colony of 1630, there was one church and one parish. "I passed twenty-five years as the minister of a small religious society in the country," he said. "The lines of my parish there were the lines also of the town. There was no other religious society in the place than that to which I ministered."[10] This

---

9. Tuckerman, *Principles and Results*, 14.

10. Ibid., 104. Even here there was an echo of Solomon Stoddard for whom church and town were more or less coincident. Marsden, *Jonathan Edwards*, 351.

sense informed his willingness to look beyond the walls of any building to see opportunities for Christian service throughout his Ministry-at-large. He never mistook a building for a church.

There were many neighborhoods, each with its own church, in the Boston of the early 19th century (and, in time, the stratifying of these neighborhoods would likewise stratify their memberships) but, as of 1820, Tuckerman could still believe Boston had only one parish and that the people who lived in that parish were as similar to one another as the residents of Chelsea.

Boston's poor, therefore, were simply people like other Bostonians, but with less capital. For this reason, Tuckerman despised the use of free seating for the poor in churches that otherwise rented or sold pews to its members. He was particularly incensed by the reservation of free benches, usually at the center of the church, for those who could not afford to purchase or rent a pew. This, he felt, called attention to their poverty, further isolated them from everyone else in church and discouraged them from attending church altogether. Peering down from a gallery at those of the poor who were not too embarrassed to sit in "free" pews could only discourage feelings of covenantal relations in those more fortunate.

Tuckerman's hope was for a church, like his church in Chelsea, in which the Christian doctrine of human equality would be the basis for congregational life.[11] Relations between rich and poor were to be as relations of one member of a congregation to another: personal and direct. His ministry, he said, was:

> an instrument for the communication of a knowledge of each other between these great classes (the rich and the poor); for bringing about a personal knowledge of each other between them; and, by calling forth a personal interest in each other, to connect them in the only bonds of permanent good and happiness, those of a Christian respect and regard for one another.[12]

Realizing Tuckerman's ideal mixture of rich and poor congregants in every existing Boston church on such a direct and personal basis was going to require a great deal more interaction among the rich and the poor than in the past. Tuckerman favored friendly visiting as the

---

11. Ibid., 48.
12. Gerando, *Visitor of the Poor*, xxxv–xxxvi.

means to that end. Friendly visiting was only one of any number of ways that the rich could encounter the poor directly and personally, but in Tuckerman's Boston, it was the most likely one at hand.

For their part—as Tuckerman soon learned from his interviews with the poor—relatively few of the poor had any intention of attending a conventional church, either because they were embarrassed to be seen sitting in free pews, or because it was their only day of relaxation, or because they were ill. It was extremely difficult for the poor to regularly attend the prayer services of the wealthy churches, even assuming there was space for them. The poor did not press against the doors of King's Chapel in discernibly greater numbers than the rich rushed to the streets near the wharfs to encounter the poor in their homes.

As a practical matter, Tuckerman would have to bring the church to them. His decision was based on his imminently pragmatic assessment of the circumstances in which the people he encountered found themselves. "What better charity can there be, than the provision at once of a ministry, and a place of worship, by which as many as possible of such of these shall be brought into a union."[13] It was not the residents of a particular street, or parish, or any other place, but "the whole body" of the poor that was to be made the object of Christian interest. The congregation, if not the building, was to be stretched to include those among the "whole body" of the poor who, through a minister's inspiration and direction, were inclined to church membership but who for one reason or another could not or would not attend a conventional church.

This did not mean that Tuckerman was indifferent to whether people went to church or not, or where they went to church. He very much wanted the poor to attend existing churches because he believed that this was the easiest way for the rich to encounter the poor.[14] He strongly resisted separate churches for the poor, pleading that nothing be done by the Ministry-at-large by which "the poor shall be made to feel that the very religion which is intended to be a bond of union between them and their fellow-men is itself an instrument of their separation from

---

13. Tuckerman, *Principles and Results,* 141.

14. The Rev. Charles Lowell, Liberal pastor of West Church, succeeded in adopting a system for families to share the ownership of pews, thereby enabling working-class families to participate fully in the life of his parish. This gained him the largest parish in Boston, but no one followed his example. Howe, *Unitarian Conscience,* 370 n. 24.

the more favored classes of their fellow-beings."[15] Yet, in the absence of an increase in the number of poor members of otherwise wealthy churches, friendly visiting was the only feasible alternative.

Tuckerman's idea that rich and poor must stand in congregational relation was an ecclesiological expression of his theological conviction that the poor and the rich were dependent on one another. The poor needed the rich for spiritual and material assistance and the rich needed the poor because only in true charity (gifts of the person, not just money) could the rich find their way to Christian fulfillment. (Indeed, it was precisely among the poor that the rich could best express Christian charity, since the poor, of necessity, so badly needed help in adapting the Christian message to their own dire circumstances.) Tuckerman understood this mutuality of obligation as a type of covenant, binding the rich and the poor together in Christian, not social or economic, terms: "I would to God that I could bring about a Christian connection between the rich and poor, the virtuous and the vicious, of all the classes among us. Christianity demands a connection of these classes…"[16] The charitable relationship among rich and the poor, engaged together in Christian work, constituted a church. The minister, by gathering rich and poor into a system of true charity, scientifically conceived and thoughtfully delivered, was the instrument of this mutuality. Support from other churches was the assurance of its realization. Tuckerman wrote, "[T]he ministry at large as I should be glad to have it constituted, should be brought into the closest connexion which can be formed of it with our churches. It should be virtually an extended ministry of these churches. It should be supported by, and taken into the bosom of these churches."[17]

For Tuckerman, it did not matter that this church had no building, nor membership book, nor endowment. The church did not exist as a physical structure, intended to serve people in a fixed geographic location. The gathered people, bound together by covenant, defined the church and established its location by their presence, not the other way around. This people being gathered from all of Boston, the city itself became a single parish, as it was at the inception of the Massachusetts

---

15. Tuckerman, *Elevation of the Poor*, 34.
16. Tuckerman, *Principles and Results*, 30.
17. Ibid., 181.

Bay Colony. Indeed, until the deliberate use of chapels as a physical alternative to conventional churches (as opposed to a convenient location in which to gather those whom Tuckerman had met on the street and more efficiently provide them with inspiration and instruction) Tuckerman's church had no physical existence at all. It existed, insofar as it had any existence, wherever Tuckerman and his associates were when they ministered to the poor—literally, where two or three were gathered together, whether rich or poor. Or, if the Ministry-at-large was to be a success, some rich and some poor.

This was the Puritans' covenant theology framed by the Unitarian idea of human nature.[18] In Tuckerman's account, traditional covenant theology's emphasis on human obedience to God's judgments became an emphasis on human obedience to the Great Commandment. As the God of judgment receded, the Unitarian moral philosophy taught at Harvard emerged in Tuckerman's theology as the foundation for covenantal commitments.

What materialized was a covenant theology that reflected the many different personal and institutional relations that characterized the Ministry-at-large itself. In this new covenant theology, some relations remained fundamentally unchanged (e.g. the covenant among members of the church) and others were substantially transformed (e.g. the minister's relation to the members of the church was less like a call than like a moral obligation.) But most important, this new covenant theology looked primarily to the commandment of love as the ground for Christian responsibility and the experience of love as the basis for Christian action. Here was the essence of a congregational church, stripped of structures, endowments and banners, existing solely, but visibly, in the covenant relation between God and the poor and in the covenant relation among the poor whom Tuckerman had gathered to his ministry.

Tuckerman did not believe that the Ministry-at-large had created a mutuality of concern and respect between rich and poor that would eliminate all social and economic distinctions between them. He hoped nonetheless for an interdependence that would radically transform their relations and the church he wished them to share: "Let there be one spot on earth other than the grave," he pleaded, "and one office be-

---

18. Tuckerman, *Letter on the Principles of the Missionary Enterprise*, 31, 36–37.

sides that of mingling 'dust with dust' in the burial of our dead, in which Christian doctrine of human equality shall be distinctly recognised and fairly acted out..."[19]

Tuckerman's acquiescence in the Benevolent Fraternity of Church's construction of chapels for the poor after the first two years of the Ministry-at-large was an acknowledgment that the rich would never find their way in any significant numbers to Friend Street and that the poor would never make any significant demands upon them. Indeed, Tuckerman was always fearful that too drastic a re-orientation of existing relations might lead to social disorder. He was convinced that, if the rich were not active in philanthropy, the poor would blame them for their hardships, become discontented and disrupt the social order.[20]

Although once the Ministry-at-large moved indoors it became more and more closely associated with the American Unitarian Association, Tuckerman himself was not interested in denominational issues as such. Perhaps this is why he was so comfortable with ecumenical efforts to help the poor and so admiring of the work of other denominations in the field. Perhaps, also, it accounts for Tuckerman's seeming indifference to the Unitarian Controversy, which raged around him during his ministry in Chelsea and during the early years of the Ministry-at-large. Channing, himself at the very heart of the Controversy, could never engage Tuckerman in the denominational conflicts that racked the Standing Order.[21]

Characteristically, Tuckerman was radical only in his theology.

Like Tuckerman's ministry, our church is ecumenical. There is no one who asks to whom we will not minister. We are ecumenical because we exist only to respond to Christ's command to actively encounter the poor, the sick, the imprisoned, the homeless and the oppressed. Methodist prisoners will not reject the ministrations of Presbyterian clergy. Congregational patients will not disdain a visit from a Unitarian chaplain. Catholic refugees will not refuse food and water from Baptist relief workers. And likewise on the streets. There are no Methodist egg salad sandwiches, no Baptist socks, no Episcopal juice boxes. There is only the Body of Christ.

19. Tuckerman, *Principles and Results*, 55.
20. Tuckerman, *Essay on the Wages*, 17.
21. McColgan, *Joseph Tuckerman*, 42–43.

· · · · ·

We are a church—not "just" a ministry, or some form of outreach, but a church. We are not a program or a mission of any one church or any one denomination.

Many different churches of many different denominations have provided us with financial and other support. Our clergy are drawn from many different traditions as well. In all the years that Bob Tobin had prodded the Harvard Square Clergy Association to create an outdoor church for homeless people in Harvard Square, the Association could never agree on a common liturgy, much less a common polity or a common theology. When we met with Bob, he suggested that we might set all that aside, in the interests of actually doing something constructive. Pat and I agreed. We will not allow denominational differences to impede the work of the Outdoor Church. We are outdoors to make the church accessible to people who are unwelcome, or feel themselves to be unwelcome, in conventional churches. How, then, could we insist on rules that would make it *more* difficult for people to attend church?

· · · · ·

Whether Lynn—for whom being Jewish in no way diminished her pleasure in attending our morning prayer service in Porter Square—was a member of our church was a question of church polity, the rules by which different denominations govern themselves. In pre-Commonwealth England, people were hanged for adhering to a congregational polity. Now, very few people give it much attention; it is the rare seminarian who has a conversion experience in the middle of a required denominational polity class.

But, for me, locating a polity in some denomination's history was an affirmation of our legitimacy and authenticity as a church. I was fortunate that I had fallen in with a denomination that had its roots in a radical insistence on a congregational polity.

At first, the intersection of historical congregational polity, especially in contrast with contemporary liberal denominations, and the reality of a street church was my opportunity to test the theoretical boundaries of our ministry. My enterprise was equal parts lawyer and grade school kid who has just stolen a candy bar from the drugstore; I'd try anything that I could justify as congregational polity, and the more at variance with conventional practice, the more satisfying it was. It was the intellectual hook on which I hung my frustration with our supporting churches, which were more eager to support us financially than to incorporate our understandings of church, sacraments and ministry in their own practice. Pat—who got to watch most of this—was amused but insistent that, whatever we did, it wouldn't force her to do anything at variance with her Episcopal training.

It became clear, soon enough, that I was cherry picking. The Outdoor Church couldn't be shoe-horned into a model of a sixteenth-century Separatist church. No homeless person had called me or Pat or Jean to be her minister. No one could dismiss us or replace us. Virtually everything about the organization and administration of our church was controlled by its staff, not its congregants.

But there was certainly enough there to satisfy me that we were comfortably within a compelling tradition. Our church was based first and foremost on a covenant, implicit but no less important for that. It welcomed all those who professed faith, keeping none from membership. It relied on the gathered community for its reality, rather than a building or a minister or a priest or a liturgical practice. And it demanded of its members that they see themselves as set apart for the joys and challenges of Christian discipleship.

And, as my need to justify our church as a church began to abate, there emerged some basic principles from the very fact of our existence. We embodied both the consolations and the challenges of the Christian project, asking our members to expect love and comfort but demanding that they extend love and comfort to one another. Most importantly, we looked to God's sovereignty as the basis for a realistic acceptance of life on the street and for hope that the renewal of a spiritual life could, in some way, counterbalance that life. With this came humility—who were we to interpose ourselves between God and the people he loved?—and great joy in a church whose primary principle was radical welcome.

• • • • •

More than anything else we hear or see on the street, violence among the people to whom we minister—especially physical and emotional domestic abuse—violates the covenant of mutual love among our congregants that we seek to keep at the center of the Outdoor Church. Nothing causes us more grief, confusion and uncertainty. Nothing creates so many conflicts and disagreements among our clergy, interns and volunteers. Nothing leads us to make so many mistakes and complicate so many boundaries. Nothing so confuses our roles as ministers to all who attend our church and as ministers to the most oppressed and abused among us. And nothing distances us more from our congregants and yet binds us to them together so powerfully. Violence among those we serve is a constant source of despair among us and a continuing threat to the survival of our church and the success of our mission. It is at once a violation of the defining covenant of our church and of the most fundamental social and ethical norms.

We would hear stories from our homeless congregants about the constant and endless violence that infected the streets. Sometimes the stories were intended to impress us with just how bad it was out there, but most often people were simply describing their lives. We heard about people putting razor blades between their fingers and slapping homeless men around in a street fight. We heard about teenagers from South Boston trolling indoor parking lots in the middle of winter and setting fire to any homeless person they found sleeping there. We heard about people making videos of homeless men fighting one another or pulling teeth out of their own mouths with pliers or running head first into street signs. We heard about an Australian who tied up homeless men with duct tape while they were sleeping and then announced to a video camera: "Very few bums were hurt in the making of this film. All were returned to their natural habitat."

We rarely see this kind of violence at first hand. Perhaps it is because we are only out on Sundays. Perhaps the people we minister to want to protect us from the worst of what happens to them, because we are clergy. Occasionally, when we come across one of our people having a seizure in Central Square, we'll be present when an ambulance or patrol car pulls up to take her to the Cambridge City Hospital emergency room. But we know that we rarely see a fraction of the violence that Cambridge police deal with every day and night.

Although Tuckerman never mentioned it in other than the most general terms, he must have witnessed the consequences of domestic violence himself. The early nineteenth century was not one of those periods in American history when public awareness of domestic abuse prompted significant regulation and reform.[22] As the workplace moved further from the household and more women gained employment in factories and other similar workplaces, the role of women within the family changed and exacerbated tensions between some husbands and their wives. Unitarianism's reaction to these changes was mixed. Horace Bushnell cautioned fathers to "not be a savage to [your children] but a father and a Christian,"[23] but his ideas about family nurture placed impossible demands on those women who were responsible for both a job and a household. Perhaps Tuckerman saw little of the consequences of these tensions because, like ours, his followers sought, out of affection and respect, to shield him from the worst of what they experienced, if only so that he would not be discouraged from continuing his visits and his assistance.

In our second year in Porter Square, a number of couples began to attend our services as couples. In each case, we were certain that the man was abusing the woman. Often, the woman would not be with us on a Sunday morning, and then explain, the following week, that she was sick or overslept or forgot. The signs of assault—black eyes, sun glasses in the middle of winter, contusions—were unmistakable.

It isn't unusual for homeless women to seek the protection of a homeless man, but there is usually a price: sex and physical abuse. We've never been able to persuade any of the abused women who attend our service—some of whom we have now ministered to for years—to file a complaint, or get a restraining order, or go into a shelter for battered women. There are often many reasons for this: fear, self-hatred, deep depression and hopelessness, the relationship is in some manner mutually dependent, perhaps even sado-masochistic, the abuse you know is better than the abuse you don't know or lack of confidence in "the system." Whatever the reason, none of these women has sought help or protection or let one of us seek it for them.

Jeannie was a little manic—she was probably bipolar—but she was equally likeable whether she was elated or depressed. Jeannie had short, curly blond hair that would have made her look like a silent movie star but for her broken nose and split lips. Her features—after so much

---

22. See generally Pleck, *Domestic Tyranny*.
23. Bushnell, *Christian Nurture*, xiii.

drinking and so much abuse—were coarse. When she was sober, her brown eyes danced. She must have been very pretty once.

Jeannie was prickly, assertive and—she wanted us to fully appreciate—a little outrageous. "This is church," she would yell hoarsely at passersby who walk through the T Station, "There's a goddamn service going on here!" She loved to take liberties with us—hugging, kissing, taking us aside for little personal revelations, making jokes laced with sexual innuendo—that very few other homeless people would dare. Then she was remorseful and worried that she had gone too far. She used to call me from time to time, often just to say hello but especially if she had just been beaten or wasn't in Porter Square the Sunday before. Jean tried to visit her often at *On the Rise*, a day shelter for women only, which Jeannie, like most of the women who spent time there, thought of as a home, a sanctuary, a community of caring women and a resource center.

If the people to whom we minister cross a boundary, they are usually too familiar or too physical. The boundary Jeannie wanted to cross was friendship. Yet Jeannie was ambivalent about getting close to any of us. If she called me when she was in trouble, she invariably called just before *On the Rise* closed, so that I couldn't get back to her until the next day. Every Sunday, Jean asked her to read the Scripture passage for the week. She would start by reading as loudly as she could and then, as she began to grasp the sense of the reading, grow quieter and more absorbed in the text as if to say, "Damn! This is good stuff." Sometimes Jeannie brought her own text—usually, a selection from a psalm that had moved her—and she read that as well, while the others shifted from foot to foot in the cold waiting for it all to end so they could have a sandwich and get back into the T station.

Jeannie was quick to take offense at small affronts: a comment about her hair, someone talking while she was reading Scripture. When clergy or interns would greet her with "Hi! Jean," she would bark, "Don't call me 'Hygiene!'" When she was upset, she would scream, storm across the street and yell insults at all of us and herself, until people stopped paying attention. Then she would circle around the station and finally rejoin us, a little calmer. More often than not, Jeannie was barred from 240 Albany Street for assaulting another guest or threatening one of the night staff. Fortunately, her father in law took her in when the weather was unusually brutal, but he was an alcoholic, too, and not very reliable.

She wasn't part of any community of homeless men and women—she was too belligerent and abrasive—and she wasn't very good at living rough. In the winter, we often found her in the McDonald's in Central Square, slowly drinking a cup of coffee with no idea about where she would spend the night.

Jeannie had a lot of history. One of her children died at the age of eight, something she blamed herself for constantly. Three other daughters were taken away from her and left in the care of her estranged husband. When the oldest of them turned eighteen and succeeded in locating her, Jeannie was surprised and delighted, but, nonetheless, she prevented her daughters from seeing her or learning that she was homeless. Jeannie was constantly in and out of prisons and hospitals, almost always because of assaults on her or by her. Most of the hospitalizations were the consequence of the tremendous physical abuse she suffered at Vic's hands. She was rarely without fistfuls of pills—most of them powerful painkillers—that she took after Vic had worked her over or which she sold on the street.

Everything Jeannie did or said was driven by shame and self-hatred. We didn't make things any easier for her. Simply by being who we are, we reminded her of the middle class life that she'd left behind. Often as not, I'd see Jeannie in Porter Square in the morning, sober, and then see her again in Central Square at the end of the day, drunk. Sometimes she'd pretend she didn't know me. Sometimes she'd rage at me, as a representative of "the system," for her difficulties and refuse to talk to me. Sometimes she'd simply weep in despair and frustration. She knew what she looked like after she'd been drinking heavily and she was deeply embarrassed when we encountered her after she had had a lot to drink.

Jeannie's most pressing problem was Vic. Vic abused her regularly, often so badly that we wouldn't see Jeannie for two or three weeks, while she waited for the bruises to fade. The violence was premeditated. Until they couldn't afford it any more, Jeannie and Vic would rent a hotel room so that the most severe and dangerous abuse was hidden from public view. Then Jeannie lost her Social Security disability benefits and Vic regularly assaulted her whenever she had recovered enough from the last beating to present an attractive target, whether on the street or not. Jeannie was always eager for us to understand just how bad the violence was. She would tell us proudly that when she was so badly injured that she had to admit herself to Cambridge City Hospital, the doctors would plead with her to get a restraining order or seek refuge in a shelter for battered women. But, she would say dismissively, no doctor was going to tell her what to do. Yet Jeannie was also very self conscious about the bruising, and wore heavy makeup and sunglasses, even in the middle of winter, if she joined us at all.

Just after Jeannie's daughters reappeared, the frequency and severity of Vic's assaults increased. Perhaps her daughters too powerfully reminded Jeannie of her inadequacies as a parent and as a person, and she allowed herself to be punished more severely. As always, Jeannie refused to press charges, allow us to obtain a restraining order for her, go into a shelter for abused women or simply leave the area. Now she was also refusing medical care. She said that the doctors in the emergency room at Cambridge City Hospital told her that they would continue to treat her after Vic's beatings but that they would inform the Cambridge police. But, she said, Vic's brothers had threatened to kill her if she went to the police. So she couldn't go to the hospital any more. The nurse at *On the Rise*, who had taken photographs of Jeannie just after one of these attacks, offered to take her to another hospital, in Medford or Winchester, but Jeannie, now out of excuses, simply refused to go.

Jeannie was an intelligent and talented woman. She learned to cook at *On the Rise*. She taught herself how to use a computer at the Cambridge Public Library. She had a lead role in a play written for and performed by homeless women. But she wouldn't leave Vic. She knew how dangerous he was and how easily he could misjudge a punch or a kick, and kill or maim her. She knew what to do and knew that we could have placed her into a safe shelter in minutes, if only she had allowed us. She had a chance to get a room at the YWCA, which would have gotten her off the street and into a secure building, but she sabotaged her chance for a room by refusing to agree to attend a program for recovering alcoholics during her first year there. "I'm not going to let them invade *my* privacy," she whispered hoarsely in my ear, so that Vic wouldn't think she was running away from him.

Jean will not deal with Vic. Just looking at him, knowing how badly he abused Jeannie, makes her physically sick. And yet Vic, in our presence and in the context of a prayer service, is attentive, empathetic and caring. Other men depend on him for sympathy and understanding.

Ministering to Vic and Jeannie together, in the same place and the same time, has been the hardest thing that I have had to do as pastor to my church.

• • • • •

When it happened, it came as a complete shock. Jean got a call from Jay Matthews, a social worker at 240 Albany Street. Jeannie had been hit by a speeding cab on the McGrath-O'Brien Highway. She died shortly after arriving at Cambridge City Hospital.

We had become so used to the idea that Vic would beat Jeannie to death, or that she would die of a seizure, that the possibility that she might die some other way never occurred to us. I had visited Jeannie just a week before in the emergency room at Cambridge City Hospital. She had had a seizure. When I got to the hospital, Jeannie was still in the clothes she was wearing when she had collapsed. She had soiled herself while she was unconscious but when she tried to use the restroom to clean herself up, other homeless men and women who were waiting to use the toilet screamed at her to get out. Jeannie was astonished that I had taken the time to find her but also defensive and self-conscious. We began with "That's it! I don't deserve to put up with this shit. I'm going into detox tonight" and we ended with "No one's going to tell *me* what to do!" Business as usual.

Jeannie had been drinking on the night she died, said Jay, who got the details from one of Jeannie's friends who was with her that evening. Vic had been abusing her and she was trying to get away from him when she and her friend stumbled onto the highway. Her friend wasn't as drunk and made it across; but Jeannie tripped, lost her balance and was hit by the cab. Perhaps Vic chased her out into the street. Perhaps, in the end as for so much of her life, it was all about drunkenness and abuse.

A few days later, Jay found Jeannie's obituary in the *East Falmouth Enterprise*:

> Jean M. Grainger, 48, of Somerville, who leaves family in East Falmouth, died on December 15 as the result of injuries sustained when she was struck by an automobile. Ms. Grainger was born and raised in Somerville, the daughter of Niki Grainger of East Falmouth and the late Robert Grainger. She was involved with the On The Rise program in Cambridge. In addition to

> her mother, she leaves her children, Joseph Grainger of Hull and Jonathan Grainger of Salem; her sisters, Debra Grainger of Dracut and Donna Casey of Hull; a brother, Robert Grainger of Hull; and three grandchildren.

So there was a whole *other* family, a family that no one in our church knew about, the one that gave Jeannie her last name. (Did they know what "involved with On the Rise" meant? Had Jeannie kept them in the dark along with her three daughters from the second marriage?)

People on the street were stunned and shocked. Jeannie was such an outsized personality, such a presence in our church. We had a memorial service on the following Sunday, but people were still talking about Jeannie and praying for her for weeks afterward.

Jeannie's life and death were a paradigm for every homeless person who ever sought God at one of our services. She could not believe that God loved her and so she could not love herself or let others love her; but she was never without hope. She wrestled with her God, prayed to him, argued with him, cursed at him and despaired of him, but she never stopped longing for the unconditional love that only he could give her. Perhaps, in time, she would have allowed her children and her friends to embrace her as they found her; perhaps time made no difference, and she would have died suddenly and unexpectedly at some other intersection of violence and substance abuse.

Wasn't this the whole point? Homeless woman finds Outdoor Church; homeless woman finds voice, finds community, finds love; homeless woman dies with the promise of salvation. So why, for months afterward, did I still hope to hear that rasping voice scream at an uncomprehending commuter who had just walked through the middle of our service, "Hey! dickhead! this is a church!"

· · · · ·

Vic is different from the other abusive men who attend our service in Porter Square. Almost all of the men we have encountered on the street are violent to a purpose, like robbery. Their violence is strategic. Vic just seems naturally violent. It is the only thing for which he seems to have any talent. He has done so much time for assault and assault with a dangerous weapon that, the next time he is convicted, he is likely to be sentenced to such a long sentence that we will never see him again.

Vic is slight and limps a little. He doesn't strike you as someone who can terrorize most of the people who know him. He drinks, but not—at least in our presence—to the point where he loses control. He has a small, pinched and ruddy face, with a pointed noise. When he is sober, his face is sharp and feral. When he is drinking, his jaw is covered with two or three days of grey beard and his features become soft and blurred.

Vic, like many men who need to drink in order to be violent, is a coward. He is drawn to people, men and women alike, who are, for one reason or another, drawn in turn to his capacity to inflict violence on them.

Steve is like that. Steve use to attend services in Porter Square regularly. Then we began to see him in Central Square. We have known Steve for as long as we have been in Porter Square—nearly five years. He is short, with a shaved nut-brown head, piercing blue eyes and no front teeth. He is a warm, humorous and generous person. Steve is a heavy drinker and very pugnacious, always, in his own telling, getting into fights with other homeless men or with the sidewalk.

One Sunday, after we hadn't seen Steve in Porter Square in a long while, we found him huddled in front of the McDonald's in Central Square. He looked as though he had been hit by a tank. His face was covered with contusions. He had been in the hospital for four days and had taken thirty eight stitches. He told me that Vic had assaulted him, the first time he had ever identified an assailant. Steve said that Vic has caused most of his injuries over the years. According to Steve, Vic follows him, waits for him to pass out on the sidewalk in Central Square, and then kicks and beats him when he is unconscious. Steve apologized for not being with us that morning but, he said, Vic had taken to stalking him after the service in Porter Square was over and Steve didn't want to risk another assault. Then Steve said something that I couldn't make out. I had to ask him three times before I could understand him: he was asking for communion.

Steve's ability to withstand pain—even when he is inflicting it on himself—is legendary. Once, after Vic had severely beaten him and collapsed his windpipe by kicking him in the throat a few times, Steve was admitted to Cambridge City Hospital. The surgeon opened his throat, performed a tracheotomy and left the tube in place while Steve recovered. When Steve regained consciousness, he panicked, not knowing where he was, yanked the tube from his throat and ran out of the hospital. Mardi saw him the next day in Porter Square, sitting on the granite ledge and drinking Listerine with one hand over his throat, as he explained later, to keep the Listerine from pouring out of the hole in his throat. The police picked him up the next day and returned him to the hospital. Steve fled again and was picked up again. This time, he stayed long enough for the doctors at Cambridge City Hospital to close the incision. While he was in the hospital, Steve said, the Cambridge police took photographs, interviewed the admitting doctor in the Cambridge City Hospital and urged him to press charges against Vic. But, like Jeannie, Steve wouldn't press charges or let the police issue a restraining order. He wouldn't let me get a restraining order for him and he refuses to go to a shelter for abused men.

·····

One blustery March afternoon, Pat, Helene, Liz and I came up to a group of six or seven men and one woman clustered on two facing benches. The young woman, Nancy, was in tears. She had beautifully permed brown hair, but her eyes—when she raised her head to talk to us—were red rimmed and puffy. Her face was swollen as well, with big red circles on her checks. She was sitting on the lap of a big guy in a Celtics pullover. Except for Jake, who was just recovering from wrist surgery, and Cal, who was enjoying Nancy's distress, I didn't recognize any of the men. They looked to be in their late twenties, hard and intimidating.

Liz, one of our interns, hadn't been in Central Square with us before. She is a tall, striking woman, with a triangular face and expressive brown eyes. Like most of our interns, she is fluent in Spanish. Hispanic men are comfortable with her. Liz is willing to take chances. She has done everything from working with sex workers in Costa Rica to juggling with the Cambridge Circus to making audio documentaries about homelessness—a lot of experience for someone just out of college in her first year at the Harvard Divinity School. Liz spoke to Nancy while I talked with Cal and some of the other men, and Pat and Helen gave out some sandwiches. Nancy said that she had been raped the night before by this same group of men and that she was certain she would be raped again this night. She said that she had tried to get into Mass General and that they wouldn't hold her there. She couldn't get into 240 Albany Street either because she wasn't a resident of Cambridge or Somerville.

Liz was upset by Nancy's incessant sobbing and by the men who kept leaning over Nancy and assuring us that she was safe with them. Wasn't there anything we could *do*? Nancy gave me the telephone number of a shelter for battered women but they didn't have any beds and asked her to call back Monday morning. Nancy wouldn't let me call 240 Albany Street or a hospital. She wouldn't go to another shelter. It was the shelter for battered women or nothing. After more assurances from the men that they would look after Nancy, we walked away.

Liz was even more disturbed after we walked away. She and Nancy had established a rapport, and Liz felt especially badly that we were leaving her at the mercy of these men. She saw that Nancy's refusal to consider any alternative to the shelter severely limited our options but she was still upset as we continued through Central Square. The issue had become not only what to do about Nancy but what to do about us. We stopped to talk through it as we headed back to the T station. The Cambridge Police headquarters was right around the corner. I thought that, if Nancy spoke with a woman police officer, she might consider choices that she had rejected before. We had never before nor since involved the police in anything that we do or see on the street—it would severely threaten the trust that people had come to have in us. Nevertheless, we persuaded ourselves that this situation was exceptional: there was a good chance that Nancy was at serious risk, that the men—most of whom we didn't know and couldn't trust —were dangerous, and that she couldn't do worse, and might do better, in the quiet of the police station away from the men who surrounded her. We walked over to the police headquarters and I described Nancy to the desk sergeant and then again to a community relations officer. They said they would get over there soon—it was only four blocks away.

As I walked down the cement steps at the entrance to the police station, I knew I had made a mistake. One of the problems with calling for help from the police is the unintended consequences. We hadn't even begun to think about them. What would happen if any of the men had outstanding arrest warrants against them? Was the situation as dire as we thought it was? Was there actually an immediate threat, one that Nancy couldn't walk away from? Hadn't she made clear that she didn't want any help beyond that one phone call to the battered women's shelter?

Worst of all, we had allowed our emotions to drive our judgment. That the emotions were a perfectly natural response to what we had seen was, sadly, beside the point. We are on the street first and foremost to minister and only in the course of ministering to offer solutions to problems. As a practical matter, this is rarely an issue. Whether as ministers or social workers, we can help a person with practical solutions only if that person is willing to accept them. Where—as with Nancy and as with all the abused women in Porter Square—if a man or women refuses to let us or anyone else—a doctor, a hospital—intervene, there is little we can do as ministers. After years of talking with lawyers and the police and doctors, nurses, street outreach workers, court officials and shelter administrators, we have concluded that no one has any clear idea about what to do when a person refuses to cooperate in his or her own protection.

· · · · ·

At any given time, two or three of our people will be at Cambridge City Hospital or Mt. Auburn Hospital because they have been badly beaten up. Other things will put them in the hospital—alcoholic seizures, falling down stairs in a drunken stupor, wandering across the street and getting hit by a bus—but fighting is usually the reason they wake up in a hospital bed. Some people, like Steve or Jake, are always victims but some, like Vic, are sometimes the aggressor and sometimes the victim.

There is a code of honor on the street, perhaps because there is so little else to give structure and meaning to daily existence. Defending or avenging women and defending or avenging friends are a very big part of it. Many men have cell phones—sometimes stolen and sometimes just picked up off the street—and stay in touch with one another until the batteries run out. If a fight breaks out, they can call in the cavalry. Some men—defenseless because of their drinking or age—somehow manage to avoid violence altogether but others like Steve are drawn to it like a moth to a flame. We hear endless talk—as if we were talking with children during recess at an elementary school—about who said what to whom and who did what to whom and who was going to get back at them for it. Some men show up every week with bruises or contusions. They say they have lost a fight with the sidewalk—they fell down while they were drunk and hit their face on the concrete—but it can also mean that they lost a fight or got rolled and don't want to talk about it.

It is astonishing to me that a human body can sustain such abuse. The doctors and nurses I have spoken with at Cambridge City Hospital say that treating men—homeless or not—who are always fighting is a very frustrating practice, like treating wounded soldiers and sending them back to the battlefield. The men, once able to walk, leave as quickly as possible, start drinking again, get into more fights and get hospitalized once more. The damage is cumulative. So—like drinking itself or living outdoors—it is only a question of time before the endless assaults and seizures are finally fatal.

• • • • •

Our church—peopled by the weak and the confused—is only a glimmer of the unconditional love that most of our congregants have never received and that only God can provide. We seek to hold the abused and the abuser within our covenanted community in the firm conviction that this is the most likely way in which all can be healed. We cannot keep those that we intensely dislike, even hate, away from the only thing that will save them.

At the same time we make clear over and over again that we are deeply wounded by the violence that persists among us. We speak of God's word and pray to him mindful that it is abhorrent to us as members of a covenanted community, as clergy and as part of the Body of Christ to know that some members of our church are physically or emotionally abusing other members of our church.

• • • • •

Whenever we hear that one of our people is in the hospital, Pat, Jean or I will try to visit. We have learned that, often as not, a story about a hospitalization that we have heard on the street—"Dave had a heart attack, fell down the stairs at the entrance to the T in Central Square and broke his collar bone"—is either completely untrue or badly distorted, so we weren't surprised to show up at Cambridge City Hospital only to find that Dave had been discharged directly from the emergency room. Now, when we show up, people are not as surprised to see us as when we first began to make hospital visits. We are not always the only visitors. When Vickie was at Cambridge City Hospital because of an attack of pancreatitis, Shaggy slept on the floor of her hospital room every night until she was discharged (and then went right back to abusing her when they were both on the street.)

Our people always seem to end up in Room 436 at Cambridge City Hospital. I have visited Room 436 so many times that I have considered offering the hospital a memorial plaque: "This plaque given in grateful memory of the care given to the chronically homeless men and women of Cambridge," etc. By now, the nurses know us well enough, but, to avoid HIPPA issues, we carry simple blank consents to disclosure that the people we are visiting can sign on the spot. Then, the doctors, nurses and other caregivers can talk with us without fear of legal liability.

A few years ago, on a frigid February Sunday, we were just finishing our walk through Central Square when Rick and Wanda told us that Dave was in the hospital. I went over to Cambridge City Hospital after we had gone back to our office at Harvard Epworth and put our coolers and knapsacks away for the week. Dave was conscious and focused but very weak. He had had another seizure. Dave had been asking me for a long time to help him obtain Social Security disability benefits. The nurse at 240 Albany Street was persuaded that Dave would only qualify for disability payments for psychiatric reasons—an extremely difficult basis on which to secure benefits—but Dave wouldn't consider having a psychiatric evaluation done by a psychiatrist.

Dave is a sweet, gentle man. He is always welcome at 240 Albany Street but he doesn't like to stay in over night. During the winter, he will bury a bottle behind the Cambridge City Bank in Central Square, stay for a few hours at 240 Albany Street for a meal and a shower, and then go back out at 2 or 3 in the morning to dig up the bottle and walk around the Square until McDonald's opens.

After a lot of persuading, Dave had agreed to talk to a psychiatrist outdoors, but I had never been able to find a psychiatrist who would examine a chronically drunken homeless guy in the middle of Central Square. Now, our moment had come. Dave is still good with the harmonica, although he doesn't play much anymore. He will play the "Mass Avenue Blues" for us if we ask. When he was in better shape, Dave played for drinks with pickup bands in clubs in Inman Square. The resident on Dave's floor liked the blues and somehow learned that Dave could play the harmonica. They had become friendly. The resident and I persuaded Dave to talk to the Cambridge City Hospital psychiatrist when he made his daily rounds; the resident would have the psychiatrist do an evaluation on the spot and we would have what we needed to submit an application for disability benefits to Social Security. But, the resident told me later, when the psychiatrist came by the next day, Dave refused to talk with him. He just couldn't acknowledge that he was "crazy." We never came that close again.

• • • • •

It is tempting—very tempting—to see in Tuckerman's street ministry a proto-urban liberation theology. To be sure, Tuckerman's experience gave him perspectives on the situation of the poor in Boston that were unusual, perhaps unique, in his time and place. He came to see their problems from their point of view.[24] Because—in the name of scientific philanthropy—he closely studied the causes of the behaviors that often lead to impoverishment and substance abuse, he understood something that, even today, is hard for many to grasp: that wealth, especially inherited wealth, does not make the wealthy person morally superior to a person of lesser means: "It is not more fair to infer of a man that he lacks principle, or is vicious, because he is poor," he wrote, "than it would be wise to infer of a man that he is virtuous, and worthy of all confidence, because he is rich."[25]

Tuckerman's willingness to withhold judgments that would prevent sympathetic relations among people, and the intensity and directness of Tuckerman's engagement with the poor, persuaded him that the mutuality of responsibilities that underlay his idea of the church implied a corresponding and equally powerful mutuality of rights. The moral philosophers at Harvard had concluded that "[T]he idea of 'right' implies the idea of 'obligation' . . ."[26] In Tuckerman's theology, it was the other way around: obligations implied rights:[27]

> And in view of the gospel of Jesus Christ, if not of the doctrine of political economists, these have claims upon those who are able to provide for them. I go further,—there are many who are comparatively unworthy of the bounty which they seek, and yet have, if Christianity be true, strong claims upon the consid-

---

24. S. A. Eliot, *Heralds of a Liberal Faith*, 116.
25. Tuckerman, *On the Elevation of the Poor*, 62.
26. Howe, *Unitarian Conscience*, 51.
27. Tuckerman, *Principles and Results*, 256.

eration of their fellow-beings in happier conditions than their own.[28]

By vesting in the poor a right of survival, in practice, a right to salvation, Tuckerman located himself in a long line of theologians running from the Church Fathers—"The earth was established in common for all, rich and poor," wrote Ambrose. "Why do you alone arrogate an exclusive right to the soil, O rich?"[29]—to Peter Maurin:

> You are in fact the ambassadors of God.
> As God's ambassadors
> You should be given food,
> Clothing and shelter
> By those who are able to give it.[30]

Tuckerman's regard for the invisibility of the poor, his willingness to see their spiritual needs in terms of their material circumstances, his conviction that the welfare and the salvation of rich and poor were interdependent and his confidence in theory tempered by experience as the basis for a reliable understanding of the condition of the poor all point toward a form of urban liberation theology.[31] There is only a small distance between Tuckerman's sense of the Kingdom and Ignacio Ellacuria's idea of the "civilization of love" displacing the "civilization of poverty": "There is a lot still to be done," Ellacuria said shortly before he was assassinated by the Salvadoran Army in 1989. "Only utopianism and hope can enable us to believe and dare to try, with all the poor and oppressed people of the world, to turn back history, subvert it, and send it in a different direction."[32]

Yet there was no part of Tuckerman's theology that he would have acknowledged as explicitly political, although he himself was active in various political causes and movements. His sympathy for the poor did not induce him to understand theology from the point of view of a particular people rather than from the ostensibly objective perspective of the Unitarianism of the first half of the nineteenth century.

---

28. Ibid., 93.
29. Ambrose, *De Nabathae*, 2, cited in Johnson, *Fear of Beggars*, 24.
30. Maurin, *Easy Essays*, 8, cited in Wolf, *Down and Out in Providence*, 75–76.
31. See for example De La Torre, *Handbook of U.S. Theologies of Liberation*.
32. Sobrino, *No Salvation Outside the Poor*, 6.

Tuckerman was, in any event, too deeply committed to the idea of the mutual responsibility of rich and poor to embrace a preferential option for either the rich or the poor. In both theology and disposition, he was as concerned for his peers as he was for the poor people that he visited daily.

Nonetheless, caring for the poor turned out to be much easier than caring for the rich. "With this people it is not difficult to be a good pastor," said Archbishop Romero.[33] But it was difficult, in the context of Tuckerman's Ministry-at-large, to be a pastor to the rich. Tuckerman rarely, if ever, was disappointed in the poor people to whom he ministered, but he was often frustrated and impatient with the unwillingness of his fellow Unitarians to translate their generous but vague universal social concerns into concrete action. He pleaded, wrote, lectured, preached, cajoled and scolded. But Tuckerman knew that the growth of the chapels and the slackening of friendly visiting toward the end of his life made clear that, insofar as it required the active participation of his peers, his covenant theology remained essentially unrealized. As with so much of Christian life, the theology was clear enough, but its actualization was very, very difficult.

33. Ibid., 92.

9

The Lord's Supper

> If men be remiss and slighty in attending upon God's ordinances, they are not likely to thrive in faith, or any other grace; it would be no wonder if they should wither away, and living in a dark discouraged condition: but, if Christians be careful to attend ordinances, and improve them for the strengthening of their faith, they are in a hopeful way to thrive.[1]

> Both the avowed enemies and the professed friends of the Christian Church talk as if you could really separate between the "spiritual" and the "material"; as if, for instance, the taking care that people are properly fed was not distinctly Church work; as if things secular and sacred were contrary to each other. They forget that it is not the bread alone, but the inward and spiritual grace of which the bread is the outward and visible sign, by which men live; that bodily food is not only a kind of parable of spiritual food, but that this food which you can see and taste is an actual means whereby not only your body but your spirit is fed, and a pledge to assure you that it has been fed. You are literally, as He himself said, feeding, clothing and housing Jesus Christ, when you are feeding, clothing, housing any human being; bad food, ugly clothes, dirty houses, not only injure the body, but injure the soul: nay, more, they do great injury unto God Himself.[2]

ONCE I DECIDED TO SEEK ORDINATION, I HAD TO DECIDE ON A DEnomination. I was drawn to the Episcopal Church. Many of the men I admired for their radical understanding of their faith in practice were Episcopalians: John Shelby Spong, James Pike, Paul Moore and William

---

1. Stoddard, *Safety of Appearing at the Day of Judgment*, 272.
2. Headlam, *Laws of Eternal Life*, 76.

Stringfellow. I imagined that it was the very weight and substance of the Episcopal Church as an institution that allowed, even encouraged, its adherents to take radical political and theological positions in opposition to it. Also, I loved the Book of Common Prayer, the music and the architecture that awakened the sense of spirituality that had first led me to the conviction that I was called to a religious life. So I began to read, to study and to talk to Episcopalians that I knew.

A friend suggested that I speak with the Reverend Anne Carroll Fowler, an Episcopal priest and Rector of St. John's Church in Jamaica Plain, Massachusetts. We met at her office in Jamaica Plain, where a little waterfall bubbled soothingly in the background. Anne listened patiently as I described my indecision about which denomination in which to seek ordination, and said, "If you intend to be an Episcopal priest, you had better have a very powerful sense of the sacramental." I had no idea what she was talking about.

• • • • •

Every now and then, Jeannie would appear in Porter Square without Vic for two or three weeks in a row. Sometimes Vic was in prison for yet another assault; sometimes he felt he didn't need to keep track of Jeannie on Sunday mornings; sometimes he felt abashed because of something he had done that he thought we would particularly abhor. When Jeannie was by herself, she could speak more freely about the incredible physical and emotional abuse Vic heaped on her on an almost daily basis. Following one such two or three week period, Jeannie and Vic showed up together, in the middle of an argument about which one of them owned a hat that Vic was wearing. Vic was on a bike. Jeannie joined the circle of worshipers. Vic kept riding around us in a circle, snarling at her and insulting her. We have grown used to many different kinds of noise from outside our circle of worship and had no trouble ignoring him. But when, in order to press his argument, he rode his bike right up to Jeannie—right into the middle of church, as it were—people were outraged. That space—the concrete apron in front of the Porter Square T station—is a sacred place for the one hour in which homeless men and women gathered to worship. Even Vic—who had once required four undercover T police to subdue him when they arrested him on an outstanding warrant for dealing drugs—could respect that. He immediately backed off, and the argument stopped until the serviced ended.

What makes our space sacred for one hour every week is our mutual agreement that it be so, our congregational commitment as a church to invoke Christ's presence. Communion is the promise and realization of that mutual agreement.[3]

• • • • •

Communion at the Outdoor Church is a moving target. We always offer communion at our services in Porter Square and on the Cambridge Common. Before the service begins, we set out the grape juice and stale wheat wafers the size of a quarter, with a little white ceramic pitcher and a handful of thimble-sized clear plastic cups. The grape juice comes in juice boxes and tastes more like apple juice than grape juice, but the juice box is convenient and we don't have to worry about refrigerating whatever is left over. One of our interns squirts the grape juice into a pitcher. Using the plastic straw that comes attached to the box is an art; if you miss, the juice ends up in your lap. We fill the pitcher with juice far away from the cart.

The weather is a big part of our communion service. The wafers and the cups blow off our serving plate in the slightest breeze. Light rain, or even mist, makes them moist and soggy, so that they don't snap when they are broken during the communion liturgy. In freezing weather, the cups crack. When they do, the grape juice seeps out, so our communicants gulp down the grape juice as soon as it is served. One frigid February morning, a thin film of ice formed over the grape juice in its pitcher.

Serving communion is a corporate event. It takes one person to set out the wafers and grape juice, another to say the words of institution, another to serve the wafers, another to carry the plastic cups, another to pour grape juice into the plastic cups and serve them, yet another to collect the used cups and, finally, someone to serve communion to all those people who are not within the immediate circle of our communicants but who are lurking a few yards away, wanting to stay warm, waiting for the sandwiches or too self conscious to be with us directly.

---

3. Communion, the Lord's Supper and the Eucharist are more or less the same name for the same event; I use them interchangeably in this chapter.

We try to involve everyone in every aspect of the administration of communion. Pouring the juice into the little cups, handing them to our worshipers and collecting the used cups is a much coveted job, especially among the most violent of our congregants. Vic, in particular, loves to participate when he is there. Why someone whose life is filled with violence, both as abuser and abused, should be so captivated by the administration of communion continues to confound us—unless we are witnessing an unanticipated argument for the Lord's Supper as a converting ordinance.

Ursula, a vocational deacon from Nottingham, England, in Boston for Ecclesia's annual "Come and See" conference, was aghast to find that we were serving grape juice and not wine during the Lord's Supper. (We, in turn, were amazed that she could contemplate serving wine to people virtually all of whom had been or were alcoholics.) Under duress—one of us misplaces the key to our storage area at St. James's or we forgot to put grape juice boxes into our bin—we have used apple juice or orange juice for wine and an egg salad sandwich for bread.

There is a long history to the argument that the communion table should be open to all, whether church members or not or even whether baptized or not.[4] Pat, Jean and I, and all the interns and volunteers who help us, are fully agreed: we are outdoors to welcome those who will not or cannot enter a conventional church, and the Lord's Supper is both the symbol and the fact of our welcome.

But we haven't all agreed that anyone can *administer* the Lord's Supper. I see no reason why, in a gathered church, any member of the congregation cannot administer communion if he is called to do so. Pat has generously suppressed any misgivings she has about this, although she remains adamant that, in her own case, she, a deacon, cannot and should not administer communion.

When Tom Lenhart and I were student ministers at North Prospect Church, one of our parishioners was dying of cancer of the liver. Brian had just gone through a very bitter divorce. He had lost custody of his boys, Benjamin, twelve, and Andrew, eight, whom he loved passionately. Brian was in denial. He wouldn't acknowledge that he was dying and he wouldn't do anything to prepare his boys for his death—he wouldn't even allow them to see him when he was in the hospital, lest they see

---

4. See generally Fabien, "Patterning the Sacraments After Christ," and Tanner, "In Praise of Open Communion."

him looking wasted and frail. Tom had been counseling Brian, but despaired of helping him to acknowledge the severity of his cancer so that he could spend more time with his boys before he died.

One very rainy Sunday afternoon, Brian, his two boys and a large group of people from North Prospect came down to join us on the Cambridge Common for our afternoon prayer service. By then, Brian had relented. He wasn't hiding his illness from his family anymore. His daughter from an earlier marriage had come up from Maryland and his sister had flown in from Hawaii.

The rain drove us across the street and onto the covered porch of Christ Church. The first part of the service was wet and dreary, and the boys were starting to get antsy. During the peace, Brian asked how much longer the service was going to last and—without giving it much thought—I said, why don't we have the boys read some of the service? Scott Campbell, who was leading the service, was taken aback—I could feel him stiffen next to me—but he didn't say anything. Brian thought that might work. Andrew was persuaded to give it a try. He could barely get his nose up over the edge of the cart so Brian propped him up with one hand and turned the pages with the other. Andrew began to the read the prayer of invitation. Every third word or so, he would look up at his father for help with a big word. Brian helped him sound them out—"institution"—"covenant"—"memory." Brian was in very heaven; his face was lit up; it was the first time I'd ever seen him smile. When we got to the words of institution, Scott moved forward to speak, but Andrew was on a roll. We looked at one another, and looked at Andrew, and let him rip. Scott thought:

> I wondered what the protocol was for an un-ordained eight year-old consecrating the communion elements. I decided God would be less disturbed about it than some of us would, so I decided to keep silent. Andrew pressed on: "on the night he was be-trayed, Jesus took the bread and blessed it . . . when-ev-er you do this, do it in re-mem-brance of me." "Wonderful, Andrew, just wonderful," the proud father cooed. The prayer finally ended. Jed and I served the elements. The adults in the little family instructed the boys on how to receive communion. It turned out this was their first communion. I wondered if they had ever been baptized. We all held the bread. We drank from the little plastic medicine cups. I prayed the closing prayer, pronounced the benediction and the service was over. As I walked back

across the common, I was ashamed that I had almost gotten in the way of what God was trying to do. But the cold and wet no longer bothered me ...[5]

We didn't know then that this would be the last time that Brian ever saw Benjamin and Alexander. But we knew that we were blessed to be in the presence of a family that, because of the real and powerful presence of the Holy Spirit, could find communion in its sheltering and consoling presence.

• • • • •

We do it differently in Harvard Square and Central Square. There, we walk around with our coolers and knapsacks filled with sandwiches and socks. We ask the people we haven't met before—once we have offered them a sandwich—if they would like communion. If they say yes, Pat or I administer the Lord's Supper to them individually. At first, we carried inexpensive visiting communion kits around with us, the kind that a priest might have with her if she were making a pastoral visit to a patient in a hospital or a sick parishioner at home. But managing the juice and the cups and the kit itself always seemed to require too many hands. After a while, we began to carry "Chasid Cups" with us.[6] These cups—more or less the size of the clear plastic cups we use in Porter Square—have grape juice hermetically sealed in the cup and a little wafer between the seal and a thin clear plastic cover. Lord knows how long the juice has been sitting in a factory warehouse; and we have yet to determine whether the elements have been properly consecrated before we get them in the mail—but the Chasid Cups *are* convenient.

We will not wait for people to approach our table. We take communion to them. We want the homeless men and women we encounter to understand that they are not objects in one of our rituals, but acknowledged and welcomed members of our community. This is the most definitive expression of our commitment to take the church to the streets.

Virtually every chronically homeless man or women we see in Harvard Square or Central Square will accept a sandwich but only a small number ask for communion or a blessing. The people who ask

---

5. Campbell, "Rainy Day Grace," 1.
6. Chasid (Greek): "devoted to the Lord or the work of the Lord."

for communion ask for it every time—it is now as much a part of their Sunday as it is ours, and we rarely fail to encounter every one of them each time we are out on the street—but people who ask for blessings have something quite specific and deeply troubling in mind, and are looking for comfort and consolation.

Initially, Pat or I offered communion to people in Harvard Square and Central Square and the volunteers or interns didn't. At first, I hesitated to practice the same liberality of sacramentalism that I preached in Porter Square or on the Cambridge Common. Just as people expect our clergy to wear collars, we sensed that people in Harvard Square and Central Square—possibly because the encounter is one on one—expect that communion will be administered by someone in a collar. There is something about their proactive decision to be served—compared with the passivity of waiting to be served as one of a group in Porter Square or on the Common—that had made me hesitant to ask any one other than ordained clergy to administer communion to them. But I was wrong. For this purpose, at least, our homeless congregants accepted our volunteers and interns as clergy. Recently, I have encouraged the volunteers and interns to offer communion and, so far, no one has objected. As so often happens, I didn't have the courage of my own faith.

Marilyn has been accepting communion from us from the very first day we walked through Harvard Square. She moves back and forth between Harvard Square and Central Square, whenever she thinks that there is more foot traffic in the other location. We will find her leaning against the low brick wall in front of the CVS in Harvard Square or sitting on an upturned plastic milk crate in front of the CVS in Central Square. Marilyn is a coffee-colored woman in her late 40's or early 50's. She wears an olive green canvas jacket with a matching canvas cap. She has a narrow face with very high, prominent cheekbones and a wide mouth. The cheekbones seem all the more prominent because she wears her hair pulled back tightly. Her eyes are heavily shadowed and she wears a striking scarlet lipstick. She looks like a Native American down on her luck.

Invariably, Marilyn has her headphones on. Like many people outdoors, she is very different when she believes that she is alone and when she thinks she is being watched. When she is alone, she talks to herself while she listens to her headphones, a dreamy, even beatific look on her face. Sitting on her crate in front of the automated doors to the CVS and swaying gently back and forth in time with the music, as the dark and a light snow fall in Central Square, she is in a different world. But as soon as she sees us approach, she stops talking to herself and waits for us, smiling broadly as if she hadn't seen us in a year. We offer her a sandwich, but she is fastidious about taking communion first, before she will even consider food or toiletries. She is unshakably considerate; whenever we see her, she asks after our former volunteers and interns, whom she remembers fondly.

It is rare that we see Marilyn after a few drinks. But when she has been drinking, she becomes more agitated and uninhibited. We will find her talking angrily to herself, so upset that she is unaware of our approach. Usually, she can switch it off when she sees us but sometimes the residue of the rage persists and she seems dazed with the effort of getting it under control for us. Marilyn never tells us what makes her so angry and won't even acknowledge that she is upset.

When she is feeling unusually depressed or angry, Marilyn sits in the Wendy's next to the CVS. She faces the window, oblivious to the people passing by, earphones on, slumped over a cardboard coffee cup and arguing softly but very intensely with herself. Knowing how fully she can engage us when she is calm, we are astonished as how quickly her psychological problems can remove her completely from our presence.

• • • • •

Nearly everyone takes communion in Porter Square and on the Cambridge Common. There, people are gathered in groups, and people may feel a certain pressure to do what everyone else is doing. In Harvard Square and Central Square, we encounter homeless people one at a time. Only those people with a strong feeling for the sacrament ask for communion. All of them look forward to receiving communion, remind us of the proper order of things if we offer them a sandwich first and thank us profusely for the communion itself.

Big Boy is one of those people whom I couldn't imagine receiving communion from anyone other than ordained clergy. Cambridge being Cambridge, we have more than the usual number of outdoor theologians on the street with us: some evangelicals with sandwich boards proclaiming the certainty of eternal punishment for those who condone abortions; some homeless men who have read the Bible back to front many, many times and are eager to chop theological logic with anyone wearing a collar; people who want to talk about what church we are from, what denomination we represent, are we Christians or do we believe in the literal truth of Revelation (this from the checkout girl at the 4C Convenience Store in Central Square, where we restock our juicy juice supplies when it looks like we are going to run out: "No?" she asks, "Then how can you call yourself a Christian?"). And then there are people like Big Boy.

Big Boy has staked out one of the benches near the Salvation Army. Big Boy has a dark, pitted face with brown hair that curls over his forehead in locks. He wears thick glasses with heavy black frames. In the summer, he doesn't wear a shirt. His stomach is enormous but firm. It is like a brown beach ball. It seems to have a life of its own. Big Boy sprawls across his bench, shopping carts arrayed around him so that everything is within easy reach, puts his feet up on one of his bags and reads the newspapers or his Bible. Big Boy's legs and feet are a constant source of pain and difficulty. His legs and ankles are swollen to the size of melons. His legs are columns of brown, scaly skin; his ankles and feet have no definition. Dreadful, infected sores have formed under the calluses on the bottoms of his feet, which he wraps in MacDonald's napkins. He can barely walk. For all that, Big Boy is very good natured and even-tempered. He has a mild disposition that comprehends all of the world's problems and his own as well. It is very soothing to be with him, if you don't look at his feet.

Sometimes in the summer we see Big Boy on the Common. He comes by after morning services at First Church Congregational, which he attends from time to time. First Church isn't a likely church for Big Boy; his theology is far more hard edged than anything he will encounter there. Even so, he is a welcome presence there. When he joins us, he takes communion, loads up on sandwiches and heads back to his bench in Central Square, where we will see him later in the day.

Big Boy is idealistic. He has an e-mail account, which he accesses from the Cambridge Public Library, and from there he sends out e-mails to hundreds of people whom he has gotten to know in Cambridge over the last several years. His e-mails urge solutions to worldwide problems: hunger, war, slavery, prostitution and disease. Big Boy has a Plan. It requires the investment of hundreds of millions of dollars by banks, hedge funds, brokerage firms and large corporations. Big Boy is rolling out the Plan month by month, but it never gets beyond a description of his fundraising strategy.

As a moral prescription, it is flawless. And, for that matter, it is not very different conceptually from the programs that Warren Buffett, the Gates Foundation, the World Bank and others have funded. Big Boy is philosophical about the lack of response to his emails. He sees his project as an exercise in consciousness-raising. He is more outgoing with Pat and our interns, who are invariably women, than with me. He loves to flirt with them and they—always concerned about boundary issues on the street—are delighted to be able to relax with someone who clearly wants only to talk with them.

Most people on the street won't talk about how they got there. We will hear about someone's childhood—most often, abusive, alcoholic parents and constant neglect, if not outright abandonment—and we can see for ourselves what the present is like. But we rarely learn about the transition; it is simply too mortifying for them to describe. Big Boy is unusually reticent. We know nothing about his past except what we accept as his given name. Our affection for Big Boy isn't based on a history or a resume. So why is he out there, while our friends and classmates who are heavy drinkers or mentally unstable somehow manage to make their way without falling off the edge into homelessness or institutionalization?

Maybe it is just bad luck. Some people have loving parents; others don't. Some people like Winston Churchill can live with, even thrive on, a heavy drinking habit, others can't. Some people's mental disabilities dovetail perfectly with their choice of work. The overly empathetic person becomes a nurse or social worker; a person still seeking to satisfy his over-demanding parents now seeks to satisfy the whole world. Other people's mental disabilities lead them to stand in the middle of the street and scream obscenities at passing cars.

Whatever it is, it is powerful. It is so powerful that people will choose to live on the street rather than confront it. When homeless people have a theology, it is often demonic and punitive. Mason, on the Common, thought that God wanted him to bear unspeakable suffering and hardship as a warning to other homeless men. Because many homeless men and women loathe or hate themselves, they believe that God must loathe and hate them too. Because people who are so loathsome or so hateful deserve the suffering that they endure, they believe that God is punishing them—directly, himself, or indirectly, through Satan or demons. Men and women who are in the grip of alcohol or possessed by drugs often understand their condition to be part and parcel of God's plan for them as much as it is the consequence of their own character. For many, substance abuse is a predestined part of life. They feel themselves to be possessed by something external to and greater than themselves. Now I understand what the Temperance Movement meant by Demon Rum.

If we haven't seen Big Boy on the Common earlier, Pat will offer him communion when we see him in Central Square. Big Boy talks through communion, as if swallowing the wafer and sipping the grape juice are short pauses between sentences, just long enough to catch his breath. But he is, for all that, intensely aware of the sacrament and gently rebukes us for denying it to him if we haven't seen him for a week or so.

• • • • •

One of the most difficult things we encounter in this ministry is people who bar themselves from the church—who will not take communion with us. Some of the homeless people we meet worry about whether Pat is "qualified" to offer communion, because she's "only" a deacon, or whether I am, because I'm not a priest. Some of the most sophisticated theology I have ever heard came out of an argument between Bob Tobin, who was with us in the Square one cold March afternoon, and a homeless man who refused to take communion from him because he was an *Anglo* Catholic priest and not a *Roman* Catholic priest.

It is more painful to encounter people who decline communion because they think something is wrong with *them*. Often, when we offer communion or a blessing, people will refuse it because they "were drinking last night," or because they "haven't had communion in ten years," or because they've "been bad." They have persuaded themselves that they are unworthy to take communion. They have absorbed the rules and regulations that our churches have imposed on communion—who can administer it and who can receive it—and they have internalized them. They no longer need the church to tell them that they can't have communion; they deny themselves communion without any help from us at all. No amount of arguing or pleading makes any difference.

We were deeply disturbed when we came to realize that some of the most desperate and needy among us are persuaded—even though they are professing Christians—that they are unworthy to take communion. It is a scandal that the church does not extend itself to them, so that they may share in the joy and the consolation that the church promises to all believers. If we do not bring the church to those who cannot find their way to it—if we do not extend the reach of God's Word to those who are not sitting inside listening to a Sunday morning sermon—then we are preventing those people from experiencing what I experienced during Evensong at King's College Chapel in Cambridge—a gift of God's grace that is so compelling and powerful that it cannot be resisted.

· · · · ·

Tuckerman's understanding of the Lord's Supper was informed by the Puritan history of congregationalism in America and by the many ways in which the Unitarians of his era reconceived it.

The Puritans understood communion to be a profession and confirmation of faith. As Calvinists, they believed that the church consisted exclusively of the elect—those predestined to experience salvation. The Anglican Church, from which Puritanism emerged, deemed anyone living within the geographic area served by a parish church to be a church member. This, the Puritans maintained, allowed those of little or no faith to be church members when the church, by definition, consisted only of the elect. In Puritan ecclesiology, only those who led unblemished Christian lives, had a working understanding of Puritan theology and had experienced—and could profess—a conversion experience could be church members and participate in the Lord's Supper. Thus, for the Puritans in England and during their first four or five decades in America, admission to the communion table was a sign of election and a privilege of church membership.

As the Massachusetts Bay Colony grew, this doctrine appeared increasingly impractical as more and more children of the original settlers either could not claim a conversion experience or had little interest in doing so. Children of church members were presumed to be church members as well, having been baptized into the church at birth, but—unless they were able to give convincing proofs of saving faith—they could not participate in the Lord's Supper nor in the governance of the church. But what of *their* children, that is, children of church members who were not visible saints? Could they be baptized into the church? If not, church membership would decline precipitously. In response, the Puritans acknowledged that church members who had not had the experience of saving faith but who nonetheless led lives life free of scandal, were knowledgeable in the theology and history of the church and were submissive to God and his church, while not full members of the church, nonetheless "owned the covenant"—the "Halfway Covenant"—and that their children could be baptized into the church.[7]

Solomon Stoddard, minister at Northampton, "Pope of the Connecticut River Valley" and grandfather of Jonathan Edwards, had played a leading role in the conception and adoption of the Halfway Covenant. But suspecting that the doctrine was theologically insupportable, Stoddard accelerated the trend toward an open communion table by re-conceiving the Lord's Supper itself. The Lord's Supper, he argued, was a "converting ordinance." Conservative in nearly all other respects, Stoddard sought to liberalize the doctrine of salvation by making the Lord's Supper one of the means by which God brought the unregenerate to salvation: "[T]he design of these holy ordinances is to be witnesses to us of our redemption and salvation by the blood of Christ."[8] George Whitefield, America's foremost evangelist before the Revolution and the preacher whom Nathan Cole had rushed to see at Middletown, admired Solomon Stoddard's writings but he was astonished to learn that Stoddard would permit even "unconverted" ministers to administer communion.[9]

God, said Stoddard, did not promise salvation to men as a joke: "Tis not to be imagined that the glorious God would with great seeming love to the souls of men, draw them into a snare ..."[10] Three things only—"walking blamelessly," lack of scandal and knowledge "to discern the Lord's body"—were requisite to admission to the Lord's Supper. By insisting that only God, and not men, could judge the sufficiency of a person's profession, Stoddard not only opened the Lord's Supper to all church members but also seemed to suggest that a function of the ordinance was to convert those who were only baptized to church membership. Not surprisingly, church membership, especially among the young, soared in Northampton.

7. Morgan, *Visible Saints*, 130–38.
8. Stoddard, *Safety of Appearing*, 147, 335–40.
9. Marsden, *Jonathan Edwards*, 262.
10. Stuart, "Mr. Stoddard's Way," 245.

This was too much for Jonathan Edwards, who restored the Halfway Covenant when he assumed Stoddard's pulpit in Northampton. Edwards had rightly understood that Stoddard, in redefining the Lord's Supper as a converting ordinance, was doing away with one of the few lingering symbols of the church's purity. The move was extremely unpopular. Edward's rigidity in the face of his congregants' opposition revealed his failure to see what Stoddard had intuited—that the Puritan ideal of church purity was insupportable—and contributed to his later expulsion from Northampton. Edwards was on the wrong side of history; both the theological reorientation of the church to the world and the practical result of increased church membership made Stoddard's understanding of the Lord's Supper too compelling to be denied.

The Halfway Covenant marked the high water mark of the Puritans' efforts to purify the church and its members from the world and the beginning of a movement toward an increasingly open communion table. "Thus in their different ways New Englanders tempered their zeal and adjusted their churches to a more worldly purity; and the cycle which began with the gathering of Separatist churches in London and Norwich in the sixteenth century reached its completion."[11] Stripped of its content as a privilege of church membership, the meaning of the Lord's Supper defaulted to Calvin's concept of the Lord's Supper as a formal remembrance of the Christ event.

Abandoning the Halfway Covenant had the inevitable effect of forcing a redefinition, not only of the Lord's Supper, but of the very purpose of the church.[12] By the time of the Unitarian Controversy, liberal ministers approached the Lord's Supper warily, not wanting to evoke the authoritarianism of their Puritan forebears. At Tuckerman's ordination, James Kendall solemnly charged him with a duty to administer the Lord's Supper only to "proper subjects" and then went on to say that he should not set up any condition or bar to admission to the Lord's Supper. Communion was to be extended to all baptized persons but, beyond this, "we have no authority, and can exercise no judgment; but must leave the rest to the great Searcher of hearts . . ."[13]

---

11. Morgan, *Visible Saints*, 150.

12. Holifield, "Intellectual Sources of Stoddardeanism," 373. And see generally Stuart, "Mr. Stoddard's Way," 243–53.

13. Kendall, *Memorial of Joseph Tuckerman*, 360–61.

⋅ ⋅ ⋅ ⋅ ⋅

The history of the Lord's Supper from Stoddard's tenure in Northampton to Tuckerman's in Chelsea was the history of the redefinition of the liberal churches as benevolent rather than sacramental communities.

William Ellery Channing's Baltimore Sermon of 1819 was on any reading a watershed event in the history of Unitarianism. As against doctrinaire Calvinism, Channing argued that reason and Scripture were perfectly consistent. He proclaimed the unity of Christ and identified the love of God and man as Christianity's highest purpose. Channing reiterated his intention to continue celebrating the Lord's Supper but only on rational grounds. In doing so, he not only affirmed that participation in the Lord's Supper be open to all baptized persons but suggested that the administration of the ordinance be open to other persons as well.[14]

As to the administration of the ordinance, Channing was not prepared to go so far as John Milton, who would have had it a *rule* that the administration of the sacraments was not confined to a particular man or order of men. (How could I have guessed, dozing through *Paradise Lost* as an undergraduate, that Milton had carved out the sacramental ground onto which I was to stumble?) Channing wasn't bothered by the liberality of Milton's thinking but he was determined to minimize the number and scope of rules that might impinge on the openness and liberality of the newly independent Unitarian churches.[15]

Yet, even in the midst of the Unitarian Controversy, the Lord's Supper, whatever meanings now attached to it, remained a sacramental duty among practicing Christians. "It is the duty of all persons," preached the Rev. Samuel Gilman, "who profess to be Christians in faith, and aim to be such in practice, to join in celebrating the appointed ordinance of the Lord's Supper. It is the command of Christ. This makes it a duty."[16]

And so it was for Tuckerman, although he had little to say about the Lord's Supper as such. Of its many Unitarian meanings, those which made sense on the street were part of the experience of church membership itself and would not have required a sacramental event to commemorate it. In any event, his Ministry-at-large focused on friendly

---

14. Channing, "Church," 440–41. See generally Schell, "Font Outside Our Walls."
15. Channing "Writings of Milton," 518–19.
16. Anon., "Rev. Mr. Gilman's sermon on the church of Christ," 194.

visiting. Creating a venue for the administration of the Lord's Supper would not have occurred to him.

Tuckerman's few references to the Lord Supper occurred before he began his Ministry-at-large. In the sermon he delivered at the 1819 ordination of Samuel Gilman in South Carolina, he reminded Gilman that the Lord's Supper was a professing ordinance: "[The minister] distributes the emblems of the body and blood of Christ, in partaking of which we acknowledge ourselves to be one body in Christ; members one of another; and heirs together of the same inheritance, if we are indeed his disciples."[17]

The longest and most detailed description of Tuckerman's understanding of the Lord's Supper occurred during his tenure at Chelsea. When the church in Malden refused to admit Amos Sargeant and his wife, Alice, because they could not remember the precise time of their conversion experience and because they believed in universal salvation, Tuckerman asserted: (1) it was a great thing for anyone to say that he is converted, under any circumstances; (2) God operates variously, including in the matter of conversion; (3) we cannot be the judge of what happens in another's heart; and (4) visible Christianity, or a conformity of one's life to the profession of Christian conviction, is the best evidence we will ever have that someone has experienced a work of grace in his heart.

In time, Tuckerman came to view the Lord's Supper as a converting as well as a confessing ordinance. His theology encouraged an inclusive understanding of the Lord's Supper, close, in spirit and practice, to Stoddard's aggressive openness:

> [O]ur profession of Christ at his table is not the end of religion, but one of its means, designed not for those who are certain that they believe all which is to be believed, and that no other faith than their own can be right; but by bringing us nearer to Christ and by uniting us with him in the most solemn and affectionate engagements, that it is a means as well of obtaining a truly evangelical faith as of a holy life and conversion.[18]

---

17. Tuckerman, *Sermon (Gilman)*, 10–11.
18. C. R. Eliot, "Joseph Tuckerman," VI:8.

This liberality of understanding made perfect sense on the street, where the very depths to which the poor had fallen proved that an association of the poor with the church was a conversion in fact.

* * * * *

The aspect of the Lord's Supper that we are especially eager to share with our congregants is a sense of that community. We naturally see the Lord's Supper as a converting ordinance. It is a powerful and recognizable way for all of us, clergy and congregants, to "convert" from a sense of isolation and alienation to a sense of community with others who—at least for so long as they are in church—can be trusted to understand and to sympathize. This is the Lord's Supper as an embodiment of the Great Commandment:

> It is the communal commitment of charity which is the true *res* of the Eucharist, and therefore the Eucharist aims at the building of the true body of Christ in time, his *corpus verum*, which the church both is and is meant to be.[19]

There is already a strong sense of community among some of the men and women who live outdoors; without it, many would not have survived out there as long as they have. Communion is the acknowledgement of the power of that community in a liturgical setting. It is a symbol for the Outdoor Church itself.

* * * * *

Unlike the people who attend our prayer services in Porter Square and on the Cambridge Common, most of the people we encounter in Harvard Square and Central Square are more interested in sandwiches than in the wafer and grape juice we also offer them. Many of them are not eating enough, if at all, and they are very hungry.

Apart from the meals served at shelters, there are very few meals for homeless people served indoors in Cambridge during the week and none over the weekend. These, in any event, do not reach most of our people. They are often too drunk or too befuddled to remember where and when a meal is being served and then find their way to it in time; there are conflicts with shelter schedules; they are frightened of some of the people who attend these meals; they can't bear to be indoors;

---

19. Cavanaugh, *Torture and Eucharist*, 229.

or they have had so much to drink that they believe they are not hungry. Starlight Ministries serves a meal outdoors in Harvard Square on Thursday nights. Bread and Jams used to prepare a hot vegetarian supper that they served outdoors on the Cambridge Common during the summer, but their volunteers made too much work for the churches whose kitchens Bread and Jams used to prepare the meals, and the meals were discontinued. Apart from us, that is it. If you are not in a shelter and you can't afford a meal, you are going to go hungry over the weekend.

Many of the people we encounter in Harvard Square and Central Square tell us how hungry they are and ask for two or three sandwiches. There is a temptation to take anything that is offered on the street, but it is not easy to fence sandwiches and they won't last long unrefrigerated. So we are happy to give out as many sandwiches as we can carry. We often run out before we finish in Central Square, even when we start with one hundred and twenty or one hundred and forty sandwiches.

We have always believed that giving sandwiches to everyone we meet on the street is an extension of the Eucharistic meal to all those members of our church who didn't attend one of our prayer services earlier in the day. This, theologically, has always been the ground on which we have distinguished feeding people from other needed social services that we could, but don't, provide for our homeless congregants. (On the other hand, the Rev. Jim Stewart, who has run the shelter at First Church for many years and is himself a United Church of Christ minister, has no patience with such theological fastidiousness. In his view, churches are called to provide services to those most in need; it is their spiritual orientation, he is persuaded, that uniquely enables churches to offer assistance to those, like the chronically homeless, who are not otherwise reached by secular social service agencies.)

The idea of feeding the hungry as an extension of the Eucharistic meal has found powerful expression in many settings. The food pantry established by Sara Miles at St. Gregory of Nyssa in San Francisco is a striking example. After an extraordinary career as war correspondent, cook and writer, Sara's ongoing participation in communion at St. Gregory's converted her to an understanding of the Eucharist as a meal shared by everyone who approached the table to be fed. Her conversion found concrete expression in the creation of a food pantry for Protrero Hill, the mixed neighborhood where St. Gregory's is located. Her vision was of "a Table where everyone was welcome. Our neighbors, friends and strangers, were hungry. The very least a Christian church could do, for starters, was feed them."[20] She persuaded St. Gregory's to sponsor a food pantry simply by extending her and their experience of community to the people in need just outside the doors of the church: "I long for us to welcome the poor of San Francisco to this same Table," she said when she proposed the idea of a food pantry to the people at St. Gregory. "I want to us to offer food to hungry sisters and brothers we don't yet know, so they can be fed here where we are fed."[21]

"The food pantry is a sacramental story, ritual, and sacrament shaping how we live," wrote Donald Schell, one of the rectors of St. Gregory's.[22]

We encounter ninety to one hundred chronically homeless men and women every Sunday. We try to feed them all. Where once Pat and I alone could manage all of the sandwiches and juice and socks we carried through Harvard Square and Central Square, we now require the help of two or three volunteers and interns. We are stretched almost to the limit of our physical and emotional resources. Yet, at the same time, we are deeply disturbed at the realization that, but for us, men and women on the street in Cambridge who can't or won't find their way back to a shelter will go without eating. We want to ensure that our people will be able to eat every day, even if they are too drunk or too high or too confused to find a meals program or return to a shelter. Like Sara, we have come to understand that we are called to extend the welcome of the Eucharistic table to everyone in our community who is need of spiritual and material comfort.

• • • • •

From the edge of the cobblestone that surrounds the Lincoln Monument on the Cambridge Common, we can see First Church Congregational. Every month, Sarah Higginbotham and the children from First Church make sandwiches for us as part of the Children's Worship and Arts program. This how First Church describes it: "On Communion Sundays, CW&A consists of brief worship followed by a service project before the children re-join the congregation for Communion. Since October 2005,

---

20. Miles, *Take This Bread*, 108.
21. Schell, "Font Outside Our Walls," 5.
22. Ibid.

CW&A has partnered with the Outdoor Church on the Cambridge Common to provide sandwiches for distribution after their worship service. Sandwiches prepared by First Church children are blessed alongside our Communion Feast and then delivered to the Outdoor Church community by First Church families." This is how Ernie describes it: "What?" he yells, "Peanut butter and jelly *again*?" There's no denying it: the children favor peanut butter and jelly. They put the sandwiches in waxed paper sandwich bags and add a banana and a Hershey's Kiss. Then they write messages and draw pictures with red and green crayons on the brown sandwich bags in which they are going to put the sandwich and the banana and the Hershey's Kiss. Homeless people who ask for peanut butter and jelly on First Church Sunday—Claire won't eat anything except peanut butter and jelly—look forward to the messages, and sort through the brown paper bags looking for a message they like. *I* like "This sandwich is for you!"

Once a year, in April or May, the children and their parents make the sandwiches on the altar at First Church, so that the sandwiches *are* the Communion Feast. There are tables set up around the sanctuary with jars of peanut butter and jelly, plates of ham and cheese slices and loaves of bread. When it is time for communion, Sarah brings the children in to rejoin the adults. Parents and children come up and make sandwiches. The remaining congregants join the choir in singing communion hymns. It is surprisingly calm; the kids know that they are near the altar. Then the children put the sandwiches and bananas in the brown sandwich bags, which already have crayon messages and pictures on them. After the service, they will bring the sandwiches out to us on the Common.

First Church has given this some thought. Its pamphlet on "Communion and Baptism at First Church in Cambridge" echoes Tuckerman's unwillingness to substitute his or any person's judgment for God's:

> [I]t is not our practice to inquire about whether one is baptized, or about one's specific convictions regarding the Eucharist ... [W]e know that the gift of the sacrament is not ours, but God's, and that therefore it is not up to us to restrict access to it unnecessarily.[23]

---

23. First Church in Cambridge, "The Sacraments."

Sometimes I preach at these services; sometimes I lead the worship. Every time I have been a part of this service, I am amazed at the concreteness of communion itself, the very same sense of concreteness that I have when I am offering communion to someone on the street. Here, the entire church experiences what we experience.

It was First Church, and not I, who decided to make sandwiches on their altar; I would never have thought it up by myself. Coming inside like this is wonderfully disorienting. I am there because First Church understands the Lord's Supper—the Lord's Supper as laid out in their church—as extending to and embracing all those people who will get one of their sandwiches later in the day. We have dreamed about this—bringing our ministry into a church so that the church will bring its worship outdoors. Audacious beyond anything I might have imagined, First Church has reconceived its sense of church community and the Lord's Supper to embrace those of us who are in their hearts even though we are outside their walls.

10

Death

> The burden concerning Dumah. He calleth to me out of Se'ir, Watchman, what of the night? Watchman, what of the night? The watchman said, The morning cometh, and also the night. (Isa 21:11–12a)

IN THE OUTDOOR CHURCH, DEATH PLAYS AN OUTSIZED ROLE IN THE lives of our congregants and our clergy. Death seems to be everywhere on the street, a constant, almost palpable presence, like the hooded figure in Ingmar Bergman's *The Seventh Seal*, leading the chronically homeless in a macabre dance of death.

Most churches share in all of the great events in the personal lives of their members: birth, graduations, marriage, children and death. But of these the Outdoor Church has only seen death. We have never witnessed the birth of a child to one of our congregants nor officiated at the wedding of one of our congregants. Sometimes we see snapshots of children long dead or long out of touch, or hear stories about abusive or distant family members. And, in time, although we never inquire into the personal lives of our congregants, we will learn a lot about living arrangements, prison records, problems with shelter discipline and rules, medical issues, Social Security disability payment problems—but almost nothing about a person's life before substance abuse or mental instability put them on the street. We know that Patrick used to be an attorney, that Mel used to be a commercial fisherman, and that Chrissie was a school teacher. But, more usually, our history with someone outdoors begins on the street and stays on the street, until the short, brutal arc of his life ends with a miserable or violent death.

· · · · ·

If one of our people was in the hospital, sometimes we would hear about it from a social worker or a case worker at 240 Albany Street. More often, people on the street would tell us that Dave had tripped, fallen down the escalator in the Central Square T station and broken his shoulder or that Jake had been assaulted and both of his legs were broken. Usually, what we were hearing was a wild exaggeration of what had happened; people on the street give meaning to their lives by overdramatizing them. If I heard that someone was at Cambridge City Hospital, I would drive over at the end of day. More often than not, the intake people at Cambridge City had never heard of the person I was looking for, or the person had been discharged days before.

It was a relief not to add another two hours to an already exhausting day. Yet, however tired, I like going to the hospital, especially at night. I like sitting in Room 436 with Shaggy or Vickie or whoever happens to be up there, with the hallway lights dimmed, hearing only the hum of the instruments and monitors and the susurrus of the nurses' voices. One of our congregants' hospital narratives involves our bronze cross. The hospital always asks the patient to take it off and, in the telling, our congregant always refuses—they never take it off, it would get lost, it shows that they are religious people and so on—and, invariably, the cross ends up on the table next to the hospital bed, is forgotten and then has to be replaced when the congregant returns to the street. During one visit to Vickie and Shaggy at Cambridge City Hospital, they told me excitedly about how the nurse had tried to take away the cross and how they had adamantly refused, and then showed me the cross on the table.

Most often, when I visit our people in the hospital, they are asleep. They are usually there because they have had a seizure or they have been assaulted, and painkillers are an important part of their treatment. Watching one of our people fall asleep in the hospital is—outside of church—the only time when I see a homeless person at peace.

When I am with someone who has been badly beaten or who seems to be in an endless cycle of seizures and hospitalization, I sometimes console myself by imagining that I am the Sandman, bringing the peace of sleep to the person I am visiting. It is an indulgence, but not as bad an indulgence as preaching about it. I have two sermons that I use as models when I am preaching about my ministry. The first is about the Outdoor Church. I can usually mold it to whatever text appears in the lectionary for the day on which I am preaching. I have begun to think of it as my stump sermon. The second—which is based on a sermon I gave at King's Chapel a long time ago and is intended to show that I am not a one-dimensional preacher and can preach about something other than the Outdoor Church—is based on Luke 2:29–31, which describes Simeon's encounter with the Christ child after faithfully waiting for him at the Temple. Simeon is an older man, "just and devout, waiting for the consolation of Israel," a righteous man on whom the Holy Spirit rests. He has waited all his life for the Messiah whose coming was foretold by the prophet Isaiah. The Holy Spirit has promised him that he will not die until he sees his Messiah. Now, his moment has come. He takes Jesus into his arms and says, or sings, the Nunc Dimittis:

> Lord, now lettest thou thy servant depart in peace, according to thy word; for mine eyes have seen thy salvation which thou hast prepared in the presence of all peoples, a light for revelation to the Gentiles, and for glory to thy people Israel. (Luke 2:29–31)

The Nunc Dimittis is the very heart of Evening Prayer, one of the foundations of the Book of Common Prayer that Thomas Cranmer completed in 1549. Evening Prayer is when the church says goodnight to its congregants. The church does not promise that nothing will go wrong in the coming night. It does not promise that the person will waken the next morning, or that the next day will be better than the last. Rather, the church promises that God will be present during the night and present the next day. The Nunc Dimittis concludes Evensong as a final reminder that God always keeps his promises.

Think of Hansel and Gretel, playing deep in the forest, heedless of their parents' warnings. They have eaten all the strawberries they were sent to pick. The sun is setting fast and, as it grows darker, they become more and more frightened. They realize they cannot refill their basket, and worse, that they are lost.

Now the Sandman appears, bringing the uncertain blessing of sleep. Not for nothing is Karla, the head of the Russian secret service in John LeCarré's *Tinker, Tailor, Soldier, Spy* called the Sandman by MI5, the British secret service: he puts their agents to sleep, permanently.

The Sandman puts magic dust on Hansel and Gretel's eyelids, promising sleep, but they are not completely calmed. Only when they invoke the protection of God's angels can they sleep in peace, for they know that sleep need not be feared. Whether they awake from sleep or not, God is with them and will protect them.

I don't give this sermon any more. Now, for me, preaching about death is preaching about the Outdoor Church: dying and death are at the very heart of being homeless.

· · · · ·

The mortality rate at 240 Albany Street is very high. Many of the people who die at the shelter are people to whom we have ministered. Ed, the first of our people to die on the street, stayed there from time to time and had many friends there. We asked the shelter if we could have a memorial service for Ed. They agreed and we have conducted memorial services for people who have lived at 240 Albany Street ever since.

When we have a memorial service at 240 Albany Street, the staff sets up a lectern on one of the dining room tables, drapes a sheet over it and stacks up volumes of an out of date encyclopedia on the floor so that Jean can see over the top of the lectern. If people bring pictures, the staffs pins them to the sheet or groups them on the table. The service is based on the Book of Common Prayer, but it is all about sharing memories of the deceased. All sorts of people attend these memorial services: people at 240 Albany Street who knew the person who died; social workers, nurses and staff members who provided support; family members who may not have seen him for many years; fellow workers who remember him from before he began drinking too heavily to hold his job; and us. One guy had worked at the post office and eight postal clerks showed up for his memorial service.

How can so many people learn so quickly about the death of someone who been virtually invisible for the last years of his or her life? Often the hospital at which the homeless person is to die needs an assent from a family member and attempts to locate one. At death, the hospital and the police make a concerted effort to identify family members or friends so that burial arrangements and other decisions can be made. If the person has been staying at a shelter, like 240 Albany Street, staff learn immediately about that person's death. And word spreads on the street as well—sometimes simply as rumors, but often enough when someone has in fact died. Here is an event that does not need any overdramatization to impress and awe.

What is true for memorial services generally is especially true for homeless people: friends and family from disparate parts of a person's life share memories so that each person walks away with a much richer sense of the person than he had before.

Because we only know people when they are living on the street and headed toward the end of their lives, the revelations of another life are a shock: She had three kids! He used to play golf! He went to Boston College! He was a fireman! It is unbelievable—but there are the old friends and children and former wife and their photographs to prove it.

It is hard for the shelter guests to stand up and talk in public. Many of them are drunk or mentally disabled and all are deeply disturbed by the death of someone they knew. Many are too upset to speak or even come in for the service; they stand outside and smoke. Some put on a bold face. While she was still living at 240 Albany Street, Sophronia attended all of the memorial services, whether she knew the deceased or not. She was once the model for the little girl in the ubiquitous United Cerebral Palsy Association poster. Sophronia had a round, haggard face, lined from too much alcohol and too much time outdoors in her wheelchair. When she was drinking, she was mean and foul-mouthed. She would sit in the front row and snarl, sotto voce, at whoever was speaking, "That's bullshit." When she turned to racial epithets, the staff would take her outdoors. Amazingly, Sophronia stopped drinking, started a program of physical therapy and learned to walk with only the use of a cane. She got an apartment in Revere with the assistance of Home Start and left the shelter for good.

Wanda was one of the first to have a memorial service at 240 Albany Street. She must have been very pretty once. She had brilliant light blue eyes and a sweet, lopsided grin. Her hair was short and mousy brown. She tried, ineffectually, to do something different with it from time to time. Wanda and Rick slept in the Bank of America ATM lobby near City Hall. When they couldn't, because someone had called the police to complain about Rick's aggressive panhandling or drinking and the police had rousted them, they slept behind the bank in an alley with Charlie and Wayne and Dave. If the weather was really bad, Jason, a gracious black man with a white goatee who favors colorful silk cravats (God knows where he finds them), would walk Wanda back to the shelter for the evening.

Wanda had lost all of her teeth. She kept losing the dentures she got from Boston Health Care for the Homeless whenever Rick hit her. Her lips were pulled back over her gums. She mumbled. I could never understand what she was trying to say to me, even when I knew what words she was trying to use: "tuna fish," "egg salad," "socks," "communion." Rick had to translate for me. When Wanda stood up, it was a shock to see how tall she was after seeing her week after week sitting on the stoop in front of the bank: I'm six feet tall and she was at least two or three inches taller. She could have been a basketball player, I thought incongruously whenever we found her on her feet. In Wanda's day, women played a much more constrained game of basketball than they do today. You couldn't run; you couldn't take more than three dribbles; you couldn't cross the half court line. But Wanda could barely take two or three steps on her own without falling down.

It was more likely that we would see her out cold on the sidewalk in front of the bank, with Rick watching over her. Wanda, the police and Cambridge City Hospital were partners in an endless loop of hospitalization, treatment, release and hospitalization. Wanda would pass out or have a seizure; the Cambridge police would come, put her in an ambulance and take her to Cambridge City Hospital; the hospital would hold her for a day or so, give her Dilantin for the seizures and release her, somewhat less intoxicated; she would rejoin Rick and start to drink again; she would pass out or have a seizure; and on and on. When Wanda had a seizure, she coughed up some grainy brown phlegm that clogged her esophagus. I watched Rick try to clear her throat while they waited for the ambulance, but his hands shook too much to be helpful. In the winter, Wanda would be sent off to Bridgewater Hospital from time to time for a thirty-day observation, but that was just to spare her thirty days of sitting in the slush.

Once, Wanda tried to get back to the shelter on her own and didn't make it. She fell asleep on the abandoned railroad siding behind the shelter and was badly bitten by rats. Both of her legs were swollen and inflamed for weeks, until, during one of her stays at Cambridge City, the staff saw that she was infected and held her long enough to treat the rat bites.

On the nights when Jason helped Wanda get back to 240 Albany Street for the night, Jean and I would see her there by herself, having a solid meal for the first time in a long while. She would smile beatifically at us and say something completely incoherent.

One winter, Wanda and Rick both disappeared for a few weeks and rumors began to circulate that Wanda had died of a heart attack. Soon enough, they were once again camped out on the benches in front of the Cambridge Savings Bank. Shortly afterward, the rumors began again: Wanda was dead. This time it was true. Wanda had had a seizure in a stall in the women's room at Wendy's and before anyone noticed her absence she had died. The police finally reached Wanda's sister, but she refused to get involved with the arrangements for Wanda's funeral.

The dining area overflowed with people for Wanda's memorial service. She was gentle and sweet and everyone who knew her liked her. Rick wasn't there. It was too much for him, he told me later. Rick is back in front of the bank now but he isn't doing well. The seizures have become more frequent and the shaking more pronounced. He tells me that he has only six months left. He may be right.

Not everyone from 240 Albany Street who died got a memorial service there. Chrissie, whom we knew from Porter Square, had been there for a while, but she had had her own apartment in Central Square for the last few years. Chrissie had a turned up nose, pink cheeks and china blue eyes. She had a high, scratchy voice and tightly curled roan colored hair that made a halo around her head. When she was sober, she looked like a porcelain doll. When she had been drinking heavily, her nose ran, her eyes got red and she slurred her words.

Chrissie had taught English in high school before she began to drink. Evan said that when he and Chrissie had been in a detox program together, they went to a dance sponsored by the program and Chrissie was beautiful. She was sober and she wore a gold floor length dress and jewelry. Evan was so upset at her appearance when she was drunk that, while she was still alive, he wouldn't show up in Porter Square for morning prayer service for fear that he would see her there. Chrissie had that affect on a lot of people. Tom Lenhart, when he was an intern with me at North Prospect Church, was crazy about Chrissie. He was deeply touched by the soft spoken, literate woman who was in the implacable grip of her drinking. When he became senior minister at First Church in Chappaqua, New York, he tried to keep abreast of her collapsing health but it was still a shock when she died.

Chrissie's drinking got worse as the day wore on. We would see her, relatively sober, in Porter Square at 9:00 AM but by the time we had reached her in Central Square late in the afternoon, she could barely stand. One Sunday afternoon we found her leaning against a store front on Pearl Street. She had dropped her reticule and all of its contents had spilled out onto the sidewalk. She was too drunk to lean over to pick up her things without losing her balance and falling over. I walked down the street and knelt in front of her to collect her belongings, nearly falling over myself because of the knapsack full of toiletries that I was carrying. Chrissie became very upset; she didn't want me to see her in such a dreadful state. But I couldn't easily walk away. It was a horrible moment for both of us.

Chrissie finally lost her apartment and moved into a congregate facility for disabled women. Shortly afterward, she was admitted to Beth Israel Hospital for complications from AIDS and slipped into a coma. I visited once or twice. Jean visited regularly. She met Chrissie's sister at the hospital. Jean read to her from her Psalter and Chrissie's eyelids would quiver, but the heavy drinking had destroyed her mind and her body and she couldn't recover.

Chrissie had become a regular guest at On the Rise. When Chrissie died, 240 Albany Street refused to hold a memorial service for her because she hadn't stayed there on a regular basis for a long while. Maybe they were jealous of On the Rise. One of the nurses at On the Rise urged them to reconsider, but the director was adamant. I spoke with the nurse and we agreed to have a memorial service next to the small park behind the Fire Station in Central Square. We announced it in Porter Square. When the day came, it was cold and rainy. We huddled under our umbrellas against the wall of the fire station. No one was there except Pat and me and Jean and Mardi.

· · · · ·

Sometimes we have memorial services for homeless people at conventional churches, because they had been in a meals program there or had worked there. That was how Bill Montell came to have a memorial service at Christ Church Cambridge, where Bill had been a part-time sexton.

Bill died the way lots of homeless people die—he was hit by a car—but he wasn't homeless then and that made it seem even more stupid.

Bill was crushed by a hit and run driver on Storrow Drive late one night, just in front of the Harvard Business School campus. The police never found the operator of the car but, based on what they saw, they thought that the driver had hit Bill while he was walking on the sidewalk and then dragged him into the middle of Storrow Drive to make it look like the collision was Bill's fault.

When Pat and I visited Bill at Beth Israel hospital, he was on life support. All the vertebrae in his upper spine were crushed. His brain had suffered a deep concussive shock and many of his internal organs were irreparably damaged. His face and skull were covered with abrasions. The prognosis was dismal. When Pat read to him from the Psalter, his eyes fluttered occasionally—we had read that people who are in a coma can nonetheless hear and understand more than had been previously imagined—but his facial expression never changed. The hospital tried unsuccessfully for a week to find some next of kin. After the weekend, Beth Israel and Christ Church met to consider a petition to Superior Court for an expedited guardianship hearing so that a decision could be made about continuing Bill's life support. The following day, he died.

Bill was one of our very first congregants on the Cambridge Common. He was a slight energetic black man in his mid fifties, with a square, open face, and large, dark eyes that were set close together. Bill radiated energy and optimism. He was always on the balls of his feet and he was always smiling. Sometimes he was on the street, sometimes he stayed with friends. When he was with us on the Common, Bill had a few small jobs—some paid and some didn't—but they kept Bill active and engaged. When Christ Church took him on as a Sunday sexton, he had a little money. He had an office in the Christ Church basement, where he read magazines when he wasn't on duty.

When Bill began working as a sexton, he couldn't be with us on the Common, so we would look for him at the end of the day at Christ Church where we left our extra sandwiches for the 6:00 PM Alcoholics Anonymous meeting. He would come bounding up the basement stairs and Pat would offer communion to him. It was always the end of a long day for us, and Bill knew it. He would try to pick us up by telling us what a wonderful church we were and what a wonderful ministry we had undertaken.

We learned at Bill's memorial service that he had taught yoga, that he was a carpenter, that he was an artist with a small but well earned reputation. We also learned that he had been done in by drugs. It had to be—nothing else could explain how he lived. Bill never let us see him using and never mentioned it. Perhaps he thought he was protecting us or perhaps it was all part of the confused way that all the parts of his life were patched together. What we always saw was an unfailingly serene and deeply spiritual man. He loved our outdoor services. He thought the Outdoor Church was as pure a church as he had ever encountered, because it raised up worshipful presence in a community of the faithful to a near-sacramental event.

He was a great hugger, too, and—since I'm not—he was always catching me by surprise. For a long while, he was the only person I would let hug me on the street.

And some people didn't get any kind of memorial service when they died, often because we knew them from Harvard Square or Central Square, not as part of a discreet community but simply as individuals to whom we ministered on the street. Nonetheless, we have tried hard not to forget them.

· · · · ·

Sometimes death hovers just out of reach, a hope or a fear not yet realized but still present. Sometimes it appears in the form of suicide. For the chronically homeless, life is so miserable; life is hopeless; life is without meaning—why not end it? Why not bet that the next life can't be worse than this one?

Many homeless people have a demonic theology that seems to make sense of their suffering. On one hand, God is a God of judgment, and his judgment is manifest in the hopelessness and misery of life on the street. On the other hand, God is a God of mercy, and his mercy is manifest in the certainty of release from suffering at the hour of death and of a better life to come. But theology can give way to a despair so powerful that only suicide seems to offer any relief.

I was taken aback the first time Jack knelt during one of our services. No one had ever knelt in front of me before, much less on the sidewalk. I barely resisted the urge to get him to stand up. He does it every time he attends one of our services. When he does, I am always distracted by the thought that the pavement must be incredibly uncomfortable to kneel on for as long as it takes to complete the communion service. Jack is a small, dark, lithe man with a wide face, high cheek bones and deep hazel eyes. Every winter, he wears the same long green cloth coat over a grey hoody, and jeans and work boots. He is a great and sloppy hugger, which reminds me too much of my father.

Unlike Evan, Jack only joins us when he is depressed. When he is not drinking, he can find work as a cook or a handyman. When he is drinking, he is miserable. Every time he showed up, Jack would take me aside and tell me he was thinking about suicide. He had a revolver, he said, and all he could think about was putting the barrel of the gun in his mouth and pulling the trigger. I could taste the metal of the barrel in my mouth. We will call an ambulance for a homeless person at our services if they are so sick that they can't sit up or walk, but we have never called the police for help with someone who is talking about suicide and we have never tried to commit anybody involuntarily. No one on the street would talk to us again if we did and it wouldn't stick anyway. And, with Jack, I couldn't sort through all the ways that, as a lawyer and as a minister, the duty to report and confidentiality intersected. So I didn't do anything and, after the sixth or seventh time he told me that he had a revolver and that all he could think about was putting the barrel of the gun in his mouth and pulling the trigger, I stopped worrying about whether he was really suicidal.

•••••

On one hand, our people have a powerful faith—or a fear of sudden, violent death—that keeps them from taking their own lives by shooting themselves or throwing themselves off the Boston University Bridge in the middle of January or stepping in front of a bus. On the other hand, they are taking their lives in small but decisive steps, not consciously, perhaps, but deliberately all the same; they are slowly drinking themselves to death or allowing themselves to be assaulted by younger, stronger men or sustaining a level of domestic abuse that would hospitalize a decathlete. When I am feeling melodramatic, I will tell someone who is dying slowly in front of me that I am tired of doing memorial services and I don't want to do theirs, but I don't expect that it will change anything, and it doesn't.

The person I have the greatest difficulty keeping at an emotional distance is Rick. He is only a few seizures away from dying and he knows it. Like Gregory, whom Pat knows from the meals program at Christ Church and who speaks seven or eight languages, Rick is intelligent, well educated, cultured and very, very funny. He says that the police roust him from the dumpster behind City Hall by beating on the soles of his bare feet, but he just laughs because he doesn't care anymore. He says he doesn't care because Wanda is dead, but he was doing this when she was alive.

One January Sunday we found Rick sleeping in the Cambridge Savings Bank ATM booth, barefoot and trying to warm up before a cop came by to ask him to leave. He was huddled under a small gray blanket with his bare feet sticking out. Rebecca left some sandwiches and juice next to the blanket and tried not to wake him, but he woke up anyway. At first he didn't recognize us but when he got himself focused he was glad to have the sandwiches—he hadn't eaten since Friday and he was shaking very badly, from the cold or from the drinking, we couldn't tell. I gave him a pair of heavy woolen socks but he was shaking too hard to put them on so I knelt down in front of him and put them on for him. "Don't do that, man," he said, a little embarrassed. "I'm going to die anyway. Save them for Dave or Charlie—I'm gone."

Death is leering at me over your shoulder, Rick. And all I have with me is faith and a pair of socks.

11

Salvation

> There is one lawgiver that is able to save and to destroy; who art thou that judgest another? (Jas 4:12)
>
> For here have we no continuing city, but we seek one to come. (Heb 13:14)

STUDENTS AT HARVARD AND MOST OTHER DIVINITY SCHOOLS AND seminaries are required, either by the school or by their denomination, to serve two internships. Harvard's field education handbook lists hundreds of different field education sites. Most are conventional churches. When I was seeking ordination, I did three: two at First Church in Chestnut Hill, when I was still a Unitarian, and one at North Prospect United Church of Christ, where I was in care and where I was ordained. Field education sites are all over the map: there are conventional churches of all denominations and no denomination, hospitals, schools, nonprofit service providers, rehabilitation hospitals, college chapels and outdoor churches like Ecclesia Ministries and us.

Our interns come from all over the Boston Theological Institute, a consortium of eleven divinity schools and seminaries, but primarily from the Harvard Divinity School, the Weston Jesuit School of Theology and the Episcopal Divinity School. We have had seven interns to date. They choose themselves. Prospective interns and student volunteers hear about us by word of mouth, or at the annual presentation I make at the Harvard Divinity School, or from a faculty advisor, and come out to see what we are doing. Some people stay for one morning or one afternoon, and never come back. They may be deeply moved by what they have seen and heard, or deeply disturbed, but they do not come back. Others stay for one morning or one afternoon, and come back again and again. These students ask if they can join us for a semester or two, and we have always said yes.

Our interns are invariably intelligent, earnest, thoughtful, serious (but not dour or dull), full of energy and enthusiasm and eager to take chances with their faith and themselves. They deal with all of the issues that Jean and Pat and I confront all the time. They are not often knocked off balance by what they see or hear.

Like Liz, our interns tend to fling themselves at the difficulties we encounter every Sunday; they want to make something good happen. They are, in this, much more like Tuckerman than like me. I know that our ministry is transformative for our clergy and students and also for our homeless congregants, but—at least in the terms with which our interns initially measure progress—almost all of the transformation is on our side. Invariably, our interns, on realizing this, feel selfish and egotistical. I urge them to consider how difficult it is to see grace at work in the lives of our homeless congregants, as well as in their own. It is like teaching, or preaching. Who can tell who has been listening and who has heard, and who can say when in a person's life what they have heard will change them?

The interns understand that but they don't completely accept it. They are irrepressibly optimistic. So it is always deeply disturbing when they come to know the most degraded and oppressed of our congregants. But they are also resilient and invariably return the following Sunday stronger and more committed. They are Tuckerman's children. They believe that transformation is to a purpose and to an end. It tends toward growth, improvement and happiness—toward perfection itself. Like Tuckerman, they believe that the transformation that leads to moral improvement will manifest itself in evident progress. We will all be better for the operation of grace in us and for the changes in us that grace will promote. They go together, as they did in Tuckerman's theology.

Whether we are clergy, staff or interns, we all want to believe that as works must follow faith, transformation in the life of the body must follow transformation in the heart. We may not always see it—after all, Tuckerman didn't do follow up studies to see how many of the people who attended his chapels had remained sober or stayed employed—but grace happens. It takes form as the love that virtually all of our people have never received from parents, friends and teachers. They were, for the most part, loathed and hated by their parents, siblings or anyone else who might have loved and encouraged them when they were young. As a result, they loathe and hate themselves. In our people's narratives of their own lives, all of the terrible things that happen to them are deserved, because they deserve nothing but pain and despair. For them, it is hard to learn to love God and to love others because it is so hard to love oneself.

Tuckerman's anthropology was grounded in the conviction that no one was loathsome or despicable and that everyone was loved by God and therefore ought to be loved by men. In God's creation, all the elements of his plan tended toward the natural perfection that reflected his infinite goodness. The law of that creation was a law of sympathy and love; its purpose was to fulfill God's plan by making possible its ever more perfect realization.

In Tuckerman's theology, a life of love for others—a life lived according to Christian principles—was always transformative. Tuckerman argued that the most natural and efficient engine for that transformation was benevolence. The donor is propelled toward moral improvement by his generosity; the recipient receives opportunities for material and moral improvement and the encouragement necessary to take advantage of them. Because it was so effectively transformative, benevolence toward the poor, in particular, was redemptive:

> [Was it not] the purpose for which Christ lived and died, and instituted the ministry by which his gospel was to be preached "to every creature," that from these and all other moral evils, every believer in him should now, and in this world, be redeemed, as preeminently the preparation for his final blessedness? This is a view of the Christian doctrine of redemption which I think second to no others.[1]

For their part, the poor were transformed by their escape from a material and spiritual poverty which would otherwise prevent them from improving themselves. Benevolent philanthropy, then, offered a means to salvation to all who participated in the benevolent transaction, wealthy and poor:

> God has committed [our privileges] to us for our own improvement, and as means of our own salvation. But is it not also his

---

1. Tuckerman, *Principles and Results*, 321–24.

will, that we should be his instruments for the improvement and the salvation of our fellow men?[2]

• • • • •

Not everyone shared Tuckerman's confidence in the likelihood that alms would promote the moral improvement of the poor. "Many an enthusiastic Christian man or woman," wrote Edward Hale fifty years after Tuckerman's Ministry-at-large, "who had engaged personally in the work of charity with zeal and devotion, has stopped aghast at the end of a winter, with the horrid certainty that more hurt has been done than good to the people whom he meant or whom she meant to relieve. 'I can ruin the best family in Boston by giving them a cord of wood in the wrong way.' This was the verdict of one of the most experienced and most successful of Boston's almoners to the poor."[3] Alms were not only a threat to their recipient, but also to the almoner:

> The prudent part of [our better classes] would not stand aloof from sympathy or fear, but would heartily unite against the spirit of pauperism as the worst of all possible enemies to their nearest interests. There can be no humanity in the poor laws. . .it is concluded that the bulk of mankind must be kept on the verge of necessity.[4]

Such armchair moralizing bore no relation to Tuckerman's astonishingly rich experience on the street. He was indefatigable in his efforts on behalf of those to whom he ministered, and visited six to eight families every Sunday. He kept meticulous journals of pastoral visits and lent small amounts to many of the poor people he visited, keeping a record of the loans in a small notebook which he always carried with him and collecting payments during subsequent visits. It was his willingness to fully embrace, and not ignore, the reality of his people's lives that enabled him to maintain his optimism about their spiritual potential.

Tuckerman loved to write about poor individuals or families who had been radically transformed by his benevolence. One entry in his journal recorded the repayment of ten dollars he had lent to Asa Griffin

---

2. Tuckerman, *Letter on the Principles of the Missionary Enterprise*, 34.
3. Hale, "Introduction," 13.
4. Walker, *The Original*, 252.

"to aid him in redeeming clothes and furniture, which he had pledged for a debt while he was living in intemperance."[5] Griffin, a journeyman mechanic, had begun to drink heavily and he and his wife were living in squalor. Invited to Griffin's house by his wife, Tuckerman found Griffin out cold on his bed and his wife in utter despair. But Tuckerman visited week after week, never mentioning that he had first seen Griffin completely intoxicated but, instead, urging him to sobriety and improvement and securing a pledge that he would stop drinking. After eight weeks of abstinence, Griffin's wife had acquired a new dress and stove and Griffin had acquired a shop fitted up for his business as cabinet maker.[6] Tuckerman knew that it was his developing relationship with Griffin and not the ten dollar loan that had given Griffin the confidence to stop drinking: "Had I treated this man otherwise than with respect, and sympathy, how would he have received me, and how would he have treated my endeavors to reclaim him from intemperance?"[7]

Tuckerman's *Journals* were filled with such stories. His *Gleams of Truth* was a highly elaborated, if somewhat saccharine, morality play in which the redemption of both the donor and the recipient of alms follows from the donor's benevolence. It was so clear, so easy! Tuckerman could never understand why most of his fellow ministers and their congregants didn't follow him into the streets of Boston. He never stopped trying to persuade them that a genuinely practical means to the concrete realization of the otherwise abstract Unitarian concept of salvation was within their grasp.

• • • • •

For the Outdoor Church, when it comes to the hope of transformation, it doesn't much matter what theology you subscribe to, whether apparently hopelessly optimistic, like Tuckerman's Unitarianism, or oppressively judgmental, like the Calvinists of the era prior to his. You can't spend much time on the street without fostering the hope that something better awaits those who live and die there. You could say—as I do—that the suffering we see has to be redeemed by the assurance of universal salvation, no matter how difficult it is to discern or how

---

5. Tuckerman, *Principles and Results*, 91–93
6. Ibid., 539.
7. Ibid., 109.

remote its realization might be. You could say—as Tina and Vic and many other homeless people did—that the enormity of their suffering and God's love for them, however irrational, are perfectly compatible notions and that, their suffering being a present reality, their future salvation is assured. One way or the other, something has to change for the better, in this life or the next.

When we tell ourselves that we are on the street to convey a message of hope, we are saying that we believe that our people's lives *will* change for the better, spiritually and materially. And, despite all rational evidence to the contrary, virtually all of our congregants believe it too.

• • • • •

Universalism—the conviction that everyone will ultimately be saved—developed in that part of New England that was least influenced by Harvard and the leading ministers of the Standing Order. It appealed to those people who had an intuitive dislike of the Calvinist idea of limited atonement, which condemned to eternal damnation all those who were not visible saints. Universalism was always a diffuse movement, largely indifferent to strict creedal statements. In response to Orthodox criticism, Restorationism directly addressed the question of punishment for wrong-doing by assuming that the sinner would be punished for particular sins and, once punished and finally and completely redeemed, would ultimately be saved. But most Universalists simply believed in universal salvation.

"Hopelessly optimistic" is another way of saying "convinced of universal salvation." Tuckerman was as oblivious to the development of Universalism in New England as he was to the Unitarian Controversy. But he developed his own theology of universal salvation from his direct experience with poverty on Boston's streets. For Tuckerman, there was no inherent infirmity that prevented men from improving themselves morally and there was no reason why that moral improvement should not be within reach of any one who sought it. Jesus was the exemplar of man's potential for unlimited moral improvement. Tuckerman's belief in *unlimited* potential for self-improvement, fortified by one empirical experience of self-improvement after another, led inexorably to a belief in universal salvation. In this he seems neither liberal nor conservative. His insistence on the theological significance of moral improvement seems conservative to us today, while his direct experience of poverty as the ground on which moral improvement might develop seems liberal. In this as in the other facets of his ministry, conventional notions of theological liberalism or conservatism became irrelevant. Tuckerman simply embraced as a call to discipleship his love for the poor people he came to know.

•••••

Tuckerman's stories of moral improvement were complete in the sense that his interventions in the lives of the poor resulted in professions of repentance or self-discovery. They were apparently confirmed by a corresponding material improvement as well. Thus Tuckerman did not need to *hope* for the possibility of moral improvement. Because he could see the material improvement that could only have resulted from moral improvement, the evidence of that moral improvement was before his eyes. Tuckerman did not do any formal follow-up studies to see if the improvement he had observed survived the passage of time. But where he reported a later encounter with one of the recipients of his alms, he made no mention of any failure or backsliding. In any event, his hope rested in the perfectibility of man and the assurance of universal salvation. Any discernable progress toward moral improvement, however modest or uneven, was sufficient confirmation.

That is rarely our experience. We don't often see the material improvements that gave Tuckerman and his associates such encouragement. We watch our congregants slide slowly but inevitably toward death. A few manage to halt the downward drift of their lives and a very few manage to achieve a modicum of material improvement—they secure a housing subsidy or find part time employment or enter a detox program—but such gains are infrequent.

Perhaps our people *are* different than the people Tuckerman served. In the 1820's, some of our people would have been living on poor farms or in institutions for the insane. Others would have been hidden from sight by families large enough to care for them. It may be that, in some unconscious way, Tuckerman and his associates selected people—either on the street before a first visit or immediately after a first visit—who offered some promise of material improvement, however dim or uncertain. It is possible, also, that Tuckerman's reporting was skewed toward stories of redemption and success; his own evaluation of his work was idiosyncratic and unscientific, and much of it was intended to help raise financial support for the Ministry-at-large.

In any event, we depend—far more than Tuckerman did—on faith and not on the measurable results of social work or political action to make sense of what we are doing. We have hope, not evidence. It is not a very large step from there to a belief in universal salvation.

· · · · ·

It is too easy to allow our empathy for the people to whom we minister to frame our relationships with them. It is a language that we and our congregants can understand; often, it is the language they themselves, like the culture at large, use all the time to describe their circumstance to themselves and to others.

But we are on the street to make it easier for homeless men and women to accept God's unconditional love for them. We are on the street to bring people a message of hope in the face of the most depressing and discouraging circumstances. We are on the street to tell people that a power infinitely higher and stronger than ourselves—and not we ourselves—is the assurance of that hope. If we make the strength of our empathy the ground on which that hope is built, we and they must fail, for we are also prone to failure. Why, then, should they have any confidence in our personal assurances?

We are messengers only. We point to the power of one infinitely greater than ourselves. With that, we gain a confidence that allows us to transcend our human weaknesses; but we lose any conviction that we ourselves will make the difference. This lesson—so hard that it must be relearned every Sunday—is often confusing to us and to our congregants. However great their faith, it is not God, but us whom they see, week after week, praying, handing out clean white socks, sharing donuts. It is particularly confusing for me. I have always felt that there is nothing special about what I do because there is nothing special about me, conveniently ignoring the obvious, that what we do is, in fact, extraordinary.

It is true but it is beside the point: extraordinary or not, the ministry must be in the service of something other and greater than me or else it is not a ministry. The old foundation breaks up over and over again, every Sunday.

All this has taken its toll on all of us. As the months have gone by, we have come to know and to like the men and women we serve. To see them literally dying in front of us—in slow motion, to be sure, but just as certainly as if they had been hit by a train—drains our emotional resources. The more we care, the more we hurt.

· · · · ·

Despite our hopes, what we actually see every Sunday—cannot avoid seeing—is the unremitting degradation and pain in the lives of most of our people. The immediate causes are madness, drugs or alcohol.

It is madness that most seems beyond the reach of anything we can do except keep our faith alive. Some people are so deranged that it is a miracle that the world through which others move overlaps theirs enough for them to eat, sleep and find shelter.

Andrew is a regular at the Thursday night meal at Christ Church. He is in and around Harvard Square a lot and I often see him there. Andrew lurches as he walks and slumps when he stands in front of you, but his brown eyes are bright and inquisitive. When we talk, he looks up into my face, although we are the same height. He has thinning gray hair that falls well below his shoulders, and his face is tanned and deeply lined from living outdoors. He laughs often at his own jokes. They are usually disgusting but quite clever. When he knows he is taking a chance on being too vulgar or too intimate, he cocks his head to the side and looks out of the corners of his eyes. Andrew likes plaid. He wears plaid woolen work shirts throughout the year, no matter how hot it may be during the summer. His eyes are never still. While he will make eye contact, he won't hold it for more than a few seconds at a time.

Andrew is brilliant in a very particular way. Although he is capable of speaking in simple declarative sentences, he rarely does. Instead, he speaks allusively, in complicated metaphors, puns, word plays, analogies and anagrams, seamlessly linked together. Andrew reads the Boston Globe and New York Times carefully, front to back, and it all finds its way into his conversation. He can cram the Pope, the Department of Defense, pedophilia, Moby Dick, the Red Sox, Harvard, religion, ministers, medical experiments, professional malpractice, lawyers, the courts, prescription drugs, Nini's newspaper stand and Xerox copying into an unbroken steam of consciousness, phrased as questions. If you can't answer any of the questions or just lose track, as most people do, he takes offense at your inattentiveness and stomps off.

Usually, the allusions refer to something that has disturbed Andrew and which he is trying to process. He becomes more confusing and abstract in proportion to how badly he has been hurt or scared. He is very proud, and hates to be taken for a homeless person. One winter evening, the young man behind the counter at Nini's called him a shiftless homeless bum while he was trying to read the Boston Globe and told him to get lost. The insult gave rise to endless riffs on the courts, his constitutional rights, the trash sold at most newsstands, jury selection and junk food. It took months before he could describe what had happened in a way I could understand. Many people can't abide him and won't talk to him. It is too frustrating to be asked over and over to respond to questions you can't understand, when Andrew doesn't seem to care about your answer anyway.

But if you can hang in there with him for a while, his jokes and similes and jibes begin to cluster around his mistreatment by doctors in a mental health facility, where Andrew believes he was given drugs which have made him permanently demented. He is trying to find some legal basis for a claim for damages for what has happened to him.

Andrew is never without a stack of medical journals and articles which he carries in a large brown cloth bag. He attends seminars and lectures at the Harvard School of Public Health and the Medical School, where (he says) he sits quietly at the back of the lecture hall and then asks the professor questions about his mistreatment at the end of the lecture. He is familiar with the general outlines of medical experimentation, drug protocols and research. But he hasn't yet figured out the precise nature of his affliction, which he sees as more evidence of the harm that the doctors did to his mind when he was institutionalized. Andrew is unusual this way: he has a very clear idea of the source of the problem that keeps him on the street and he is painfully aware of why he acts the way he does. It is heartbreaking to hear him say in so many different ways, "I could figure out how they damaged my mind, if only they hadn't damaged my mind."

Like Claire, like Patrick, like so many other intelligent, middle class men and women who were brought down by substance abuse or mental illness or, more usually, both, Andrew finds himself on the other side of a very bright but very thin line. He is just like us but he is a stranger in a strange land where we cannot follow him. He is as close as a handshake, but we cannot touch him.

•••••

If madness seems utterly beyond our reach, substance abuse is close behind. And, while addiction to drugs is every bit as devastating as addiction to alcohol, it is alcoholism that is destroying most of the people to whom we minister.

It took years before we learned Eugene's name. We would see him most Sunday afternoons in Central Square. He is a tiny man, with a large bald head. When he is nearly sober, he cocks his head, looks up out of bright, pin prick eyes and smiles self-consciously as if he had just been asked out on his first date. He looks like a shy pixie. He is always surprised and happy to see us, but he is never certain whether we have been away for a week or for five minutes. He accepts everything we offer him—sandwiches, juice, cookies, socks—so that he can tell us over and over again how appreciative he is. He keeps right on telling us even as we as walk away, so long as we are in sight.

Eugene is a "Listo," the most despised kind of alcoholic. Homeless people, mainly men, drink Listerine in quantity because it is cheap, always available and unregulated, although some box stores put the larger jugs of Listerine on very high shelves where it is assumed that a homeless person can't reach it. Listerine is not only cheap but very potent. Some brands have as much as 28% alcohol by volume. That's 56 proof. There are more potent non-beverage alcoholic drinks that are easily accessible, like vanilla extract, but Listerine is much cheaper in greater volume.

The Listerine has made Eugene incontinent. The first time I encountered him, he was sitting on one of the wood slatted benches in front of the record store that blasts hip hop incessantly, a few steps down from Wendy's. Eugene was just barely conscious and his eyes were unfocused, but he was smiling broadly and he seemed glad to get a sandwich and juice and socks. I was so acutely aware of the reek of Listerine that I didn't notice the puddle of urine that was forming under the bench. Eugene either didn't know that he was urinating or he knew and was too embarrassed to acknowledge it or do anything about it. I have never been able to shake that image of the urine pooling under Eugene's bench and Eugene's sloppy but beatific smile.

One Thursday night Jean and I found Eugene at 240 Albany Street, nursing a plate of Spaghetti O's. He was staring across the room at the kitchen serving window, where the plastic cups and plates were beginning to pile up. Evan had started working nights there, and he wanted to introduce us to Eleanor, who had been at 240 Albany Street for a long while and was going to begin working at Shelter, Inc., another shelter in Central Square, the very next day. Suddenly, Eugene leaped to his feet, his face lit up with his shy grin. He said, grabbing Evan by the arm and looking at me, "Here is my brother! He is a wonderful man!" We had never heard Eugene say anything other than "Thank you" before. Then he put his arm around Jean's shoulders and earnestly said to Evan, "This is my sister! She is a wonderful woman!" Then he gripped both of my hands and even more earnestly said to Eleanor, "This is my brother! He is a saint!" We were delighted that he was able to remember us, but, like the twenty or so men we see in Porter Square and Central Square who have been drinking that hard for so long, his ability to remember anything is fading fast.

• • • • •

A very few people manage to find their way to a new life. They do it by going away. Some never come back. Others come back clean and stay clean. One way or the other, you have to get away from everything that you associate with your addiction, especially your friends, because they have a vested interest in seeing you fail; when you are trying not to drink, you are a judgment on your friends' continuing degradation and you make them very uncomfortable. But, for most people who have been out on the street for a long while, their friends outdoors are the only community they have, the only people who won't kick them when they are out cold on the sidewalk or in an ATM lobby, or curse at them or spit on them. They are the only people who really understand what it means to be homeless. It gives a whole new meaning to Paul's injunction that the old man must die so that the new man can live. Among our people, it doesn't happen very often.

But Evan did it. He went away, got clean and stayed clean. Evan and his friends Pete and Meagan were the first people to attend our prayer service in Porter Square. Pete was big—maybe 6′ 2″ and about 200 lbs—but Evan is *really* big, at least 240 lbs and five or six inches taller than Pete. They both wore heavy black leather jackets and jeans.

Evan's face is meaty and worn and he has lines and creases all over it, like W. H. Auden. His jowls sag. Everything about him is big and thick. His hands are gigantic; he could easily grasp my bicep in one of them. He has enormous brown eyes that are always wide open, thick lips and brown hair that is slicked back in a fifties' pompadour. Evan is gentle and earnest and very generous. He had an apartment just outside Porter Square and he let Pete have a room there for a few dollars a week. They got into an argument once about some unpaid rent, and Pete moved out onto the street for a few weeks, but they patched it up and Pete moved back inside again. Evan was struggling with his drinking and Pete was struggling with heroin. Evan had been in and out of detox programs and different twelve step programs, but he didn't stay with them for very long. For a long while, he urged me to meet him at an AA meeting on the grounds of McLean's Hospital in Belmont, but when I finally showed up for one of the meetings Evan wasn't there.

We almost always saw Evan sober. He was embarrassed to be with us when he was drunk, although we tried to persuade him that that was precisely the time we *wanted* him to be with us. If he was drinking heavily, he would stay outdoors and we wouldn't see him for three or four weeks at a time. Sometimes he would stay with Meagan, who had a place nearby and tried to make sure he was eating while he was drinking. He found a used bike behind the Shaw's Supermarket in the Porter Square Shopping Center and rode it everywhere. When he wasn't drinking, he would ride his bike up to Porter Square by 8:45 AM so he could help us set up the altar and hand out the laminated orders of service. Evan also read the Scripture passage for the day, when he was there. He had a booming baritone voice that carried beautifully. When Evan is reading, you can hear every word, even when the T commuter rain train is idling just below us and the Cambridge sanitation workers are kicking empty trash barrels along the sidewalk.

Pete had cancer and had started treatment for it long before we met him. He was clearly in a lot of pain, but he rarely mentioned it and never complained. Week by week, he seemed to shrink. One day, he told us that the doctors had prescribed morphine for the pain and we knew that the end had come. When he died, Evan was very distraught and began drinking heavily. We didn't see him for a long while.

Then, one early Spring Sunday, he showed up on his bike and told us that he was leaving Cambridge and going to Gardner, an old city in the center of the state that went into permanent eclipse when the furniture industry moved south. He had been admitted to a detox program there that required that he stay on site for six months.

We didn't see Evan for more than a year, although we knew from Meagan, who had gotten a part time job on the night desk at 240 Albany Street, that he was staying sober. When we saw him again, he had a new bike and had lost a lot of weight because, he said, he rode his bike everywhere. He couldn't be with us, because he was still in the same program on an outpatient basis and they had meetings every Sunday morning, but he was around. He got a part time job at 240 Albany Street—Meagan's old job—and a room at the YMCA in Central Square, and we see him down there sometimes at the end of our walk through Central Square. You can't miss that foghorn voice.

• • • • •

And sometimes—but rarely, very rarely—it all comes together. It all came together when Sally decided that she wanted to be baptized.

In most churches, baptism precedes communion. Even a relatively liberal formulation like "Our communion is open to all people who are baptized" makes baptism a precondition to admission to the Lord's Table. But some churches—like St. Gregory of Nyssa in San Francisco—do it the other way around.

If I attended an indoor church, I would want to go to St. Gregory. One of its founders, Fr. Rick Fabian, was a year ahead of me at Yale, although I didn't know him there and I have never met him. I have been to St. Gregory, though, where I met Sara Miles and saw her food pantry. St. Gregory was designed to reflect the theological convictions of Rick, Donald Schell, its other clergy and its congregants. It is famous for its dancing icons. The icons are painted in rows around the rotunda that rises above the communion table at the center of the church. The icons show two circles of saints—some are traditional saints, like Mother Theresa, and some are people that St. Gregory deems to be just as saintly, like Anne Frank.

St. Gregory is second best, an indoor church that is designed—at least in part—to be outdoors. Its baptismal font is a waterfall located just beyond the rear doors of the church. You enter the church directly in front of the communion table; to reach the baptismal font, you must walk past the table to the rear of the church and then go outdoors again.

The ecclesial point is that communion should precede baptism. This underscores the openness of the Lord's Supper to the converted and unconverted alike, offering an invitation to the church and to Christian life that will be confirmed in baptism.[8] In this account, communion is a converting ordinance and baptism is a professing or confirming ordinance. Solomon Stoddard would have been very pleased with St. Gregory.

• • • • •

Treating communion as a converting ordinance made sense of a question raised by Tuckerman's accounts of the people he visited: the poor people to whom he ministered weren't anything like our congregants. Tuckerman didn't seem to be ministering to the same kinds of people that we met on the streets of Cambridge. The arc of the lives of the people that Tuckerman visited was unfailingly up; but the arc of the lives of our people was almost invariably down.

If the perfectibility of mankind was the road to salvation, how would we ever find it on the street? The street was like reality television, except that it was real. How, then, could any of our people be saved?

It was Tuckerman's understanding of human nature, and not his theology, that was the problem. But I didn't have to follow Tuckerman everywhere. On the street, people are good and bad, not just good or almost good. They are failed people who need to transcend themselves. That they don't give up—that Jack never pulls the trigger—is itself hopeful, even if they will never achieve the material success that Tuckerman took as a sign of progress toward redemption.

A steady march toward moral perfection is not the only path to salvation, notwithstanding Tuckerman's passionate belief in the perfectibility of man and in Jesus as the exemplar of that perfectibility. Our God's love extends even—especially—to those who have never had or no longer have the resources to find that path, much less follow it. We need not move toward Jesus on the street; he is already with us. Nothing our people can do will stand against the persistence of his mercy.

Tuckerman felt that he needed to find proof of the merit of his Ministry-at-large in the individual success stories that he so diligently

---

8. Fabian, "First the Table, then the Font," 4. And see Schell, "Breaking Barriers: Rethinking our Theology of Baptism"; Waldo, "Baptism and Eucharist"; Schell, "Font Outside Our Walls."

recorded in his Journal. We have very few proofs like that. Instead, we must rely on the same faith that we preach to our congregants: the substance of things hoped for, the evidence of things not seen.

• • • • •

Just as unexpectedly as when attendance fell off on the Cambridge Common, it picked up again. There was Ernie, of course, and Howard, and a few kids wandering up from Harvard Square in a daze. But we began seeing people that we hadn't seen on the Common for a long while: Gil—a lanky, tall blue eyed man in the mold of Rick in Central Square or Steve at Christ Church—witty, intelligent, hopelessly drunk, resigned to his alcoholism and unwilling to do anything about it; Pete, his snow white hair falling below his shoulders and a satchel crammed with neatly organized medical journals; Tim, now at the shelter at First Church Congregational, always raging about his latest social worker but about to get a job and an apartment at the same time; and Henry, still binge drinking but determined to get into detox. Students were walking over from Harvard Yard. The police presence on the Common abated and people who were sleeping nearby in pup tents and under tarps roused themselves to join us.

And couples: Duncan from Porter Square and his new partner, Rosemary, and Glenn and Sally. Couples where—as best we could see—the man was not physically or emotionally abusing the woman.

I knew Duncan from Porter Square. He is very tall, with a long face and long teeth, and gray eyes and gray hair. He looks directly at you and can hold your gaze. His speech rattles like a playing card in the spokes of a bicycle wheel. When he joined us in Porter Square, he was one of those people who had a redemption story to tell and told it over and over again. Duncan had a drug problem, he was sick, his girl friend committed suicide. He has hinted that they shared some very pure heroin and she took an overdose. Soon he couldn't pay the rent and he was on the street. Then he found God, and then he found us. There were occasional slips—he let an abscess develop under his left arm and it became badly infected, he thought he was in love with Fran and let her into his apartment but she was doing drugs and he didn't want to go back to *that*—but he never stopped coming to Porter Square and he never stopped testifying. Now he is content to sit back a little and listen to Kyle; he has been there, done that. He is our elder statesman, helping with communion, praying for the soldiers in Iraq and making sure that people don't dive into the plastic bin with the juice and socks all at once. He comes to Porter Square alone but he brings Rosemary to the Cambridge Common. She is very quiet, very composed, pretty and nicely made up. Duncan is very, very proud of her. Our prayer service on the Common is just right for Rosemary, he says, not like Porter Square, with Brad wandering in and out, playing his boom box and all jacked up or Lynn muttering about the Obama sign in the front window of the building she thinks she owns. Family friendly, he means.

Glenn and Sally are also pretty regular now on the Cambridge Common. Pat and I met Glenn the very first time we took our extra sandwiches into Harvard Square. He was walking up and down Garden Street where it meets Mass Avenue, panhandling. This was Glenn's spot for a long while. Then, he was unkempt and his long gray hair hung over his very pale gray eyes. His cheeks were drawn and pallid and he coughed in loud, hacking bursts. There was something the matter with his lungs, he said. No one could figure it out. He would go to Cambridge City Hospital and get some medicine and that would work for a while, but not for very long, and soon he would be back in the hospital for something else that might help. The doctors were saying that they were running out of different kinds of medicine to give him.

The automobile exhaust from the idling cars couldn't have helped much. Nor did his constant smoking. Glenn would walk up and down that little stretch of Garden Street, holding his sign and coughing heavily. He liked to talk with us and always took a sandwich. He was pessimistic about his lungs but optimistic about his soul. Then he disappeared for a while, and reappeared in the rotary where Routes 2, 3, and 16 come together. Even though the State Police regularly roust panhandlers from the rotary, it is always a desirable place to ask for money. Cars have to stop for an unusually long time waiting for the light to turn green and the medians are wide and safe. I would often see Glenn as I drove through on the way to Cambridge, and stop to talk and give him a McDonald's gift certificate. If I was wearing a collar, I would pull up on the median, get out and talk with him for longer than one traffic light cycle; I figured I would get away with it at least once, but no one ever stopped to giving me a citation or a warning. Glenn's lungs were worse but, if anything, he was more upbeat than ever. Then I didn't see him at the rotary any more and I thought that his lungs had finally given out.

At least a year went by. Then Glenn appeared on the Common with Sally. He had been trying to find us. He looked wonderful. His hair was clean and cut short in a crew cut. His eyes were just as pale as ever, but clear and bright. The doctors at Cambridge City Hospital had found a drug that cured his lung disease. He had got on Social Security and found a place to stay. He introduced us to Sally. She is very short, two heads shorter than Glenn, and looks up at him fondly. She has a triangular face and luxuriant thick brown hair, coiled at the back of her neck, high cheekbones and gray eyes. She has a very slight East European accent. Glenn rarely says anything during the services himself but afterward, when we are sharing sandwiches, he never fails to tell me that I had helped him just by stopping to talk with him, when no one else would. Then he gets a little teary and I get a little teary until Ernie breaks it up by asking for another sandwich or chastising Pat for not bringing any cans for him that week.

Sally didn't want to take communion. She thought she had to be baptized in order to take communion and she had never been baptized. I told her that I was from the "communion-first-baptism-second school" and she understood what I was talking about but she had talked with Glenn and she wanted to be baptized first. That was fine with me.

Pat and I had never done a baptism at the Outdoor Church (nor a wedding nor a confirmation nor an ordination nor lots of things) and, not wanting to encounter a mother with a child so young as to be baptized, we almost hoped that we never *would* do one. But we had forgotten about adult baptism. So, without giving it too much thought, we agreed that we would baptize Sally the following Sunday.

I didn't remember that we had agreed to baptize Sally until that morning, when my wife wished me a wonderful baptism as I walked out the door to drive to Cambridge. Pat had remembered, though. She brought oil and some cotton and the Book of Common Prayer. (We forgot to bring out any water and had to rush across Garden Street to Christ Church to get a bowl. The bowl had a white ceramic glaze and read "Allons-y à Paris" around the inside of the rim.) Pat had been very forgiving of my endless reinventing of our ecclesiology, so I thought it would be nice if we did our baptism exactly as it was in the Book of Common Prayer. Pat would lead almost all the prayers but I was to splash water on Sally's head three times and then anoint her forehead with oil, from the ball of cotton that Pat had soaked and put in a little dish.

It was a gorgeous early fall day. After weeks of humidity and rain, the weather had turned cool and dry, hinting at the end of summer and the beginning of the academic year. Ernie was there, of course, and Howard, and Glenn and Sally and Duncan and Rosemary and Marianne, our new intern, and Bruce, Pat's partner, who had come up from Rhode Island. Sally stood with us next to our cart, now covered with a felt altar cloth—green for ordinary time—that the children at Pat's church, Christ Church in Woonsocket, Rhode Island, had made for us. Ernie immediately fell asleep, as he always does when our prayer services began. Glenn was grinning broadly. Howard read the Scripture for that Sunday. Now that once again we have a large number of people with us on the Common, he has to stand beside the altar and read as loudly as he can so that everyone can hear him over the traffic on Garden Street. There was a group of teenagers behind us singing along with an amplified keyboard and practicing a synchronized dance. At the other end of the cobblestone apron, Fran, Doug and some other homeless men were standing around shouting at one another and waiting for sandwiches and juice. ("I know that guy, he's no good," Ernie had whispered hoarsely when he arrived, pointing at Doug, "he was at Dever!") Passersby stopped for a minute or so to see what we were doing.

The baptism went beautifully. Sally was a little nervous and very solemn. I tried not to drench her. We all applauded at the end and finished our regular service. Ernie woke up and took two egg salad sandwiches and a juice box. Glenn was so teary, he didn't even try to tell me that I had helped him just by stopping to talk with him when no one else would, and he didn't try to say anything to Sally. But he wouldn't stop looking at her and he wouldn't let go of her hand. Ernie announced that he was going back to Boston. Then we had chicken salad sandwiches and tiny stale lemon squares and—much to Marianne's horror—Devil Dogs, Pat's only real indulgence.

As Lynn says, "You can't beat that."

12

Conclusion

> For this commandment which I command you this day is not too hard for you, neither is it far off. It is not in heaven, that you should say, "Who will go up for us to heaven, and bring it to us, that we may hear it and do it?" Neither is it beyond the sea, that you should say, "Who will go over the sea for us, and bring it to us, that we may hear it and do it?" But the word is very near you; it is in your mouth and in your heart, so that you can do it. (Deuteronomy 30:11)

THOSE WHO KNEW TUCKERMAN AT A DISTANCE VIEWED HIM WITH UNrestrained admiration. Cyrus Byrtol, writing in the *Christian Examiner*, called the Ministry-at-large "the noblest expression of that idea of moral culture which more than any other [conception] marks this age."[1] In Europe, he was appreciated as an exemplar of a new, scientific method for addressing the problem of the poor. Baron de Gerando, himself an expert on "pauperism," said: "[*Principles and Results of the Ministry at Large*] throws a precious light upon the condition and needs of the indigent, and the influence which an enlightened charity can exert."[2] Mary Carpenter, whom Tuckerman met in England during his 1833 visit, was influential in the reform of prison and reformatory conditions in her own right. She claimed that Tuckerman had inspired her to pursue a career of social reform. Her memoir is nothing less an extended and wildly enthusiastic encomium to Tuckerman's memory.

Nor did time diminish enthusiasm for Tuckerman's example. Years after his death, the AUA had nothing but praise for the founder of the Benevolent Fraternity of Churches. Tuckerman was "one of the first to

---

1. Byrtol, "Review," 220.
2. McColgan, *Tuckerman*, 265, 343 n. 41.

make an intelligent study of poverty, and to whom, perhaps, more than to any one else, the poor of Boston, the State and the Nation, are indebted for sympathetic comprehension of their condition."[3] Rev. Samuel. A. Eliot, at the 75th anniversary of the founding of the Ministry-at-large, wrote: "There was nothing imitative in his enterprise. . . . You may, indeed, say that it was nothing more than the application of the teaching and example of Jesus Christ to the conditions of a modern American town. Nevertheless, even that was a daring novelty. . . ."[4] Twenty years after his death—and, not coincidentally, after friendly visiting was no longer central to the work of the Ministry-at-large—Tuckerman's street ministry was fully embraced by the ministers who followed him: "The doubtful enterprise on which he then entered," said Frederick T. Gray, his first associate, "has become a recognized and cherished instrumentality of Christian beneficence."[5]

Yet some of Tuckerman's contemporaries were ambivalent about him. They were puzzled by his insistence that the poor would be better served if the people seeking to help them did so in person, face to face, in their own homes or on the streets where they lived or in chapels in their own neighborhoods. Tuckerman's insistence on encountering the poor where and as they lived was, in a Boston dominated by Harvard's moral philosophy, thought to be more the result of his enthusiasm than of a sufficiently reasoned philosophy. For Channing, Tuckerman's "heart" and not his mind best explained Tuckerman's commitment to the Ministry-at-large:

> The truth is, that his heart was in his work . . . His heart was his great power . . . Much of this success was undoubtedly due to his singleness of heart . . .His constant experience of God's goodness awakened anticipations of a larger goodness hereafter. He would talk with a swelling heart, and in the most genuine language, of immortality, of Heaven, of new access to God. In truth his language was such as many good men could not always join in.[6]

3. Cotton, "Joseph Tuckerman Loved the Poor."
4. B. Tuckerman, *Notes on the Tuckerman Family*, 71.
5. Gannett, "Joseph Tuckerman."
6. Channing, *Discourse on Tuckerman*, 29, 34, 44, 56.

It was much the same for Story who, by the end of Tuckerman's life, had substantially upgraded his estimate of Tuckerman's stature: "I do not know any one," he wrote in response to Channing's request for a valedictory, "who exemplified in his life and conduct a more fervent or unaffected piety, than Dr. Tuckerman did. It was cheerful, confiding, fixed, and uniform. It was less an intellectual exercise than a homage of the heart."[7]

His contemporaries found ample evidence of Tuckerman's "emotionalism" in aspects of his personality. Even in encomiums to his achievements, Tuckerman could not escape condescending assessments of his character. His nephew, Henry Theodore Tuckerman, described Tuckerman as nervous and volatile:

> His thin, aquiline face, and hair combed back from the brow, his benevolent manner and habit, on all occasions, of expressing sentiments and taking a stand instantly suggestive of his calling, made him more distinctly clerical to the casual observer than is usually the case with ministers now. . . . His motions, when in health, were nervously rapid, his flow of words ready and free, his tone usually pleading; he was capable of great cheerfulness, and an excitable temperament lent freshness and cordiality to his address. . . . Indeed, the basis of his character was a peculiar ardor of feeling, in which consisted both its strength and its weakness. All my recollections exhibit him as an enthusiast; and the reserved manners and somewhat formal tone of mind, which used to prevail in New England, made him a striking contrast to those with whom I came in most frequent contact. . . .[8]

And yet in public, he was thought to be excruciatingly dull. His hosts in England complained that he would talk of nothing except the poor. His preaching in Chelsea was disparaged as tedious, uninspired and boring. Tuckerman's brother in law, the Rev. Dr. Francis Parkman, was typically critical: "At first, my brother was far from being a popular preacher, having some peculiarities (perhaps I must say affectations) of manner and utterance, which were painful and disagreeable, and from which, I think, he was never entirely free."[9]

---

7. Channing, *Discourse on Tuckerman*, Appendix, 71.
8. Tuckerman, *Notes on the Tuckerman Family*, 106–7.
9. Carpenter, *Memoirs*, 11.

Tuckerman's willingness to credit his feelings would—in the minds of contemporaries schooled in the reasoned convictions of the Harvard moral philosophers—have impaired his capacity for serious thought. Indeed, his intellectual capabilities were suspect from the very beginning. Story wrote of Tuckerman's undergraduate years: "During his college life he did not seem to have any high relish for most of the course of studies then pursued.... In poetry he was more attached to those who addressed the feelings and imagination...."[10] Channing shared Story's low opinion of Tuckerman's prospects: "[Tuckerman was] unconscious of his privileges, uninterested in his severer studies, surrounding himself to sportive impulses, which, however harmless in themselves, consumed the hours which should have been given to toil."[11]

Even as an adult, Tuckerman seemed not to have the gravitas that was expected of a leading Unitarian of his age. His attempts at intellectual work were thought to be, at best, indifferent and, at worst, undisciplined. Channing judged Tuckerman's valedictory book, *Principles and Results of the Ministry at Large*, to be ill conceived and hurriedly written:

> As to the great ideas which ruled over and guided his ministry, and as to the details of his operations, they may be gathered best from the reports which he was accustomed to make to the societies under whose patronage he acted. He published indeed a volume on this subject [*The Principles and Results of the Ministry at Large in Boston*]; but it is hardly worthy of his abilities or his cause. It was prepared under the pressure of disease, when his constitution was so exhausted by excessive labor, that he was compelled to forgo all out-door duties. He wrote it with a morbid impatience, as if he might be taken away before giving it to the world. It ought in truth to be regarded as an extemporaneous effusion ... as might be expected, it fell almost dead from the press.[12]

To be sure, Tuckerman acknowledged that *Principles* was "written under much weakness."[13] The book did not sell many copies, either in America

---

10. Channing, Appendix, *Discourse on Tuckerman*, 65.
11. Channing, *Ministry for the Poor*, 27.
12. Channing, *Discourse on Tuckerman*, 36–37.
13. Carpenter, *Memoirs*, 105.

or in England.[14] But Tuckerman believed nonetheless that *Principles* had succeeded in making clear that the philosophy that framed the work of the Ministry-at-large was carefully considered and not prompted by "strongly-excited emotions."[15]

For Channing, Tuckerman's lack of appreciation for the great theological movements of his time was additional evidence of his intellectual limits. "On such a mind, religious controversies could take but a slight hold. He outgrew them, and hardly seemed to know that they existed."[16] Tuckerman himself shared in this assessment: "There are certain speculative questions in theology upon which some decide very authoritatively, but which I am accustomed to think but little, and say nothing."[17] But this was unnecessarily self-deprecating; the Unitarians of the era, unlike the Orthodox Congregationalists from who they split, had no appetite for theological debate; in this respect, Tuckerman was in excellent company.

• • • • •

But Tuckerman's work and his dedication to it were too compelling to be dismissed as arrested intellectual development. To be sure, Tuckerman, in public, was constrained and formal and, in private, excitable and idiosyncratic. Yet when he was among the poor or describing his encounters with them, his enthusiasm was irresistible. Tuckerman was a very different man among the poor than he had been in Chelsea: "In his sermons written for common congregations he had never been very attractive; but his free, extemporaneous, fervent address drew round him a crowd of poor who hung on his lips; and those who were not poor were moved by his fervent utterance."[18]

So unsettling was the strength of Tuckerman's feeling for his work that Channing, describing it, could become emotional himself:

> Dr. Tuckerman was a martyr to his cause. That his life was shortened by excessive toil cannot be doubted. His friends forewarned him of this result. He saw the danger himself, and once

---

14. Ibid., 106.
15. Ibid., 105.
16. Channing, *Discourse on Tuckerman*, 54.
17. Carpenter, *Memoirs*, 92.
18. Channing, *Discourse on Tuckerman*, 96.

and again resolved to diminish his labors; but when he retreated from the poor, they followed him to his home, and he could not resist their supplicating looks and tones. To my earnest and frequent remonstrance on this point he at times replied, that his ministry might need a victim, that labors beyond his strength might be required to show what it was capable of effecting, and that he was willing to suffer and die for the cause. Living thus he grew prematurely old.[19]

• • • • •

"Emotional" or "enthusiastic," as used by Tuckerman's Unitarian contemporaries, were other ways of saying "experiential."

Harvard's moral philosophers were engaged first and foremost in the development of the theoretical underpinnings of modern liberal Christianity. Channing, for example, when he thought about the poor, had little interest in the practical application of Unitarian theology to their problems. He was more concerned with the general principles that could be adduced from Tuckerman's ministry:

> Over the years, William Ellery Channing encouraged, cajoled, and criticized Tuckerman into increasing the scope and effectiveness of his friend's work. But unlike Tuckerman, Channing seldom discussed the material needs of the poor, the finances of poor relief, or the quandary of discriminating between deserving and undeserving. Instead, he defined the moral and intellectual sources of Tuckerman's "higher charity." In one letter of encouragement, Channing urged his friend to find ways to express "distinct, substantial truths, which the intellect may grasp, and which answer to the profoundest wants of the spiritual nature.[20]

Because Channing's thinking was so general and Tuckerman's work so concrete, some have seen the Ministry-at-large as no more than a practical and particular application of Channing's more abstract contributions to Unitarian theology.[21] Even Conrad Wright, in an otherwise

19. Ibid., 57–58.

20. Wach, "Unitarian Philanthropy," 545; Channing to Tuckerman, 13 May 1835. Channing Papers, Massachusetts Historical Society, cited by Wach, at 545.

21. Wach, "Unitarian Philanthropy," 540: "William Ellery Channing was Joseph Tuckerman's closest friend. Probably the best-known Unitarian of his time, and certainly the pre-eminent spokesman for Boston Unitarianism, Channing reawakened

admiring assessment of Tuckerman's achievements, suggested as much: "Tuckerman believed in the worth of every human soul, and sought to unfold the latent powers of the individuals with whom he worked. His purpose was the moral and intellectual development of men. It was a practical application of Channing's great seminal idea, the dignity of human nature."[22]

Although Tuckerman used the language of the Harvard moral philosophers, his theology was inextricably entwined with the concreteness and immediacy of his day in and day out experience as a minister-at-large: what the liberation theologians would much later call *praxis*. What distinguished Tuckerman's Unitarianism from Channing's was his emphasis on experience. Experience framed every part of Tuckerman's thinking. "I might there have continued my ministry [in Chelsea] for centuries," he wrote of the radical understanding he had gained in his encounters with the poor, "society around me continuing what it was, and I could not have obtained the view of human life, and of the moral conditions and claims of multitudes of our fellow beings, to have been obtained in a year of the ministry to this city."[23]

Channing anticipated a liberal Protestant theology in which, if a choice had to be made, faith in reason could take precedence over faith in God. Liberal Christian ministry, in his understanding, was the practical application of a well conceived system of ethics and morality. But Tuckerman's ministry was mandated by the Great Commandment; he was called by God to minister to the poor: "Ah, my friend," he wrote, "our danger lies, not in our liability to erroneous conceptions of Christian doctrine, but in our defective sensibility to Christian obligations, and in our poor and low standard of Christian duty."[24]

· · · · ·

early nineteenth-century Unitarian theology with a deepened spirituality which spoke eloquently to contemporaries in Europe and North America. Their English colleagues greatly admired both men. Channing's theology and Tuckerman's philanthropic work struck a chord in England. On both sides of the Atlantic, their practical example of social immorality, or religiously inspired ethical ideas about social organization and social relations, provided a compelling model for addressing the problems of the urban poor."

22. Wright, Review of *Joseph Tuckerman: Pioneer in American Social Work*, 391–93.
23. Tuckerman, *Principles and Results*, 16.
24. Carpenter, *Memoirs*, 93.

We hadn't seen Rick all winter, but that wasn't necessarily cause for alarm. He usually spent a few weeks around Christmas time with his sister. She would take him in on the condition that he not drink in the house. After a few weeks he would drink in the house and she would throw him out. It was a surprisingly warm day for mid-April—the temperature would reach record highs in the middle of the following week—the day we saw Rick again, stretched out across his accustomed bench, with no shoes or socks on. His long face was unshaven, but his thin, almost translucent hands weren't shaking any more than in the fall. His hair was cut very short and I was surprised to see how white it had become; I thought, incongruously, of sitting in the barber's chair and watching my hair fall into my lap and thinking, "Wow! That's really white!" as if I hadn't noticed staring at myself in the mirror every morning.

Rick was happy to see us, especially Pat. He likes to tell her how much he loves her—but ironically. Our two interns, Emma and Marianne, bustled about finding some sandwiches and juice for Rick, but, as usual, he refused everything but socks and a bag of toiletries, which he always calls a "Hurricane kit." Then he looked up at Pat and said, "Pat, I've got to stop this, I've got to get off the street." This was a first. We all perked up. Hardly pausing for breath he told a joke on himself about not giving up drinking even if he got off the street. Same old Rick. Then he said, "Pat, I've really got to stop this, help me, tell me what to do." But when we told him we would help him with an application for Social Security disability benefits, so he could pay for a subsidized apartment or even a room in an SRO, he told another joke about drinking so much that he wouldn't be able to see the application form, much less fill it out. It was getting harder to hang in there with him.

A part of our justification for not judging the homeless people we encounter or attempting to intervene uninvited in their lives is that, when someone actually *does* ask for help, we go to great lengths to provide it. Here was a corollary that we encountered all the time: Rick was clearly asking for help but he was just as clearly refusing it by making a joke of his own cry for help before we could even respond to it. Contradictory, but clear enough. He really wants to get off the street and he really doesn't want to engage anyone directly in order to do it. We like Rick a lot. Even if we didn't, if he asks for help, we should fall all over ourselves to help him. But how?

Rick also told us that Dave had been approved for Social Security disability benefits. This was news to me. I was irritated. Dave's case worker and nurse at 240 Albany Street had told me that he had been rejected when he filed an application for benefits on the basis of his bad back, and that the only way to get benefits for him was to claim that he was disabled for psychiatric reasons. I had been trying to persuade Dave to see a psychiatrist for nearly two years, so that he could document a claim for benefits based on a psychiatric disorder. Dave wouldn't admit that he was a "looney." But all the while he complained bitterly that his "Social Security situation" was stalled, not going forward fast enough or being mishandled by the Social Security Administration. I thought he was fantasizing, but he wasn't. Without telling me, one of the social workers at 240 Albany Street had helped him prepare a new application, once again based on his injured back, and this time the Social Security Administration had approved his application. I couldn't very well sulk now that Dave had a reliable source of income but—at least in my view of myself as a lawyer—I felt stupid and incompetent.

Rick said that when the weather was bad Dave was spending his days at the Pearl Street Branch of the Cambridge Public Library, but, when the weather was nice, he would stay out with Rick and Charlie in front of Citizens Bank. Rick also said that Dave was carrying around all of his monthly benefit—about $1,000—and drinking even more heavily than before. Now, users and dealers knew Dave had a lot of money on his person. He had already been rolled once. But he refused to make CASCAP his representative payee.

The interns spent the week reflecting on what to do with Rick, and I spent the week trying to find Dave and persuade him to use a representative payee.

The interns did better than I did. They both concluded that it might help if Pat could spend more time with Rick by herself than the five minutes or so that we usually spent with him. We agreed to try it.

I stopped by the library a few times. I wouldn't normally spend so much time trying to find Dave during the week—it is usually impossible to find anyone on the street at any particular time and place—but I was a little angry with myself and I felt I ought to be doing something. The branch was a modern building made of cement modules, with little corridors and rooms running in different directions under very low ceilings. It got a lot of use, to judge by the number of people there. People knew Dave, and knew that he stayed there, but he was never there when I showed up and he wasn't outside Citizens Bank either.

The following Thursday, I went over to 240 Albany Street by myself. Jean was writing papers—she had enrolled in the MSW program at Boston University, where she worked the switchboard at night and where the tuition was free—and Marianne and Emma were getting ready for exams. Evan was behind the desk. He showed me some pictures he had taken in Maine of bears that wandered right up to his car. I asked him if he had seen Dave. He was there, sleeping. Mark woke him up for me. It took Dave a little time to get his bearings, but soon his pale blue eyes began to focus. A flesh colored growth that hung from one of his nostrils seemed to have disappeared. He was less drunk than I had seen him in a long while. We sat at one of the dinner tables. I told Dave that I was very worried that people on the street knew he was carrying a lot of money and that he had become a target. I wanted him to talk to Diane Griffiths at CASCAP about getting a representative payee. That's OK, said Dave, I can handle myself. Dave is slight, weighs about 150 pounds and is never completely sober, so we both knew that was a joke. I said, Rick says you've already been beaten up once since you've got the money. Oh, that, said Dave. I wasn't beaten up by a drug addict. I was sleeping in the Bank of America ATM lobby and a cop I'd never seen before came in and started rolling me over with his foot. So I got up and pissed on his shoes. That's how I got beaten up. Knowing Dave, this was as plausible as getting assaulted by an addict. Dave said, I need to carry about $500 with me, so I can rent a room if I find a good one. You don't have to carry around that kind of money for that, I said. You can put down a deposit, go back to the bank and get the rest. I don't have a passbook, he said. You don't need a passbook, you already have a debit card. I forgot the PIN, said Dave.

This wasn't going anywhere. Dave didn't want to give up control of his monthly benefit and he wanted to be able to drink any time he wanted to, now that he could afford it. But at least he agreed to carry less cash and ask the bank to tell him his PIN, so he could use his debit card.

And that was as much as I was going to get. I didn't feel a lot better about myself as a lawyer. I didn't feel a lot better about myself period. Dave stared at the Formica table and I stared at the Formica table. It had some spaghetti on it, from dinner. I couldn't think of anything else to say.

We saw Rick again the following Sunday. It was very hot and humid, in the high eighties even though it was still April. Rick was sitting on the same bench, even though it put him directly in the early afternoon sun. Sweat was running down his face. He had some color in his cheeks. Marianne persuaded him to accept a peanut butter and jelly sandwich with his usual socks and Hurricane kit. We had agreed that Pat would stay behind and talk with Rick, alone, for fifteen or twenty minutes, while we headed further up Mass Avenue toward City Hall and then back again past the Post Office. After about ten minutes, Pat rejoined us across Mass Avenue. She said that Rick couldn't stay focused. He kept asking her if she would marry him. Pat reminded him that he had asked us for some help, but he either didn't remember or he didn't care. Pat was despondent. But we agreed to keep trying.

Rick had told us that Dave was sleeping behind City Hall, so, while Pat stayed to talk to Rick, Emma, Marianne and I hauled our coolers up Inman Street to look for Dave. Dave was there, curled up and fast asleep. Emma and Marianne stayed on the street and I climbed up the embankment behind City Hall to get to where Dave was sleeping. I said hello, standing a few feet away so I wouldn't frighten him. He woke up and shook himself, dropping the pint of vodka that he had tucked in his pants. "Oops!" he said, "Sorry about that, Pastor."

"That's OK," I said. I offered him a sandwich, which he took, and a Juicy Juice box, which he didn't.

"I didn't mean to lean on you so hard Thursday night," I said.

Dave said, "Pastor, you're not leaning on me. You've come out every Sunday for five years, looking for me, talking to me. I know you want things to be right with me. I know what's in your heart."

· · · · ·

Stripped of its implicit condescension, Tuckerman's critics were right: he led with his heart. But his heart was self effacing. He was confident—he was always a man of his time and place—but it was not the confidence of self-absorption. His heart's primary object was always those mired in poverty. The depth of his regard for the poor was great enough to encompass all of the pain he was going to encounter among them. He could continue, even grow stronger, in his ministry, however difficult it was to see the people he had come to love suffer in front of him, because he was able to focus on them and not himself.

Tuckerman's experience on the streets of Boston was the source of all the strength he would need to attend to the people he sought to help. The facility with which he allowed that experience to inform his work gave his ministry an authenticity and a concreteness that saved it from sentimentality and superficiality. The actual experience of hearing, really hearing, voices other than his own, of hearing people in their own homes and surrounded by their own families and their own belongings, talking about their own lives, had been utterly transformative. Channing thought that Tuckerman was the victim of his ministry. In fact, Tuckerman gained from his encounters with the poor all the strength he would need to continue in the Ministry-at-large for more years than he ever imagined he would live.

Tuckerman was not a martyr; he was a disciple. In the universe of Christian possibilities, he found a vibrant form of discipleship that completely energized him. Tuckerman's contemporaries always tried to make sense of him and his ministry by looking at him rather than at the people he wanted to help. Just like today, the people Tuckerman sought out were virtually invisible even to those who believed they had an obligation to help them. His peers subscribed to liberal Christianity just as whole-heartedly as Tuckerman. But love for others without the others is love in the air and not on the ground. That was why it was so easy for Tuckerman's contemporaries to see him as an emotional rather than a thoughtful person. That was why Channing's overheated language about how Tuckerman's ministry needed a victim and how he was willing to suffer and die for the cause always sounded more like Channing than like Tuckerman. Tuckerman didn't write like that and he probably didn't talk like that either. Tuckerman's ministry was never about himself.

Harvard's moral philosophy could be about you and it could also be about someone else. In that philosophy, one life—one march toward moral perfection—was as important as any other. It was *forward* looking but it wasn't necessarily *outward* looking. Tuckerman's theology had the same ethical content but it was a *theology*. It was predicated on a call and it demanded discipleship. The rule of that discipleship was simple and it was mandatory: it could be about you but it *had* to be about someone else. It was the Great Commandment itself.

When Tuckerman went out to the streets in 1826 to find a ministry, his heart burned within him to help the poor. Because it did, he had no difficulty finding them or discerning how to minister to them:

> At first [Tuckerman] entered almost tremblingly the houses of the poor where he was a stranger, to offer his sympathy and friendship. But "the sheep knew the voice of the shepherd." The poor recognized by instinct their friend, and from the first moment a relation of singular tenderness and confidence was established between them. That part of his life I well remember, for he came often to pour into my ear and heart his experience and success. I remember the effect which contact with the poor produced on his mind. He had loved them when he knew little of them; when their distresses came to him through the imagination. But he was a proof that no speculation or imagination can do the work of actual knowledge. So deep was the sympathy, so intense the interest, which the poor excited in him, that it seemed as if a new fountain of love had been opened within him.... How often have I stood humbled before the deep spiritual love which burst from him in those free communications which few enjoyed beside myself! I cannot forget one evening, when, in conversing with the late Dr. Follen and myself on the claims of the poor, and on the cold-heartedness of society, he not only deeply moved us, but filled us with amazement, by his depth of feeling and energy of utterance; nor can I forget how, when he left us, Dr. Follen, a man fitted by his own spirit to judge of greatness, said to me, "*He is* a great man."[25]

---

25. Channing, *Discourse on Tuckerman*, 586.

Bibliography

Amon, Michael. "Numbers of homeless drop, but some question data." *Newsday*, July 30, 2008. http://www.endlongtermhomelessness.org/press_center/numbers_of_homeless_drop.aspx.
Anon. "Mr. Gilman's sermon on the church of Christ." *The Unitarian Miscellany and Christian Monitor* (January, 1822) 194.
Barnard, Charles. "First Semi-Annual Report, Postscript." In *Joseph Tuckerman: Pioneer in American Social Work*, 341. Washington, DC: Catholic University of America Press, 1940.
———. "The Ministry to the Poor." *Christian Examiner* 17 (1835) 345–56.
Berger, John. *From A to X: A Story in Letters*. London: Verso, 2008.
Blanchard, Joshua P. "Address Delivered at the 2nd Anniversary of the Association for Religious Improvement." In *Joseph Tuckerman: Pioneer in American Social Work*, by Daniel T. McColgan. Washington, DC: The Catholic University of America Press, 1940.
Bremner, Robert. *American Philanthropy*. Chicago: University of Chicago Press, 1960.
Buckminster. Joseph S. *Works*. Boston, 1839.
Bushnell, Horace. *Christian Nurture*. Cleveland: Pilgrim, 1994.
Byrtol, Cyrus. "Review of Tuckerman's *Principles and Results of the Ministry at Large*." *Christian Examiner* 25 (1838).
Cambridge Continuum of Care. "2008 Cambridge Homeless Census Update." April 24, 2008. No pages. Online: http://www.cambridgema.gov/deptann.cfm?story_id=1620.
Campbell, Scott. "Rainy Day Grace." *Zion's Herald*, March 21, 2004, 1.
Carpenter, Mary. *Memoirs of Joseph Tuckerman, D.D.* London: Richard Kinder, 1849.
Carroll, Marianne Daigh. "The Sabbath and Christian Discipleship." MA thesis, Harvard Divinity School, 2009.
Casaldaliga, Bishop Pedro. "Sermon." In *No Salvation Outside the Poor*, by Jon Sobrino. Maryknoll, NY: Orbis, 2008.
Cavanaugh, William T. *Torture and Eucharist: Theology, Politics, and the Body of Christ*. Challenges in Contemporary Theology. Malden, MA: Blackwell, 1998.
Chadwick, John W. *William Ellery Channing*. Boston: Houghton Mifflin, 1903.
Chalmers, Thomas. *Christian and Economic Polity of a Nation*. 3 vols. Glasgow, Scotland: J. Starke, 1821–1826.
Channing, William Ellery. "The Church." In *The Works of William Ellery Channing*, 440–41. Boston: Franklin, Burt, 1971.
———. *A Discourse on the Life of the Rev. Joseph Tuckerman, D.D.* Boston: W. Crosby, 1841.
———. *Memoirs, Vol. III*. Boston: American Unitarian Association, 1868.

———. *The Ministry for the Poor, a Discourse.* Boston: Russell, Odiorne & Metcalf, 1835.

———. "The Writings of Milton." In *The Works of William Ellery Channing,* 518–19. Boston: Franklin, Burt, 1971.

Cole, Nathan Cole. "Spiritual Travels." In *Some Aspects of the Religious Life of New England.* New York: Silver, Burnett, 1897.

Collison, Gary. "A True Toleration: Harvard Divinity School Students and Unitarianism." In *American Unitarianism, 1805–1865,* edited by Conrad Edick Wright, 219. Boston: Massachusetts Historical Society, 1989.

Cooke, George W. *Unitarianism in America.* Boston: American Unitarian Association, 1902.

Cotton, Edward H. "Joseph Tuckerman Loved the Poor." *The Christian Register* 11 (1921) 58–59.

Cotton, John. *Moses, His Judicials.* Boston, 1636.

Cummings, Preston. *A Dictionary of Congregational Usages and Principles.* Boston: Whipple, 1853.

De La Torre, Miguel A. *Handbook of U.S. Theologies of Liberation.* St. Louis: Chalice, 2004.

Drummond, Chester A. "The Report of the Minister-at-Large, 1943–1944." *The Benevolent Fraternity Bulletin* (May 1944) 3.

Eliot, Christopher R. "Joseph Tuckerman: Pioneer in Scientific Philanthropy." *Proceedings of the Unitarian Historical Society* (1935) 1–29.

———. *Chapters in a Biography of Joseph Tuckerman.* Andover-Harvard Theological Library, Depository boxes, bMS 428/1 (1)—(7), 1924.

Eliot, Samuel A., editor. *Heralds of a Liberal Faith.* 4 vols. Boston: American Unitarian Association, 1910–1952.

———. "Mr. Tuckerman's *Eighth Semi-Annual Report of his Service as a Minister-at-large in Boston.*" *Christian Examiner* 12 (1832) 116–24.

Fabian, Richard. "First the Table, Then the Font." Association of Anglican Musicians, 2002.

———. "Patterning the Sacraments After Christ." *Open* 40 (Fall, 1994).

Forsyth, P. T. *The Church and the Sacraments.* 1947. Reprint, Eugene, OR: Wipf & Stock, 1996.

Frothingham, Octavius Brooks. *Boston Unitarianism, 1820–1850.* Boston: Regina, 1889.

Gannett, Ezra S. "Joseph Tuckerman." *The Benevolent Fraternity Bulletin* 16:1.

Garlow, Stephanie S. "HUD: Homeless population declining." *Associated Press,* July 29, 2008. http://www.usatoday.com/news/washington/2008-07-29-homeless-report_N.htm.

Gerando, Joseph-Marie. *The Visitor of the Poor.* London: Simpkin & Marshall, 1833.

Gladwell, Malcolm. "Million Dollar Murray." *New Yorker* 82 (2006) 96–107.

Gray, Frederick T. "The Origin of the Ministry-at-Large." *The Christian Examiner and Religious Miscellany* 49:2 (1850) 204–14.

Griffin, Clifford S. "Religious Benevolence as Social Control, 1820–1865." *Miss. Valley Historical Review* 44 (1957) 425–44.

Hale, E. E., editor. "Introduction." In *On the Elevation of the Poor: A Selection from His Reports as Minister-at-Large in Boston.* Boston: Roberts, 1874.

Headlam, Stewart D. *The Laws of Eternal Life.* London: Reeves, 1897.

Heimert, Alan, and Andrew Delbanco. *The Puritans in America: A Narrative Anthology.* Cambridge: Harvard University Press, 1985.
Holifield, E. Brooks. "The Intellectual Sources of Stoddardeanism." *New England Quarterly* (1972) 373–92.
Hooker, Richard. "Hooker's Survey, Part I." In *Dictionary of Congregational Usages and Principles*, 130. Boston: Whipple, 1853.
Howe, David Walker. *The Unitarian Conscience.* Middletown, CT: Wesleyan University Press, 1988.
Jencks, Christopher. *The Homeless.* Cambridge: Harvard University Press, 1994.
———. "The Homeless." *New York Review of Books* 41:8 (1994).
John, Glynmor. *Congregationalism in an Ecumenical Age.* London: Independent, 1967.
Johnson, Kelly. *The Fear of Beggars: Stewardship and Poverty in Christian Ethics.* Eerdmans Ekklesia Series. Grand Rapids: Eerdmans, 2007.
Jordan, Daryl M. "He Hath Filled The Hungry With Good Things: Early Developments in Anglo-Catholic Social Theology." No Pages. Online: http://www.anglocatholicsocialism.org/acsocialtheology.html#3.
Kantor, Ira, and Eva Wolchover. "One Roof at a Time: Gov Pledges More Than $1B for State's Spiraling Homeless crisis." No pages. Online: http://www.bostonherald.com/news/regional/general/view.bg?articleid=1112075.
Kendall, James. *A Memorial of Joseph Tuckerman.* Worcester, MA: Franklin P. Rice, 1888.
Larkin, Jack. *The Reshaping of Everyday Life, 1790–1840.* New York: Harper & Row, 1988.
Laws, John Wallace. "American Unitarian Eucharistic Faith." BA diss., Meadville Theological School, 1938.
Malthus, Thomas. *The Works of Thomas Robert Malthus.* 8 vols. Edited by E. A. Wrigley and David Sonden. London: Pickering & Chatto, 1986.
Markowitz, Deborah. "Diagnosing the Cause of a Hyperosmolar Aniongap Metabolic Acidosis." *Journal of Intensive Care Medicine* 18 (2003) 160–62.
Marsden, George M. *Jonathan Edwards: A Life.* New Haven, CT: Yale University Press, 2003.
Maurin, Peter. "To the Bishops of the U.S.A.: A Plea for Houses of Hospitality," and "Superfluous Goods." In *Easy Essays.* Chicago: Franciscan Herald, 1977.
McColgan, Daniel T. *Joseph Tuckerman: Pioneer in American Social Work.* Washington, DC: The Catholic University of America Press, 1940.
Miles, Sara. *Take This Bread: A Radical Conversion.* New York: Ballantine, 2007.
Morgan, Edmund S. *Visible Saints: The History of a Puritan Idea.* Ithaca: Cornell University Press, 1963.
Nunley, Jan. "'We are all homeless': an interview with Bishop Geralyn Wolfe." *Episcopal News Service Archive* 21, February, 2003.
Patterson, Randall. "Beggars Can Be Choosers." *New York Magazine* 13, December, 2004. No Pages. Online: http://nymag.com/nymetro/urban/features/10608.
Peabody, Ephraim. *Pauperism in Boston: a Sermon before the Society for the Prevention of Pauperism.* Boston: J. Wilson, 1849.
———. *Sermon on the Occasion of the Death of Rev. Frederick T. Gray, 1855.* The Boston Athenaeum, Tract, B1216, No. 11.

Peabody, Francis G. "The Place of Joseph Tuckerman in the History of Philanthropy." *Christian Register*, December 16, 1926, 1133–42.

Pleck, Elizabeth. *Domestic Tyranny: The Making of American Social Policy against Family Violence from Colonial Times to the Present.* New York: Oxford University Press, 1987.

Posey, Trisha Diane Carter. "Poverty Encounters: Unitarians, the Poor, and Poor Relief in Antebellum Boston and Philadelphia." PhD diss., Graduate School of the University of Maryland, 2007.

Punchard, George. *A View of Congregationalism.* Andover, MA: Allen, Morrill & Wardwell, 1844.

Richardson, Peter Tufts. *The Boston Religion: Unitarianism in its Capital City.* Rockland, ME: Red Barn, 2003.

Romero, Oscar. "Homily of November 18, 1979." In *No Salvation Outside the Poor.* Maryknoll, NY: Orbis, 2008.

Schell, Donald. "The Font Outside the Walls." No pages. Online: http://godsfriends.org/vol12/no2/Font-Outside.

Schlesinger, Arthur M., Jr. *The Age of Jackson.* Boston: Little, Brown, 1945.

Schwartz, Joel. *Fighting Poverty with Virtue: Moral Reform and American's Urban Poor, 1825–2000.* Bloomington: Indiana University Press, 2000.

Sell, Alan P. F. *Saints: Visible, Orderly & Catholic: The Congregational Idea of the Church.* Allison Park, PA: Pickwick, 1986.

Sobrino, Jon. *No Salvation Outside the Poor: Prophetic-Utopia Essays.* Maryknoll, NY: Orbis, 2008.

Stoddard, Solomon. *The Safety of Appearing at the Day of Judgment in the Righteousness of Christ.* Boston: 1687.

Stuart, Robert Lee. "Mr. Stoddard's Way." *American Quarterly* 24 (1972) 243–53.

Tanner, Kathryn. "In Praise of Open Communion." *Anglican Theological Review* 86 (2004) 473–85.

Thornburgh, Nathan. "Defining 'Homelessness Down.'" *Time,* July 30, 2008. http://www.time.com/time/nation/article/0,8599,1827876,00.html.

Tiffany, Francis. *Charles Francis Barnard: A Sketch of his Life and Work.* Boston: Houghton Mifflin, 1895.

Tuckerman, Bayard. *Notes on the Tuckerman Family.* Cambridge, MA: Riverside, 1914.

Tuckerman, Edward. "Letter." In *Heralds of a Liberal Faith*, vol. 2, edited by Samuel A. Eliot. Boston: American Unitarian Association, 1910–1952.

Tuckerman, Joseph. *Address on the Obligation of Christians to become Ministers of Christ.* Boston: Blackwell, 1834.

———. "Diary." In *Joseph Tuckerman: Pioneer in American Social Work,* 31. Washington, DC: The Catholic University of America Press, 1940.

———. *An Essay on the Wages Paid to Females for Their Labour.* Boston: Carter & Hendee, Cummings & Hillyard, 1830.

———. *First Annual Report.* Boston, 1835.

———. *Gleams of Truth.* Boston: James Munroe, 1835.

———, *Letter to the Executive Committee of the Benevolent Fraternity of Churches Respecting Their Organization for the Support of the Ministry at Large in Boston, 1834.* Boston Athenaeum, Tract C311, No. 24.

———. *Letter on the Principles of the Missionary Enterprise*, 1st Series, No. 6. Boston: Gray & Bowen, 1831.

———. "Letter to Dr. Bowring, Secretary to the British and Foreign Unitarian Association." In *Joseph Tuckerman: Pioneer in American Social Work*. Washington, DC: The Catholic University of America Press, 1940.

———. *Letter to the Executive Committee of the Benevolent Fraternity of Churches*. Boston: 1834.

———. *Letter to "*"*. In *Memoirs of Joseph Tuckerman, D.D.* London: Richard Kinder, 1849.

———. *Memorial of Rev. Joseph Tuckerman, 1888*. Boston Athenaeum, Tract, 3Z5. T795.

———. *Mr. Tuckerman's Quarterly Reports on His Service as Minister at Large in Boston*. Boston: Isaac R. Butts, 1832.

———. *Mr. Tuckerman's Semiannual Reports on His Service as Minister at Large in Boston*. Boston: Isaac R. Butts, 1833–1836.

———. *On the Elevation of the Poor: A Selection from His Reports as Minister-at-Large in Boston*. Boston: Roberts, 1874.

———. *On the Validity of Presbyterian Ordination Delivered in the Chapel of Harvard University, in Cambridge, on the 8th of May, 1822*. Harvard Archives, HUC 5340.122.

———. *Principles and Results of the Ministry at Large in Boston*. Boston: James Munroe, 1838.

———. *Sermon Delivered at the Ordination of the Rev. Samuel Gilman*. Charleston: A. E. Miller, 1819.

———. *Sermon Preached at the Ordination of the Rev. Orville Dewey*. New Bedford, MA: Andrew Gerrish, Jr., 1824.

———. *Sermon Preached on the Twentieth Anniversary of his Ordination*. Boston, 1821.

———. *Sermon Preached on the Ordination of Charles F. Barnard and Frederick T. Gray*. Boston: Russell, Odiorne & Metcalf, 1834.

Wach, Howard M. "Unitarian Philanthropy and Cultural Hegemony in Comparative Perspective: Manchester and Boston, 1826–1848." *Journal of Social History* 26 (1993) 539.

Walker, George Leon. *Some Aspects of the Religious Life of New England*. New York: Silver, Burnett, 1897.

Walker, James. "Conscience." In *Sermons Preached in the Chapel of Harvard College*. Boston: Harvard University Press, 1861.

———. "Reason, Faith and Duty." In *The Unitarian Conscience*, 237. Middletown, CT: Wesleyan University Press, 1988.

Walker, Thomas. *The Original*. London: Renshaw, 1836.

Walker, Williston. *The Creeds and Platforms of Congregationalism*. New York: Pilgrim, 1991.

Walsh, Michelle A. "The Dual Missionary: Revisiting the Depth and Intent of Joseph Tuckerman's Theological Vision and Work." MA thesis, Boston School of Theology, 2007.

Ware, Henry, Jr. *On the Formation of the Christian Character*. Cambridge: Hilliard & Brown, 1831.

Wolf, Geralyn. *Down and Out in Providence: Memoir of a Homeless Bishop*. New York: Crossroad, 2005.

Wright, Conrad Edick. *Congregational Polity*. Boston: Skinner, 1997.

———. Review of *Joseph Tuckerman: Pioneer in American Social Work*, by Daniel T. McColgan. *The New England Quarterly* 14 (1941) 391–93.

———. *The Unitarian Controversy*. Boston: Skinner, 1994.

———, editor. *American Unitarianism, 1805–1865*. Boston: Massachusetts Historical Society, 1989.

www.ingramcontent.com/pod-product-compliance
Lightning Source LLC
Chambersburg PA
CBHW051638230426
43669CB00013B/2354